Introduction

SPENDING EACH SUNDAY AFTERNOON IN WESTVIEW, THE HOME OF my paternal grandparents Livingston and Eugenia Biddle, I became fascinated with family lore. My grandfather was the son of the financier Anthony Drexel's eldest child, Emilie, and her husband, Edward Biddle. The history of the Drexel and Biddle families was omnipresent in portraits, sepia-toned photographs, silver and china adorned with family crests, and furniture passed down through generations. Each piece was imbued with a story, and the tales, recounted over long luncheons, wove a tapestry of names, events, and indelible personalities.

Westview was in Bryn Mawr, on Philadelphia's Main Line, as it's still known, and contiguous to Wooten, the estate of George Drexel. The youngest son of Anthony Drexel, founder of Drexel University, George was close in age to my grandfather; in fact, my grandparents' house was a wedding gift from Uncle George. Although Anthony died in 1893, the sense of him as a distinct and present person continued during my childhood and youth; he was always spoken of in glowing terms, not because of his philanthropy or professional legacy, but because he and his wife, Ellen, had reared my grandfather following Emilie's death. As a result, the modest man who had quietly ruled a global banking empire and created an institution of higher learning where men and women were treated as equals became a living entity to me, not someone memorialized for his sagacity and reticence. A man capable of high spirits and fun, Anthony Drexel enjoyed indulging his children—and grandchildren—with every material possession he'd been denied as a child.

Anthony also opened his home to his brother's daughters, the infant Katie Drexel and her elder sister, when their mother died following Katie's birth. They lived with Uncle Tony and Aunt Ellen for nearly three years before being reunited with their father and his new wife. As an adult, Kate, as she was then called, would come to depend upon her uncle as mentor and friend.

When I heard tales of my grandfather Biddle's upbringing, or how President Ulysses S. Grant and his family had attended Emilie Drexel's wedding to Edward Biddle, I was given a unique view into Katharine Drexel's childhood, too. Emilie was her adored and high-spirited older cousin, an example of who she would become when she reached maturity. Katie was an impressionable young girl during the Civil War; its tortured aftermath of prejudice and deprivation, which would ultimately inspire her life's work, remained a singular event in the lives of my own grandparents. Both of my grandmothers shared their memories frequently. My maternal grandmother's father had lost a leg fighting for the Union's cause; she remained a confirmed Republican all her life because "Lincoln freed the slaves." My paternal grandmother's family were Carters from Virginia; she recalled being labeled "a damn little Yankee" when she visited relatives there. History, therefore, wasn't the stuff of dry textbooks; it was alive in the voices I listened to every week. The interwoven narratives of the Drexel and Biddle families and the events of past decades were as real to me as the roses and dahlias gracing the dining table at Westview.

Katharine Drexel underwent an extraordinary transformation, from a pleasure-loving young lady of privilege during the Gilded Age—"the prettiest of the sisters"—to a woman passionately committed to aiding and uplifting the poorest of the poor. Born in 1858, she inherited a fortune when her father, Frank, died in 1885. Throughout the nation, newspaper headlines trumpeted the sum; his estate was worth $15.5 million. It was unthinkable for a woman to possess such staggering wealth. While her affluent sisters followed the conventional route of marriage, and the charitable activities accepted within their sphere, Kate shocked her family and friends by choosing a path of self-sacrifice and service, first taking religious vows in the Roman Catholic Church and then forming her own teaching order. Her cousins, ensconced in their sumptuous residences, considered her choice dangerously radical.

Katharine combated racial prejudice and fought the Ku Klux Klan as she traveled through the country establishing schools for African and Native Americans. She considered Xavier University in New Orleans a crowning achievement, but of equal importance was her tireless work on behalf of the Navajo and Pueblo nations. Her focus was on education rather than religious conversion. She believed that the genocide of the nation's indigenous peoples and abasement of African Americans would not cease until there was parity in educational opportunities.

At a time when journeys to the Dakotas, Wyoming, Arizona, and New Mexico were fraught with peril because of the government's repressive policies, she overcame bigotry, distrust, and threats of murder. She died in 1955, having devoted her considerable energies to uplifting America's forgotten peoples.

Her story has haunted me as long as I can remember. I've always wanted to know more. What was this woman like as a person? Who was she as a child? How did her personality and strength of character evolve; and how did she come to make her remarkable decisions? In the midst of this new era of vast wealth, crushing poverty, and desperate need for social justice, her work among the poor and disenfranchised is especially pertinent. I view Katharine Drexel as a model for all who seek to make the world a better place.

The archival materials I used for my research revealed a girl and young lady of society whose ebullient nature was at war with the serious woman who would one day be canonized by the Roman Catholic Church. Equally, her life reflects the nation's history: the tumultuous years leading to the Civil War, Lincoln's assassination, Reconstruction, Jim Crow, the movement for women's suffrage, and the equal rights movement.

Toward the close of her long life, Katharine Drexel was already viewed as holy. During her last days, she believed she saw the myriad students and young people she'd encouraged, and spoke to their phantom forms, saying: "The children . . . Oh, the children."

I dedicate this book to her living memory.

one

HEREDITY

KATHARINE DREXEL DIDN'T BEGIN LIFE WITH SAINTHOOD IN MIND. As a young girl, she would have been shocked and dismayed by the notion, or suspected someone was pulling her leg. Saints were special. They were beautiful pictures in a book. They were holy, and, more important, they were always, always good. Besides which, as any church-going child was instructed, they were different from mere mortals; they were perfect. Even after Katharine Drexel had accomplished the greatest of her life's works, she still viewed herself as an ordinary human being trying to achieve the extraordinary.

Instead of aiming for sanctity, Katie's was a normal American childhood full of pranks, laughter, and high spirits, the drudgery of schoolwork—especially French, which she toiled in vain to master—the exuberance of summer holidays, and times of teenage angst and rebellion. She discovered boys and vanity and heartache, too. It was her wealth and place among the elite of Philadelphia that set her apart, not religious fervor.

Raised with every luxury provided by the late Victorian era, she enjoyed European travel, a debut into society, and summers at fashionable resorts. By rights, her path should have been the reverse of the one she chose. Her sisters and cousins married into Philadelphia's oldest and wealthiest families, establishing households of their own and continuing the cycle of affluence and leisure. It would have been easy for her to follow the example of her relatives. Young women of her era were expected to wed, and Katie, or Kitty as she was sometimes called, was the prettiest and most vivacious of her sisters; she had no dearth of gentleman admirers. Instead, she broke ranks, cleaving to a practice of self-deprivation and hard labor that most of her extended family found incomprehensible.

What were the origins of this iconoclastic spirit, her strength of will, and nonconformist nature? Her journals and letters, and those written by her paternal grandfather, Francis Martin Drexel, reveal uncanny connections across the generations. Both were mavericks, unwavering in their drive and commitment. Once they focused on a goal, they were tireless in achieving it. Lassitude and self-defeat were unknown. Francis's terse description of his decision to quit Austria for a new home in an unknown land reveals his sense of adventure and resolve. He knew what he wanted, and nothing was going to stop him: "I left my native place again for the wide world to make a fortune."

And a fortune it was. Francis was the genius who created Drexel & Co., the financial institution that built the vast wealth Katharine inherited. From him, she acquired indispensable characteristics of fearlessness and hope. Although he died when she was only five, and their relationship never moved beyond that of stern patriarch and small child, the two shared a commonality. In the world of banking, Francis Martin Drexel was a visionary who turned practicality and audacity into success. His granddaughter was his equal; in her hands the signature Drexel attributes of boldness and decisiveness were adapted into a new model of conviction and intent. Francis's goal was creating wealth; Katharine's was transforming lives.

Born to Magdalena Willhelm and Franz Joseph Drexel on Easter Sunday April 7, 1792, in the town of Dornbirn in Vorarlberg in the Tyrol, Francis Martin entered the world at a time when peace reigned in western Austria. Maria Teresa, Archduchess of Austria, eldest daughter of Emperor Charles VI, wife of Emperor Francis I, Queen of Hungary and Bohemia, had been dead twelve years, but her four decades of pragmatic leadership, and her wisdom in marrying her daughters (Marie Antoinette being the ninth) to other ruling princes had produced beneficial political alliances among the reigning families of Europe and the land she loved. In turn, stability brought prosperity to bucolic Vorarlberg. Although most of its inhabitants worked the land, the region's proximity to Switzerland, Germany, and Liechtenstein made trade a crucial element in the economy. At the time of Francis Martin Drexel's birth, his father was a successful merchant.

The family home lay in Hatlerdorf, formerly its own village but by then subsumed within the greater municipality of Dornbirn, whose population of about five thousand inhabitants made it the largest town in Vorarlberg. Above Hatlerdorf rose Mount Karren, its brooding presence hovering over towns, hamlets, farms, and fields. From atop Karren it was possible to see the long arm of Lake Constance seven miles in the distance and the Rhine curving northward into it, building up silt walls as if to challenge which was more potent, river or lake.

The house where the baby was born reflected his father's prosperity: a solid wood construction, punctuated by numerous broad windows, each hung with intricately carved shutters, the steep roofline a necessity owing to the winter's heavy precipitation. Oxblood, employed to preserve wooden surfaces, gave the exterior a warm, reddish hue. The interior had dark, coffered ceilings; enameled stoves heated individual rooms; in each, the oak furnishings were spare but handsomely functional and burnished with scrubbing and polish. The baby's low cradle was softened with an eiderdown and crisscrossed by several straps to keep him safely tucked inside. His sister, Susanna, who was born in 1789, slept in a trundle bed close by. The parents' bed lay against the wall, its mattress constructed to accommodate a reclining position rather than a fully horizontal one. (Tradition dictated that only in death did a body rest in a supine state.) Outside the residence, a large well-tended garden lent the home a country air. Barns and live-stock were common additions to Dornbirn homes, practicality being a vaunted regional characteristic.

Francis's birth was duly recorded in Dornbirn's book of inhabi-tants, a document listing deaths as well as births and dating back to the 1500s. The *Familien Buch* also listed orphaned children and those adults legally responsible for their care. The signatures affixed to each page bore witness to the gravity attached to these family matters and to the common sense and pragmatism of the town's residents. Even the name Drexel—variations are Drachsl and Dråxl—found its root in the utilitarian; a *drechsen* is a wheel-wright.

During the late eighteenth century, the residents of Vorarlberg cleaved to pastoral ideals, the majority farmers and herdsmen as their ancestors had been. Shepherds and cowherds summered flocks in the high pastureland; hamlets dotted the steeply sloping hillsides, their churches' onion domes prominent against the sky, an additional reminder of the virtues of a plain and pious life. Within the towns of Dornbirn, Bregenz, and Bludenz commercial industry consisted of the spinning and weaving of cotton, which was often carried out in the damp subterranean environment of the cellars in private homes. The cultural extravagances of distant Vienna were viewed by the Tyrolese of Vorarlberg as just that: the glittering city might as well have been in another nation altogeth-er. Until Napoleon changed the face of Europe, the land in which Francis Martin Drexel was raised was a place caught out of time.

The plentiful forests of oak, beech, elm, ash, and pine, the tilled fields and orchards, the medieval village of Feldkirch with its walled castle and tile-roofed houses, the peaceable hamlets and the fertile terrain might have seemed like an unlikely region to kindle an adventurous spirit like Drexel's, but it did. Standing on Mount Karren and gazing down over the town and then out into the vast panorama of the horizon, the boy saw the craggy profile of the Swiss alp Mount Sântis on his left-hand side, and the German village and island of Lindau on Lake Constance on his right. Landlocked Liechtenstein was out of sight, but also accessible. His father had regular trade connections in Italy, which meant that the thrill of exploration was ever present. Francis had only to look at the mountains or rivers or the lake to realize that the broader world was within reach.

The year 1799 jolted staid Vorarlberg. In March the battle of Feldkirch pitted eighteen thousand French troops led by one of Napoleon's greatest generals, André Masséna, against four thousand Austrians led by Hotze and Jellachich. The town and thirteenth-century Schattenburg Castle perched above it had been of military importance since its inception. A narrow, rocky gorge on the Ill River permitted entrance into Tyrol from the west. When Masséna's troops entered the treacherous defile, the outnumbered Austrians were able to drive back the detested French invaders and win the day. The battle of Feldkirch was the beginning of what became a protracted and devastating war, but for the time being peace returned to the region, and with it a false sense of power and autonomy.

When Francis turned eleven in 1803, his father decided to send him abroad to study. It was a mark of stature that young Drexel's educational opportunities expanded rather than remained limited to local tutoring by a parish priest. Full of self-importance, as well as trepidation at leaving home, he departed for the prestigious Convent della Madonna in Saronno, Lombardy, thirteen miles north of Milan. The journey followed a familiar route: south along the Rhine, through the ancient Swiss town of Chur, across the St. Gotthard Pass, before descending to Swiss Bellinzona with its fortified castles and long crenellated wall that stretched across the Ticino River valley. After Bellinzona came Lake Como and finally Saronno.

Although the route was customary, the St. Gotthard Pass could be a lethal place. Sheer rockface plummeted into the roiling waters of the Reuss River. Mist produced by the raging currents billowed upward, obscuring visibility along the narrow, twisting trail. For the lone child in the company of adults accustomed to the rigors of the trek, this was a life-altering experience. A process began that enabled him to choose adventure and uncertainty over security.

One of the objectives of his foreign schooling was that Francis gain fluency in Italian and French in order to take over the family business. He proved so successful a linguist that he needed to reacquaint himself with his native tongue when he returned to Austria. In Saronno, he discovered more than proficiency with languages; he discovered art and a future career, not as a merchant but as a painter. Frescoes by Gaudenzio Ferrari and Bernardino Luini graced the pilgrimage church of Madonna dei Miracoli with its handsome dome and early sixteenth-century campanile. The Luini works executed around 1525—The "Marriage of the Virgin, The Adoration of the Magi, The Presentation at the Temple, and Christ Among the Doctors—had special appeal, aside from their mastery and the serene grace of the subjects' poses and expressions. Luini's history was a dramatic one: after supposedly killing a man in self-defense, he appealed to the monks for asylum; in exchange, he created the frescoes. To a preteen boy, the tale was compelling in its sensationalism. Countrified Dornbirn couldn't compete with the potential thrills found in Lombardy and Milan.

The Italian idyll was short lived. Thirteen months after Francis began his studies, his father was forced to discontinue his son's education and bring him home. Napoleon's Austrian campaign and the nation's subsequent economic woes had finally affected Vorarlberg. The elder Drexel's business partner had suffered irretrievable losses, resulting in near ruin for Francis' family. Rather than complete a course of studies in Italy and France, Francis returned a poor boy with few prospects. On December 2, 1805, Napoleon vanquished the Austrians at Austerlitz. On December 26, the Treaty of Pressburg granted Tyrol to Bavaria, a Napoleonic state. The impoverished Drexels now lived under foreign rule.

Without funds to afford even a meager local education, and with an artistic predisposition as his sole resource, Francis was apprenticed to an artist in Wolfurt five miles from Dornbirn, near lakeside Bregenz. The date he began his apprenticeship was New Year's Day, 1806. Although Vorarlberg was distant from Vienna, the visual arts played an important part in the region's culture in the eighteenth century. Johann Joseph Kauffmann and his daughter, the classicist Angelika Kauffmann, were from the Bregenzerwald as was the genre painter Jakob Franz Zipper, whose fame, like Angelika Kauffmann's, had also spread to the courts of Italy. Francis recognized that he was following a tradition of artistic excellence, which may have softened the blow he received when the career he and his father had envisioned collapsed.

In a memoir prepared for his children, "The Life and Travels of F. M. Drexel, 1792–1826," his comment was brief: "I was able to follow my natural inclination for painting which I had from infancy. I never had any inclination for mercantile affairs." Despite the offhanded manner of the disclaimer, the words echo with bitterness. There's irony, too; "mercantile affairs" rather than "painting" became Drexel's ultimate livelihood. The traits that brought him his future triumphs were emerging. Faced with a situation he couldn't alter, he changed direction and declared the alternative the better option. Obstacles became opportunities; disappointments were ignored or touted as beneficial.

While he applied himself to his new craft—diligence being another facet of his character—war continued to rage throughout the continent. In 1809, when he was seventeen, the Tyrolese revolted against the occupying Bonapartist troops. The charismatic Andreas Hofer led the uprising; naturally, young Drexel joined the cause. When the revolt was brutally crushed on August 4 of that year, every able-bodied man and boy aged sixteen to forty-five became liable for conscription into Bonaparte's forces. To avoid service in the French army and the agony of fighting against his own countrymen, Francis fled across the Rhine into Switzerland on the night of August 9. It was a risky endeavor both physically and politically.

The next several years he roamed Switzerland, France, and Italy finding employment when he could and going hungry when he couldn't. He was robbed, became an unrepentant gambler, dropped the vice, took it up again only to renounce it a second time. His peripatetic nature took him to Basel, Paris, and Milan and numerous large and small towns and villages in between, seeking the fame and fortune he desperately desired. He bought elegant clothes when he could afford them, or bartered work for lodgings and a meal when his money ran out. He experienced loneliness and hopelessness, but the freedom and autonomy he found were addictive. Even if his father's former prominence had returned, Francis wouldn't have been satisfied within the confining routine of Dornbirn; he'd grown accustomed to the thrill of the unknown. With his chiseled cheekbones, bold eyes, and a mouth curving in worldly humor, he'd become the romantic ideal of an adventurer.

In January 1812, with sufficient earnings to purchase a new suit of clothes, he decided to visit home. He'd been absent two and a half years. Of necessity, the sojourn was undertaken in secrecy. The night of his return a masked ball was being held in Dornbirn. The handsome stranger dressed in fashionable attire was rumored to be the governor, which pleased Francis no end.

The next day, he was forced to flee his homeland again. Bonaparte had begun recruiting for his Russian campaign, and all young men were ordered to present themselves for physical examination prior to enlistment. As the borders were closed, Drexel and his father bribed a ferryman at Buren to the west of the city to leave his boat unlocked at night. In silence, father and son rowed across the darkened waters of the Rhine to Switzerland while the boatman and a guard ate their evening meal. Hoping to avoid suspicion, the elder Drexel returned on another ferry. The following week, though, he was arrested and fined, and his vanished son was stripped of his citizenship and rights to inheritance.

Francis' fugitive life continued for another year and a half until Napoleon was defeated, and Vorarlberg again became Austrian. By this time, he had honed his craft with additional instruction in

Lausanne. In his 1815 conversation piece portrait of his two siblings, parents, and himself—with the family dog—Francis looks
directly out of the canvas at the viewer, inviting us into the orderly home. The family patriarch sits at a table, a book held before
him; Magdalena, in a starched, white cap, is to her husband's left;
Susanna, in traditional Tyrolese garb, sits opposite her father.
Anton, wearing an Alpine hat, appears newly arrived on the scene;
he covertly studies his brother with a mixture of awe and envy,
which glance Francis ignores. The clan looks prosperous but
thrifty; it's also clear that the artist is an outsider, welcomed back
into the family but a stranger now, as if Francis has already intuited the future.

Upon his return to Dornbirn, he was commissioned to create a
triumphal, life-size group portrait of the Austrian Emperor Francis,
King Frederick William III of Prussia, and Alexander of Russia—
all three men kneeling in gratitude following the Battle of Leipzig.
The medium was watercolor; Drexel had less than twenty-four
hours to complete it before the emperor and his entourage arrived
in the city. During the abbreviated royal visit, the young artist was
presented to the monarch. He hoped the introduction would lead
to an appointment to an arts academy, and was crushed when that
failed to transpire; his proud, prickly nature took umbrage at what
he perceived as unfair treatment.

Disillusioned, he quit his home in February 1815, then achieved
minor success painting portraits in Germany and Switzerland until
dismay with his future prospects took its toll; he determined to set
out for the promised wonders of America.

> The prospect being a novel one to go to such a distant place,
> several whose acquaintance I made went also, and above all one
> fool makes many, I resolved to go too and see that other half of
> the World or at least a portion of it, I reasoned to myself since
> my native place having but five thousand inhabitants would
> never employ me professionally, and being obliged to be from
> home it would be a no wether I was One Hundred or Ten
> Thousand miles off. . . . If I did not do well [I] would return after

six months, but if on the contrary six years, but by no means stay.

On April 2, 1817, he embarked on a journey down the Rhine to Amsterdam, and six weeks later across the Atlantic to Philadelphia. The contract for his passage aboard the *John of Baltimore* cost eighty dollars and listed the promised fare: "Mondays Potatoes with dried Codfish, Tuesday, Pork and Sauercraut, Wednesday, Codfish and Potatoes, Thursday, Beef and Rice. Fryday, Pork and Beans, Saturday, Pork and Souer Crout, Sunday the same as Thursday; One quart Water, 1 lb Ship Bread and two glasses Gin per day; Beer the first 3 weeks, One pound butter and quantity of cheese per week." Seasickness made him unable to eat for the first twenty days of the voyage; thereafter, all passengers, including children, were put on half rations due to the ship's masters' miscalculation—or greed. When Drexel protested this ill treatment, he was threatened with imprisonment for the remainder of the journey.

Having departed Amsterdam on May 18, the *John of Baltimore* anchored at the foot of Callowhill Street in Philadelphia on July 27 at 11:30 at night. Prior to arrival the ship had been quarantined, as was customary, at the Lazaretto on Tinicum Island south of the city. After the calamitous yellow fever epidemic of 1793, and reoccurrences of the disease in 1797, 1798, and 1799, all arriving vessels spent a minimum of a day and sometimes several months in quarantine before being permitted to journey to Philadelphia proper. For every incoming passenger, it was an anxious time; the final destination was torturously near, but unattainable. Drexel was fortunate; reaching the Lazaretto at 9 A.M. July 25, he and the other passengers were held for only twenty-four hours.

Cleared to proceed, the ship continued upriver. Now the landscape the young man saw wasn't limited to a series of sedate hospital buildings surrounded by leafy walks, it was a cacophonous commercial port.

Philadelphia was no longer William Penn's "Greene Countrie Towne" with tidy brick buildings and demure facades. Marble, classical ornamentation, a plethora of Ionian and Corinthian columns and porticos altered the face of the metropolis. The Chestnut Street Theatre emulated the Palladian architecture of Bath, England; the newly constructed Washington Hall at Third and Spruce streets accommodated 6,000 audience members. The arts and sciences were burgeoning; the Pennsylvania Academy of the Fine Arts had opened in 1805, the Academy of Natural Sciences in 1812, the Athenaeum of Philadelphia in 1814. They joined the long-established American Philosophical Society in "promoting useful knowledge." Additionally, the city was the nation's financial center. The Second Bank of the United States had been chartered in 1816; Philadelphia was also home to private banks that met the needs of merchants dealing in foreign trade. Thomas Biddle ran a private bank, as did Stephen Girard, whose international reach would be surpassed by Drexel and his heirs.

On that hot July day, however, Francis Martin Drexel was a poor émigré who'd endured a grueling seventy-two-day sea journey. Like many other passengers spilling onto Philadelphia's wharves and joining the throngs moving toward the fish market on High Street, or the covered sheds selling produce, poultry, and livestock, he had no prospects other than his vaunting ambition. In his coat pocket was a single letter of introduction to an artist named Rieder living at Spruce and Seventh streets, a block from Holy Trinity Church. Established in 1789 when the city's German Catholics numbered half the city's Roman Catholic population, the church's stylish Flemish-bond brickwork was a reminder of his impecunious status.

Other neighborhood structures reflected the chasm between wealth and poverty. Mikveh Israel's burial ground, which contained the remains of noted figures from the nation's inception, was two blocks west of Holy Trinity. St. Mary's, then the Roman Catholic Cathedral, located on Fourth Street, and St. Joseph's were the resting places of equally famous men and women. St. Peter's Episcopal Church and The Third Presbyterian Church on Pine and Third and Fourth streets, respectively, counted Philadelphia's leading families among their parishioners. To those seated in the handsomely equipped carriages that traversed the area—the ladies holding parasols to protect them from the summer sun and the gentlemen in fitted coats and gleaming linen—Drexel, underfed and dirty, looked like a vagabond, which he was.

Rieder was too ill to take in the émigré, but he sent his visitor to the Grundloch family on Broad Street. As the hour was late, Drexel found temporary shelter before presenting himself to the Grundlochs with whom he lodged for six weeks before establishing a studio at 131 South Front Street. His portrait of Mrs. Grundloch was his first painting done in Philadelphia. The sitter appears reassuringly old-world, dressed in garments similar to those of Drexel's mother. There's no hint of fashionable Philadelphia; instead, a note of apprehension in Mrs. Grundloch's eyes suggests she wasn't altogether certain that it was necessary—or wise—to create her likeness.

Commissions soon followed. As Drexel wrote in his journal, he "continued to do middle well." Mastering the English language was an early priority. He attacked his studies with zeal, keeping a copy-book in which he penned what he considered to be fine examples of prose and poetry, as well as creating his own maxims:

> Men are subject to various inconveniences merely thro' lack of a small share of courage, which is a quality very necessary in the comen occurrence of life, like in battle . . .
>
> Whatever you do do right and diligently, which will safe [save] a great deal of trouble and vexation . . .
>
> There is but one way of doing Business, and that is the right way.

In 1817–1818, he painted George Washington Morris, who was active in the Dutch Reformed Church, and his wife, Jane Walters Morris. Explorer George Rogers Clark (elder brother to William) and silversmith Henry Erwin sat for him the same year, twin portraits of merchant James Paul and his wife followed in 1819, and the wife of a silk merchant, Madame Jacques Pointe de la Montagne, and her niece Virginie Buchy in 1820—both outfitted in costly silks and laces.

In addition to individual portraiture, Drexel created family group conversation pieces and miniatures. In one family grouping, thirteen figures are on display, all consciously revealing the status possessions of the period: a new patterned carpet designed to fit the space, *a la mode* clothing, a pianoforte, and artwork adorning the room's walls. Drexel exhibited at the Academy of Fine Arts yearly salons, and created popular genre scenes like *A Young Beggar, Two Beggars at a Window,* and copies of historical canvases by John Trumbull *Death of General Warren at the Battle of Bunker Hill* and *Death of General Montgomery in the Attack on Quebec.* In 1824, he made his first inroads into painting Philadelphia's blue bloods with portraits of Edward and Laetitia Biddle. And he had commissions for religious scenes, too: one being a large Crucifixion scene to serve as altarpiece for Holy Trinity Church. He was tireless in his quest for success.

Socially, he established himself within the German-American community, and was elected into the Deutschen Gesellschaft of Philadelphia on December 26, 1822. He also became engaged to Mary Fisher, whose family embraced him until the young woman suddenly died and her mother turned against her daughter's fiancé. Whatever grief he felt over Mary's death was mitigated by the rejection he experienced. Drexel was never one to blame himself: "The family before her death treated me like a son of their's but after the sad catastrophe Mrs. Fisher did me the honor to detract from my conduct and honor, as she had admired and praised before."

Incapable of remaining introspective or inactive for long, he met and wooed Catherine Hookey shortly thereafter. Catherine was a daughter of grocer Anthony Hookey, one of the founders of Holy Trinity Church. The couple was married on Easter Monday, April 23, 1821, and established a home at 40 South Sixth Street where Drexel also maintained his studio.

For the émigré, this was the true beginning of prosperity and happiness. Their eldest child, Mary Johanna, was born a year later in 1822; Francis Anthony was born January 20, 1824, and Anthony Joseph on September 13, 1826. An 1825 portrait of a young Mary Johanna, Catherine, and Francis shows the painter seated at his easel, his gaze penetrating, his manner pleased and a bit vain. His wife, as well attired as Francis, stands behind him. Their little girl is perched on the rolled arm of a camelback sofa, a costly piece of furniture to place in close proximity to oil paints and brushes.

The peaceable existence wasn't without problems. Catherine's eldest sister, Mary, had previously eloped with a swaggering Irishman named Bernard Gallagher, who was a self-styled army captain from the West Indies. By the time of her younger sister's marriage, the scapegraces had been forgiven and Gallagher entrusted to work in the grocer's shop at Third and Green streets. He considered the career a mundane one and took out his frustrations on his new brother-in-law.

> I did not escape his infamous tongue, and Writings of letters anonimously even long after Marriage, my Wife he did the same favor, emploid others to write anonimous letters for him, went to places where I was emploid to traduce my Character, and succeeded at Mr. Bazeley's who had emploid me as a teacher of Drawing in his Seminary at the rate of $72 per quarter, but Mr. B. would not listen to a traducer when he began to traduce to Parents Mr. B's establishment for having such a imoral teacher . . . an action for Damages was the result where when it came before the court and jury on the April 1824 his lawyers—Duane and Ingersol seeing the desperate case and fearing the jury would give the full amount of Damages [Drexel had requested a payment of $10,000], proposed to my attorneys terms of paying $2,100, and that he Gallagher should acknowledge before Court and Jury that he wronged me knowing nothing disadvantageous against me or Wife. . . . Not wishing to ruin his Wife & children I directed my attorneys to accept the proposal.

Following this litigious battle, Drexel lost his employment at Bazeley's establishment and was replaced by Rieder. His commissioned work also suffered. In 1826 he decided to journey to South America, and paint the newly emerging grandees and their wives. The reactive nature of the decision was an established behavioral pattern, but this time it wasn't parents and siblings he left behind, but a wife and young children who were then forced to rely on the Hookeys, and of course, Mary and Bernard Gallagher.

For his son, Frank, two years old when his father departed, it was the beginning of a life-long emotional rift. Anthony, born four months after Drexel's departure, didn't meet his father for nearly four years, but Francis's absence also molded his character; he became preternaturally serious, quiet, and responsible, traits that remained with him always.

The impact on his family notwithstanding, Francis Martin Drexel sailed on the brig *Navarre* on May 15. In his luggage were uncolored aquatint portraits of General Bolivar depicted quarter length and wearing full dress uniform. Published by I. B. Longacre at a cost of $2,500, they represented a considerable investment. Drexel intended to sell the engravings of the Liberator to loyalists and reap a tidy profit. The plan went awry when the political climate in South America changed. Simon Bolivar was accused of attempting to unite Colombia, Peru, and Bolivia into a single confederacy of which he would become dictator for life. Naturally, his popularity plummeted.

Drexel's account of his sojourn in his "Journal from Guayaquil, Pacific Ocean, to Different Parts of Chili" didn't reveal his disappointment or mention the family he left behind. With characteristic bravado and a sense of derring-do, he described near mutinies, lavish seaside entertainments, sumptuous dinner parties—with voluble young noblewomen, conflicts with police officials, thefts of personal belongings, earthquakes, bullfights, political unrest, squabbles over lodging, treks into and over the Andes, fortuitous meetings with powerful governors, generals, and the newly elected president of Chile, Francisco Antonia Pinto, as well as distances traveled, expenses, and completed art works.

[November 29] I embarked on the Peruvian Brig Confianza. . . . Night came on and with it such a quantity of cockroaches out of every crack that I was glad to go on deck, and even took my bed there to sleep unmolested . . .

[December 16] [The captain and I] had a few words, when he brought his sword on deck to fight with me. I told him if he wished to settle in that way, I had a good pair of pistols below and would give him satisfaction . . .

[December 20] General of the Mariners, Don Lose Bivero, invited me most cordially to come on shore and live with him . . . Said he was very glad a gentleman like me had come, who was in this part of the world very much wanted, and I would do very well, make a great deal of money, etc . . . but how different after one hour every thing appeared! . . . I was requested to open my trunk which was completely ransacked . . . (the General) told me that he had orders more than two months ago to arrest as a spy a German or Frenchman, who would give himself out for an artist, or painter . . .

[January 4, 1827] Made a beginning on the portrait of Mrs. Thwaites a lady from Buenos Ayres, with which I had very bad success, altho' a very good likeness. She was very vain, and thought herself much handsomer . . .

[January 26] A revolt of the Columbian soldiers headed by Colonel Bustamanti. . . . The 27th at 12 o'clock numerous citizens, officers, and soldiers went to the Cabildo, proclaimed the Bolivar Constitution void . . .

[February 26: a sea-bathing party and beach picnic with General Bivero's party] I undressed, and went into the water with but a borrowed pair of pantaloons on, and found white and black, masters and servants, and ladies and gentlemen all together, enjoying the fresh and cool sea water, splashing each other, and making plenty of noise, playing about and washing their skins. However, I most plainly saw that the blacks in spite of their rubbing would not get white. . . . At four o'clock dinner was ready. . . . More than ten different dishes followed each other; vegetables, salad and pudding, pastry, and melons, grapes with figs . . . the wines were Madeira and port both of which went the rounds briskly . . .

[March 11] I received the first letter of my wife . . .

[May 11] The Prime Minister Vidauri ordered that all the Portraits of Bolivar in the Public buildings should be taken down to forget him and his deeds. . . . Some gentleman for whom I painted portraits of Bolivar, begged me by all means not to tell it to any person . . .

[October 29: Santiago] Arriving at the top of the Questro de Prado, beheld at once the whole range of the Andes. . . . There could certainly not have been a more splendid and imposing view . . .

[March 19, 1828] . . . with little regret I left Santiago for Valparaiso with my sword on my side, on horseback, with a Frenchman who had a coffee house at Valparaiso, and was armed with pistols . . .

[May 21—May 23: Coquimbo] A quarter before 8 in the evening had a most severe earthquake. . . . The bells in the steeple of St. Augustin tolled involuntarily. It certainly was very awful. . . . Many persons slept that night in the open air, others made tents . . . Had before 12 p.m. another. 22nd at 3 a.m. and at 7 1/2 a.m. others. The sea was roaring very much that night but looked beautiful in the moonlight. The 23rd at midday another severe shock. At one another . . .

[September 28—September 29: La Paz] . . . at 8 at night, the only company of soldiers (Peruvian) . . . left their quarters, loaded their muskets . . . with the resolute and dreadful object to divide themselves to the four principal streets, and murder every person they met, and for their recompense to rob the principal houses. . . . Three times the most and principal citizens have been murdered and robbed . . .

[June 8, 1829: Arequipa] I was in his house (Major Don Jose Palma) seven months in which time I painted the portrait of Dr. Gonzales his friend, his own portrait, a miniature of his Lady, altered a portrait of a son of his, made him a present of a large painting, "The Burial of Christ," and lent his lady $30—not returned to me.

[July 16: Valparaiso] . . . smuggled my gold on board the ship
Orbit of Baltimore, and gave it in the hands of Mr. Thomas G.
Smith of Boston to deliver to Mrs. Drexel at Philadelphia . . .

Drexel's journey concluded by sailing around Cape Horn on the
ship *Lafayette*, heaving to for thirty-six hours during a severe gale,
being becalmed for ten days near the northern Brazilian coast, and
eventually arriving in Baltimore on April 4, 1830. He was cleared
by customs and left by steamboat for Philadelphia on April 9:
"Arrived the 10th in the morning half past 7 o'clock at my house
after one month less than four years' absence."

———————

The homecoming wasn't as euphoric as he'd envisioned. In his
absence, his brother-in-law had continued to malign "that damned
Dutchman," even declaring that the extended Hookey family
would never set eyes on the painter again. For Catherine and her
three children, the damage caused by Gallagher's allegations
couldn't be overcome quickly. Nor could Drexel disregard the crit-
icism. He'd left behind his wife and young children, after all, and
though he returned he'd been in peril on a weekly basis and proud-
ly recorded each harrowing detail. On paper, his labors had earned
$22,610; $12,545 he had sent home to Catharine; his expenses
were $3,260. For an extended absence, his profit wasn't as great as
he'd hoped; artistic recognition had eluded him, too.

Dutifully, though, he resumed his craft, supplementing the
income by selling trimmings and other dry goods from his home,
an activity suggested by his father-in-law. He briefly tried his hand
at being a brewer, taking on a partner named Partenheimer and a
staff of four Irishmen. The couple had a fourth child, Joseph
Wilhelm, who was born on June 24, 1831.

Five years of struggling with the mundane and quotidian ended
in 1835. Francis was now forty-two, and in a hurry to make a significant mark on the world. He left his family and Philadelphia
again and traveled to Mexico City. This time his sole focus was

business; he didn't have the time or inclination to keep a journal. A sole handbill survives from this period. It announced the artist from *Filadelfia* available to render portraits in either full-size or miniature form, and promised a faithful and tasteful likeness. The address given was 18, Calle de Tiburcia.

Early 1837 found him home again, and as frustrated by his lack of financial success as before. The same year the nation began teetering on the brink of financial chaos.

————

In the twenty years since Drexel had emigrated, the Industrial Revolution had brought irreversible changes to Philadelphia and its populace. Manufacturing rather than trade was becoming the city's life blood; textile mills, steam-powered sawmills, foundries and sugar refineries consumed swaths of once verdant farmland, and the Delaware and Schuylkill rivers, which had been rife with fish and game, and lined with birches, oaks, and willows, now bristled with commercial docks and coal depots.

Oliver Evans had helped introduce steam power to Philadelphia during the late eighteenth century; Matthias Baldwin gave the invention its widespread, practical use. In 1831, Baldwin built a miniature working engine capable of pulling two cars and four passengers. The following year he built the full-sized "Old Ironsides," a steam locomotive that chugged along a horse-car track built by the Philadelphia and Germantown Railroad. By 1835, his expanding locomotive works relocated from the city's center to Broad and Hamilton streets. Coal was the driving force of this transformed, mercantile landscape. The Schuylkill Navigational Company transported it from anthracite beds near Port Carbon down the river in flat-bottomed barges to the city's steam-driven manufactories. Coal powered the manufacture of firearms in Henry Deringer's manufactory located in the Northern Liberties. His eponymous "derringer" became the stuff of legend; his larger weapons were sold to U.S. government arsenals. William Cramp, shipbuilders, became the world's largest producer of iron ships.

Naturally, all this machinery and the businesses that housed them required capital. Chestnut Street was the center of the nation's financial institutions—most conspicuously the Second Bank of the United States. Chartered in 1816 with the vast sum of $35 million, the Second Bank went though some rocky years, weathering the Panic of 1819 until it came under the leadership of Nicholas Biddle, whose proactive measures prevented a financial crisis then engulfing Britain from spreading to America's shores.

Biddle graduated from the College of New Jersey, now Princeton University, in 1801 at the age of fifteen, serving as class valedictorian. He became secretary to John Armstrong, United States minister to France, prior to practicing law, and was ensconced in Paris in 1804 during the time of Napoleon's coronation. Subsequently, he acted as secretary to James Monroe, then United States minister to the court of St. James, returning home in 1807. He edited the literary compendium *The Port Folio,* and *The History of the Expedition Under the Commands of Captains Lewis and Clark.* The Greek-Revival style of his country estate, Andalusia, was influenced by his extensive European travels. It was at Andalusia that he hosted some of the city and nation's most notable residents. Biddle, erudite, cosmopolitan, and courtly, was bound to have his detractors among the new breed of self-made men. So, increasingly, did the central bank.

When Andrew Jackson was elected president for a second term in 1832, his vice president on the ticket was Martin Van Buren. They made an interesting pairing. Jackson had enormous personal courage and had proven himself in battle; his personality was fiery and charismatic, his temper as famous as his bravery. Like Jackson, Van Buren was from humble origins, but where "Old Hickory" had fashioned himself into a grandiose version of the common man whose tenacity and political savvy had won for him the nation's highest honor, Van Buren maintained a low profile. He preferred private deals to public display. Both men loathed the Second Bank; they believed it was governed by the elite, and inherently dangerous to Jacksonian democracy. The president's opinions regarding the institution verged on the violent. His feelings were deeply personal; he had experienced near bankruptcy twice.

Prior to winning a second term, he'd warned Biddle not to make the Bank's recharter an issue. Biddle refused. He prevailed on friends in Congress to push through the recharter in July 1832—only to have Jackson veto it. In a letter written to Henry Clay on August 1, 1832, Biddle responded to the veto by comparing it to "the fury of a chained panther biting the bars of his cage." The battle between the two men was now engaged. The fight escalated with Jackson's reelection.

By then, the Second Bank had become a nationwide entity, maintaining branches in Baltimore, Boston, Buffalo, Burlington, Charleston, Cincinnati, Fayetteville, Hartford, Lexington, Louisville, Mobile, Nashville, Natchez, New Orleans, Norfolk, Pittsburgh, Portland, Portsmouth, Providence, St. Louis, Savannah, Utica, and Washington, D.C. For the traveler or merchant with business in multiple states, the system was a boon. Jackson, though, felt that local banking institutions and local economies should take precedence. In September 1833, he ordered that United States funds be withdrawn from the Second Bank. Local and state banks took over the business of lending money. Speculation increased, and inflation ensued because of the issuance of banknotes not backed by silver or gold reserves.

In Philadelphia, the feud between the president of the United States and the president of the Second Bank had additional relevance, because Biddle was Philadelphian born and bred. City newspapers divided themselves along class and party lines: Jacksonian Democrats reviling and berating the supposedly lordly Whigs and vice versa. The mudslinging was vicious. Jackson was ridiculed in broadsheets depicting him in royal garb: "King Andrew The First: Shall he reign over us or shall the people rule?" Biddle was vilified as "old snatch and grab." Undeterred, and urged on by his illustrious friends, he shot back salvos to his political allies, writing to Joseph Hopkinson, then Judge of the United States Court, Eastern Division of Pennsylvania on February 21,

1834: "This worthy President thinks that because he has scalped Indians and imprisoned Judges, he is to have his way with the Bank. He is mistaken—and he may as well send at once and engage lodgings in Arabia."

For his part, Jackson vowed to "kill" the bank. On both sides of the argument, it was all-out war.

In 1836, the president issued the Specie Circular of 1836, requiring that purchasers of government lands be required to pay in hard currency. The result was a run on the banks, and the Panic of 1837 that precipitated the Great Depression. "Another One Gone" became a common newspaper headline as local bank after bank throughout the nation collapsed.

This was the economic maelstrom in which Francis Martin Drexel found himself when he decided to finally end his overseas journeys. It wasn't unlike the abrupt reversals of fortune his father and other Austrians had suffered, but his reaction to the national upheaval was to seize it as a moment of opportunity. Brio, not hesitation, was his watchword. In Louisville, Kentucky, in 1837, Drexel's career began a stunning transformation when he started using his South American connections and trading in the stable species of Spain and Germany, as well as in gold. In Philadelphia in January 1838, he opened offices—not as an artist, but as "F. M. Drexel, Exchange Broker."

By 1847, the artist-turned-banker had become so prosperous that he was able to float the U.S. Treasury a loan of $49 million to finance the Mexican War. The same year, his sons Frank, twenty-three, and Anthony, twenty-one, were made partners in the family concern. F. M. Drexel, Exchange Broker, was now Drexel & Co.

"Men are subject to various inconveniences merely thro' a lack of courage," Francis had declared in his notebook shortly after his arrival in America. His granddaughter Katharine, equally brave and equally forceful, had a similar attitude: "Our Lord likes courage. Get it from Him."

two

A CHILD OF PRIVILEGE

CATHERINE MARY, WHO WAS NAMED FOR HER PATERNAL GRAND-mother, was born to Hannah and Frank Drexel on November 26, 1858. In future, the appellation would cause confusion among bishops and attorneys when she took the religious name of Mary Katharine while maintaining the legal designation of Catherine. As a baby and later as a child she was called by the diminutives Katie and Kitty and sometimes Kitten, all of which reflected her lively personality. As she grew older she assumed the forthright Kate.

Four years prior to her birth, Philadelphia had made a giant leap in growth by expanding its boundaries; the Consolidation Act of 1854 added outlying boroughs and districts to the densely packed, original core of William Penn's "City of Brotherly Love." No longer could a criminal escape from one borough into another; no longer did police officers and fire companies confine themselves to single wards like the Northern Liberties or Southwark, Kensington or Fishtown. The modern city, sprawling between its two rivers, was a single, bustling unit. Horse-drawn streetcars served the ever-expanding populace. Everywhere was production and vitality. Everywhere money was being made and spent.

Except for the very poor who lived in increasingly crowded tenement dwellings, Philadelphia exuded an aura of opportunity, which extended to the city's cultural institutions. At its resplendent year-old opera house the American Academy of Music (now the Academy of Music), the American premiere of Verdi's *Il Trovatore* was presented on February 25, 1857. That evening new wealth mingled with old. Imagination and tenacity, rather than family connections, were the era's requirements for personal success.

On the raw November day when the infant girl arrived, her parents resided at 433 Race Street. Comfortable though the brick home was, and fitted out with fashionable French-polished furniture, dark-hued draperies, and the greenery-filled "parlor gardens" then in vogue, the neighborhood was an odd choice: half residential, half the backbone of Philadelphia's industrial hub. One block east toward the Delaware River, a sugar refinery sprawled across several lots that stretched between Race and Crown streets; facing the refinery to the south was a manufactory of lamps and gas fixtures; a dress trimmings company and salesroom stood at Fifth and Cherry streets; G. Goebel's Hotel and Lager Beer Saloon also fronted Cherry Street; and Philadelphia's tanneries, manufacturing chemists, and ironmongers could be found in the vicinity.

At 172 North 4th, between Callowhill and Willow streets was the office of *The Free Press*, a weekly newspaper that published German and English editions; it served the large and prosperous German population that had been fundamental to the city's growth. The city's commercial docks with their ancillary warehouses, ropewalks, and sail makers lined up along Front Street, and laundry lines stretched between upper windows of crowded streets and narrow alleyways. From these, nightshirts, step-ins, sheets, and corset covers flapped, sending shadows over the unpaved roadways below. For the eldest son and daughter-in-law of one of the United

States' most powerful financiers, the pleasant tree-lined streets surrounding Rittenhouse Square, two miles distant, would have been a more fitting address. It was there that Frank's parents had their lavish palazzo.

Despite his gentle, bewhiskered features and pensive eyes, Frank had an independent streak. The elder Francis's ambitions and peripatetic nature had put more than physical distance between the two men. It was hard for Frank to forget a childhood where he and his siblings had been virtually fatherless for four years, or to forgive being denied a formal education during his teen years when he and Tony had been forced to labor as counter boys and night watchmen at the Drexel brokerage house. In those days, Frank's love of music and need for financial and emotional independence had impelled him to walk a twelve-mile round trip each Sunday in order to play the organ at St. John's Church in the mill town of Manayunk. His annual earnings were one hundred fifty dollars, a significant sum to a poor boy, but a paltry amount to the son of a rising banker. Although now a partner in Drexel & Co., he never enjoyed the same rapport with his father that his younger brother, Tony, did. In choosing to live on lower Race Street, Frank challenged every one of his parents' aspirations, and Francis made his displeasure known. On this raw November day, though, the home's location was immaterial. Catherine Mary was a newborn; in five weeks she would be motherless and Frank would be a widower.

Hannah Langstroth Drexel had been born in 1826 to Piscator and Eliza Lehman Langstroth. She came from long-established German stock, the maternal side of her family being descended from the Leverings, who had emigrated in 1685. The quest for religious freedom had induced her ancestors, German Baptist Brethren (or "Dunkers" as they were commonly called because of their immersive baptism practices), to settle in what would become part of Germantown in the hilly outskirts of Philadelphia. Their faith revolved around the Bible and hymnal as teaching tools; the home, they believed, should be a sanctuary. In manner and outlook, Hannah's female relatives were the antitheses of her Drexel in-laws. Not for them gowns with triple skirts, or the latest styles known as the Longjumeau or Cherbourg, or advice in popular books on etiquette that dictated that jewelry was de rigueur when a lady was being driven in an open carriage.

Underweight and frail, the infant was baptized at once; it was uncertain whether she'd survive. Her mother's life also hung in the balance. Midwifery at the time was an imperfect science. Puerperal fever and peritoneal inflammation were wrongly believed to be infections passed along by wet nurses, monthly nurses—even friends calling upon the new parents. Sometimes the conditions were blamed on the mothers themselves, who were chided about not being sufficiently passive patients. In 1848, the Hungarian physician Ignaz Semmelweiss estimated that between one in ten and one in three women died of puerperal fever according to the season. He ordered his students to wash their hands in a disinfectant solution of chloride and lime when assisting at childbirth, but the regimen was not widely adopted. In Philadelphia, it was unknown.

With Hannah's health worsening daily, the household became an anxious place. Relatives came and went bearing somber expressions, their postures tense, their words muffled and filled with foreboding. Lizzie, the two-year-old elder sister, felt their fear without understanding its cause or why she and her infant sister were relegated to the nursery, while Frank, caught up in concerns for his wife, grew more and more distant. Dread mounted as the days stretched into agonizing weeks. Hannah drifted into delirium, then became comatose. Helpless, the doctors and adult members of the family could only watch at her bedside and wait.

On December 29, 1858, Catherine Drexel was publicly baptized at the Roman Catholic Church of the Assumption. The following day, her mother died. The death notice that appeared in the daily *North American and United States Gazette* on Saturday, January 1, 1859, stated only the facts: "On the morning of 30th inst. Mrs. Hannah J. Drexel, youngest daughter of Mr. Piscator Langstroth and wife of F. A. Drexel. The relatives and friends of her family are respectfully invited to attend her funeral on Sunday morning at 9 1/2 o'clock."

The wording, though succinct as was customary, contained a glaring break with tradition; immediately below Hannah's was another death notice for an eighty-nine-year-old widow, Margaret Whelen. In the latter's case, the rules of the mid-nineteenth century were strictly observed. Only *male* friends and family were encouraged to attend her final rites. Frank's rebellious streak had again surfaced; anyone reading the newspaper would have been surprised at his choice not to limit the attendees to men only.

Despite the rigidity of bereavement practices during the Victorian era: the regulations governing clothing styles, formal and informal visits, and appropriate home ornamentation, death was embraced rather than avoided. Inspirational pieces extolling the departed were published on an ongoing basis. "Guardian Angels" by Daniel Jay Sprague appeared in the November 1858 issue of *Godey's Lady's Book*. The outpouring of emotion found an echo in Frank's desolate soul: "Each heart has its own Necropolis, filled with the memory of the loved and forgotten. The blessed dead! How free from stain our mutual love! . . . The glorious dead! How glorious are they! How reverently we speak their names! How fondly cherish their words in our remembrance! . . . The immortal dead! How joyous are they mid the fountains of undying pleasure! . . . How they earnestly entreat us to holiness, and touchingly chide the sins and follies of our lives."

While Frank gave in to his awful grief, Anthony and his wife, Ellen Rosét Drexel, offered to take the motherless girls into their large and airy home where they would join their young cousins. Frank's misery must have been acute to relinquish his children, but that's precisely what he did. Every hope he'd had for stability, for the sheltering world of wife and little ones, was gone. The sense of abandonment he'd experienced when still a child had returned, and his introspective nature grew more brooding.

Without knowing her mother and with little Lizzie as her companion, the baby was sent to live with her uncle and aunt. The day was frigid, the streets slick with ice and grimy snow. Lizzie, baffled and fearful, whimpered and wouldn't be consoled. Her tears caused her sister to wail, but Lizzie didn't explain why she was crying. Hannah's name wasn't mentioned, not by Frank who clung hopelessly to his children, nor by Ellen and Anthony, or by Lizzie even when she grew older. From that time forth, Hannah Langstroth Drexel became a nonperson. Katie wouldn't learn of her existence until she reached her teens.

Ellen Rosét Drexel and Anthony had been married eight years when Hannah died; they had also left the chic confines of Rittenhouse Square, building a new home in what city directories designated as "W.P." (West Philadelphia). The decision to decamp to the unfashionable west bank of the Schuylkill River was ostensibly an issue of space; the rambling two-and-a-half story stone house at William and Walnut streets—between 38th and 39th—was built on a property that took up most of a city block, and cost an extraordinary $20,000. The truth was more complex. Like Frank, Tony had been denied a formal education, a fact that embarrassed him deeply and later provided the impetus for creating the university that now bears his name. Moving west of the Schuylkill allowed him to escape the tightly knit clan of old-money Philadelphia, and with it any perceived censure of the Drexel family as arrivistes, or worse, *unsophisticated* arrivistes.

Frank's infant daughter and the toddler, Lizzie, joined the couple's three children: Emilie, seven, Frances, five, and Mae, three. Emilie was the leader of the group, and a tomboy in the making. The spacious, sun-filled home that was the antithesis of Frank's house was her realm, and her sisters and cousins her adoring subjects. Until 1862 and the birth of the first of four sons, Tony and Ellen's home was female-centric. A warm and smiling mother and aunt, Ellen was sensible, compassionate, and unfailingly patient; her husband was equally indulgent and generous. Despite his public appearance of reticence or even sternness, in private he was another person altogether. He believed in spending his money, providing his family with the material goods he'd lacked as a child. If his wife declared that only pure, white flowers should grace her tables—and she did—no expense was spared in procuring them. Decades later, during the early years of twentieth century, when his youngest child, George, owned the largest privately held steam yacht in the United States, the 287-foot *Alcedo*, it was outfitted as sumptuously as a palace; aboard George entertained European royalty, including Tsar Nicholas, on the grandest possible scale. The son of a one-time itinerant portrait painter denied his own offspring nothing.

In this permissive and carefree environment, Katie and Lizzie blossomed. Because Tony had gone to work for his father at the age of twelve, he'd developed a reverence for education of every type. The home was filled with books. To him, reading wasn't a duty; it was pleasure. For the children, there was *McGuffey's Newly Revised Eclectic Fourth Reader*, its pages brimming not only with lessons in elocution, science, and mathematics but also with adventure stories, poetry, and plays of high adventure like *William Tell*. A favorite form of entertainment was amateur theatrics, which were performed in an upstairs sitting room that served as an impromptu stage, its furnishings, jardinières, and flowering plants adapted to various real or fictional settings. Trunks of costumes and props were sources of wonderment for the five children, spilling forth exotic robes and headgear of riotous colors. The productions were so popular that generations of Drexel descendants carried on the tradition, each new wardrobe trunk containing favorite pieces of inherited clothing.

As the eldest, Emilie assumed the role of star actress, dictating the rearrangement of the room's furnishings: chairs and tables being clustered together to form snow-covered mountain passes, and ferns and flowering plants transformed into forests, primeval and otherwise. The smaller children were supplied with lesser roles, or sometimes leapt about in unconstrained glee while Emilie soldiered on. She liked reciting poetry. Longfellow's "Hiawatha" was a favorite:

> *Swift of foot was Hiawatha;*
> *He could shoot an arrow from him,*
> *And run forward with such fleetness,*
> *That the arrow fell behind him!*
> *Strong of arm was Hiawatha;*
> *He could shoot ten arrows upward,*
> *Shoot them with such strength and swiftness,*
> *That the tenth had left the bow-string*
> *Ere the first to earth had fallen . . . !*

Then there were lines like "Give me my bow and quiver!" from *William Tell*, a story that found special appeal because it reminded Tony of his father's youthful adventures in Switzerland.

The fable about the spider and the fly, or William Cowper's humorous "The Nose and The Eyes," were both in *McGuffey's*, one of the books most requested to be read aloud, a task Tony relished. This was the beginning of the close bond between uncle and niece: Katie nestling close, then asking to have the story reread again and again.

As with most affluent Philadelphians, education was undertaken at home, and governesses and tutors hired for specific duties. In Tony's household, a backlash against his purely practical instruction caused him to place a strong emphasis on the glories of language. Katie, at this highly impressionable period, learned to revere the power of words.

As nurturing as this insular world was, by 1860 Philadelphia had began spiraling into a state of crisis. The cause was slavery in the South. Commerce in the city had close links to that of the Southern states. Philadelphia textile mills depended upon southern cotton, which was woven into "cottonade," a cheap, sturdy fabric that was resold to slave owners. Calico printed in factories in the Northern Liberties was shipped to Africa and traded for boatloads of slaves that were carried on an oblique route to the islands, and thence to the mainland. Additionally, wealthy Northern families had married into Southern slave-owning families, and nearly half of the students attending Philadelphia's prestigious medical schools were from slave states.

With John Brown's raid on Harper's Ferry in late 1859 and subsequent execution, tempers on both sides of the abolition argument reached a boiling point. Public rallies either vilifying or defending slavery were met with threats of violence or actual attacks. Rage and reproach roiled across the metropolis, even threatening the inviolability of its houses of worship. At St. Peter's Episcopal Church at Third and Pine streets, a vestryman and respected attorney, Sydney George Fisher, published an incendiary, pro-slavery tract entitled "The Laws of Race" in 1860. He found willing adherents to his views among members of his congregation, and an equal number who decried the work.

Like Sydney Fisher, Tony and Ellen were Episcopalians, members of the newly built Church of the Savior. Ellen had been raised in the Episcopal Church; marrying her, Tony chose to leave the Catholic Church and embrace her religious practices. Given the sometimes-lethal clashes that had occurred between Philadelphia's Protestants and Catholics beginning in the 1840s, it's a testament to the bonds of family that the brothers were able to support each other's separate theologies.

Tony's and Frank's parishes survived the battle over abolition, but St. Peter's, which had been founded in 1761 and had stood firm during the Revolutionary War and British occupation of the city, came close to closing its doors during the years leading up to the Civil War. Fisher's publication may not have been responsible for the chasm splitting the congregation, but his opinions in "The Laws of Race" widened the gulf:

> The white race must of necessity, by reason of its superiority, govern the negro whenever the two live together. . . . Herein lies the difficulty of the case . . . [an evil] that arises from the nature of the negro, and not from slavery. He makes no spontaneous moral or intellectual progress, whether a slave or free. . . .

He acquires no arts, he builds no cities or ships, he invents no machinery, he paints no pictures, he writes no books, he makes no laws, he cannot appreciate truth or beauty. . . . He must therefore be governed, guided, cared for; and slavery which gives him a governor and caretaker does not oppress, but elevates him. . . . We therefore maintain slavery, not because we do not love liberty, but because we believe the negro unfit for it.

The Wide-Awakes, a political phenomenon that sprang forth in 1860 and attracted thousands of northern young men to largely silent nighttime marches, created a glorified, pseudo-military masse in support of Abraham Lincoln. Wide-Awakes wore specially designed uniforms, fashioned from enameled cloth that shimmered in the torchlight that accompanied their processions. It was a popular belief that the Republican Party could claim half a million Wide-Awake "soldiers." Before true war arrived, the nation's northern youth were already gearing themselves for battle.

Katie, though still a toddler, couldn't have helped but overhear her adult relatives and family servants discussing the racial crisis engulfing the nation, and that would soon develop into the Civil War. "Why?" is a two-year-old's favorite question. Given her personality as an older child and adult, she would have been certain to demand answers.

———

During the autumn of 1860, issues of race weren't paramount for Kate and her sister. Their father, Frank, had married Emma Bouvier on April 10 of that year. Following a European wedding trip he'd returned to Philadelphia to establish a home at 1503 Walnut Street for his bride and his children. Katie and Lizzie were taken away from their aunt and uncle and brought to live with their father and stepmother. It had been twenty-two months since they'd seen him. Lizzie could scarcely remember him, and Katie not at all. Making the reunion more difficult, the residence, which was three blocks east of Rittenhouse Square, was nothing like Tony and Ellen's cheerful abode. Stylishly decorated with dark Renaissance Revival furniture, draperies and carpets in somber colors, stiff arrangements of preserved flowers displayed within bell jars, and clusters of objets d'art covering every surface, the place had an austere, untouchable appearance, especially for a child. Emma had also installed a private chapel, and an organ for Frank, who regularly filled the house with thunderous, melancholy melodies.

A daughter of Louise Vernou and Michel Bouvier, a French émigré and cabinetmaker turned successful real estate speculator— Bouvier at one point owned fifty thousand acres in what became West Virginia—Emma was nothing like the girls' ebullient aunt. Her father had arrived in Philadelphia in 1810, then established a shop with a steam mill on south Second Street where he specialized in the veneers and marbles popular in Europe. Early customers included financier and fellow Frenchman Stephan Girard and the Comte de Survilliers Joseph Bonaparte, brother of Napoleon Bonaparte, who had built a palatial chateau on the banks of the Delaware River north of the city. Jacqueline Bouvier Kennedy Onassis was the great-granddaughter of Bouvier's son John.

Devout Roman Catholics, the family carried with them a certain Continental élan. They spoke French at home, and Emma relied almost exclusively on her mother and sisters for companionship and advice. She had no need to reach out to her in-laws, and she didn't. The snub earned her a reputation for arrogance. Rigorous in her devotional practices, she regarded her Episcopalian sister-in-law with dismay. Frank's sister Mary met equal displeasure as she had also married out of the Roman Catholic Church when she wed John Diederich Lankenau, a leading Lutheran layman. The Drexel family's pluralism reflected the polyglot nature of the country and represented William Penn's ideal of religious tolerance, but Emma mistrusted such liberality.

On the day the girls arrived at their new home, the elegant if exacting Emma and formal, à la mode surroundings bewildered the children. Wide-eyed, they huddled together in their matching dresses with large, utilitarian pockets that were so very un-Parisian, staring at a woman attired head to toe in imported taffetas and Lyons lace, her hoop skirt voluminous, her waist pinched, and her hair arranged in a complex coiffure of false braids, cushions, and pearls. Despite her smiles, she was an unknown quantity. So was their father. Would the two be fun-loving like Aunt Ellen and Uncle Tony, or strict like their grandparents? Katie, usually garrulous, clung to her sister's hand and said nothing; Lizzie dropped a polite curtsy then hung her head. When asked by their father to say "Mamma" they did so in two small whispers.

During the initial weeks of settling into the Walnut Street house, the sisters were bombarded with painful emotions: the sudden loss of Aunt Ellen and Uncle Tony and their cousins, fear that "Papa" and "Mamma" wouldn't love them, and fear of not obeying the rules of their new home. Despite Emma's efforts to draw them out, the girls remained shy and uncommunicative, behavior they'd never evinced before. When a nursery maid accompanied them to statuary-filled Rittenhouse Square, three blocks from their new home, they yearned for the garden at their uncle Tony's, and the games of hide and seek they'd played with their cousins. They didn't want to act like perfect little ladies while strolling the manicured paths. They wanted to have fun.

Whatever domestic dramas were being enacted or secretly endured as Emma and Frank established the routines of family life, a national tragedy was looming. In 1861, President-elect Abraham Lincoln arrived at the State House, now Independence Hall, to commemorate George Washington's birthday. The crowd lining Market Street on that icy February day blocked the thoroughfare. Abolitionist and pro-slavery rhetoric had reached a fever point. An assassination was rumored to await the President-elect during his journey by train through Baltimore; at the inauguration, sharpshooters were ready to be deployed. The words Lincoln spoke inspired an uproar of patriotic fervor that drowned out the naysayers. Those listening were ready to do battle for the cause of justice and freedom for the enslaved.

I have often inquired of myself, what great principle or idea it was that kept this Confederacy so long together. It was not the mere matter of the separation of the colonies from the mother land; but something in that Declaration giving liberty, not alone to the people of this country, but, hope to the world for all future time. It was that which gave promise that in due time the weights should be lifted from the shoulders of all men, and that all should have an equal chance. This is the sentiment embodied in that Declaration of Independence. Now, my friends, can this country be saved upon this basis? If it can, I will consider myself one of the happiest men in the world if I can help save it. . . . But, if this country cannot be saved without giving up that principle—I was about to say I would prefer to be assassinated on this spot than to surrender it.

Lincoln's speech and ideology were widely discussed within the larger Drexel family, just as the issue of abolition had been. Part of the fortune Francis Martin Drexel and his sons had amassed served to promote the Union's cause when hostilities commenced. Drexel & Co. floated a loan in the amount of $60 million to the United States Treasury to aid the war effort. An obligation that size wasn't entered into lightly; although business was conducted at the firm's marble-fronted edifice on Third Street, private conversations weighing the pros and cons of the loan, its inherent risks and moral imperative, were heard in every Drexel household.

Back-stairs conjecture also focused on Lincoln's message, providing another forum for information for Katie and Lizzie who spent a good deal of time with the maids and cooks, listening to their talk and comparing it with what they overheard above-stairs. Despite the rigidity of Emma's managerial style, her staff was as loquacious as any other. Popular ballads like those of songwriter and musician Henry Clay Work were sung, warbled, and whistled by everyone from the laundress to the men delivering coal or groceries or milk to the sweeps hired to clean the chimneys along Walnut Street. For a child with a vivid imagination, the bitter reality of battle was confronted on a daily basis when she heard "Brave Boys, Are They," or "Our Captain's Last Words":

May the bright wings of love
Guard them wherever they roam;
The time has come when brothers must fight,
And sisters must pray at home . . .
"Boys! you follow now another;
Follow till the foe shall yield;"
Then he whisper'd, "Tell my mother
Stephen died upon the field."

Because Philadelphia was the largest industrial city north of the Mason-Dixon line, the metropolis often resembled an armed camp. During the war years 900,000 men passed through Philadelphia. Disembarking at the port, they were fed at hastily erected "Refreshment Saloons" before being marched westward to meet southbound trains. On their way, they were cheered. The returning wounded were nursed at facilities specifically constructed for that purpose; they were the largest military hospitals in the country; Satterlee General had 3,124 beds; Mower General, 4,000 beds. At the height of the conflict, all were filled. On Gray's Ferry Road, the Schuylkill Arsenal served as principal depot for the Quartermaster's Department; the Frankford Arsenal manufactured munitions; warships were built at the city shipyards. Rittenhouse Square became a drilling ground for the University of Pennsylvania Light Infantry. Even the State House wasn't exempt; rows of tents fronted it, the soldiers' laundry stretching on ropes strung between the trees.

Despite all the activity, the outcome was far from certain; the loss of loved ones was a constant. When General Robert E. Lee's troops entered Pennsylvania, approaching Harrisburg in late June 1863, many Philadelphians assumed it was only a matter of time before the Confederate Army conquered the Army of the Potomac. They understood that the city would not be spared.

In the Drexel households, the threat of the Union's defeat intensified a personal tragedy. Francis Martin, the family patriarch, died June 5 at the age of seventy-one. Ever impetuous and impatient, he'd been returning home aboard the Reading Railroad following a visit to Pottstown, Pennsylvania, when he attempted to alight as the train began to slow at 18th and Willow streets. His foot slipped and he fell across the track while the moving locomotive rolled forward and crushed both thighs. Carried home in agony, he underwent an emergency amputation but survived the surgery by only a few hours. Family lore subsequently maintained that Drexel had been pushed by a Southern sympathizer angered by the financier's political leanings. Whatever the truth behind Francis Martin Drexel's death, it's certain that had he lived he wouldn't have adapted well to his physical impairment. Shrewd, iron-willed, brilliant in his fiscal speculations and calculations, he had always been a man in a hurry. An editorial in the *North American and United States Gazette* extolled him thus:

> In his personal habits Mr. Drexel was plain, simple, frugal and unostentatious. From his diversified experiences, he had acquired great stores of information and a keen insight into human nature, which contributed greatly to his success. He was possessed of a strong, clear intellect, was diligent in business and was gifted with a remarkable ability in piercing to the innermost the merits and demerits of every plan or scheme submitted to him. . . . This community is deprived of one of its most valued citizens.

So prominent a public figure was he that the newspaper broke with the tradition of respecting the deceased's family's privacy and reported on the funeral, describing the choral music, "Kyrie Eleison," "Dies Irae," and Requiem Mass by Ohnewald, and a hymn "Angels Ever Bright and Fair" "excellently sung by Miss. P. A. Donnelly." For the staid *North American*, the attention was unusual; the columns devoted to Drexel's fatal accident, death, and interment competed for space with the news of the siege of Vicksburg.

What wasn't mentioned was that Holy Trinity, the Roman Catholic Church at 6th and Spruce streets where he was buried, had—and still has—an impressively large altarpiece painted by the youthful Drexel when he was trying to establish a lucrative career as an artist. It's tempting to ponder his reaction to that Crucifixion scene when he became older, a man whose life had carried him in a direction he could never have envisioned when he'd perched on a ladder, palette and brushes in hand and filled with creative ardor. When he worshipped at Holy Trinity (to this day referred to as "the Drexel church"), did he gaze at his work in wonderment at his transformed status? Did he feel a niggling sense of regret at relinquishing those earlier dreams? Or did he simply nod his head: the successful gentleman of affairs acknowledging the necessary demise of the young romantic?

The prescribed year-long period of mourning in Frank and Emma's house was lessened with the birth of Louise on October 2, 1863. It was the same day as a massive rally for factory workers and shopkeepers in support of the Union, as well as the hanging of a condemned Yankee spy in Richmond. The nursery atmosphere that filled the Drexel home helped deflect the anxious mood pervading the rest of the city.

An infant to dote upon and an increased rotation of visitors dispelled gloom. Far from being the cause of sibling rivalry, Louise was considered a gift. She made her parents smile and her father laugh, which was a great relief to his two older daughters. Coddled and encouraged, "Lou" outpaced Katie as the family clown. Even when she was learning to talk, she shouted out whatever she wanted and whenever she chose, and Emma, so determined to make proper young ladies of Lizzie and Katie, did little to stem this wild behavior. Below stairs, the staff was equally indulgent. The kitchen might be bustling with activity, the doors of the iron stove swinging open and shut as coal was added, or cakes set to bake, or poultry to roast, but there was always time for the baby of the family who, despite Emma's disapproval of candies and sweets for children, developed a sweet tooth from being bribed with sugared biscuits.

On April 9, 1865, the seemingly interminable war finally ended when Robert E. Lee surrendered at Appomattox Court House. For several days prior, every newspaper and weekly magazine led with the story: the occupation of Petersburg, the occupation of Richmond, and subsequent visit by President and Mrs. Lincoln. Even the battlefield correspondence between Grant and Lee was reported in full. When victory was declared, the dailies erupted in exclamation points: "Peace!!! Lee Surrenders. The Rebellion Crushed! End Of The War!!" "Victory!! Victory!! Gen. Grant's Sun at Austerlitz! Lee Finds His Waterloo."

Philadelphians celebrated wildly. Patriotic bunting and flags decorated every house; the demand for bunting was so great that importers ran out of stock, and those who couldn't afford to purchase new fabric ripped up old clothing and petticoats and refashioned them into flags. Brass bands, fireworks, one-hundred-gun salutes, bonfires combusting on street corners, church bells pealing continuously and a howitzer firing at the State House shook the city, terrifying the horses, setting the dogs baying and sending every hawk, sparrow, and pigeon aloft in startled flight. The rain and unseasonably cold wind couldn't dampen the enthusiasm, or quench the bonfires, or curtail mass gatherings of people who flooded the streets. Determined though she was to keep her stepdaughters away from rowdy crowds, Emma couldn't prevent Frank from taking Lizzie and Katie to watch the ebullient displays.

On April 14, jubilation turned to despair when the president was assassinated. The news reached Philadelphia the following morning, and the reaction, as it had been to the declaration of peace, was swift. To a nation supposedly accustomed to bloodshed, the act was unimaginable. The president murdered: how could such a heinous deed be perpetrated, and by what deranged psyche? The residents of the southern and northern states may have been divided politically and philosophically, but they considered themselves civilized peoples who didn't shoot presidents in cold blood as they sat enjoying the theater. Reports about John Wilkes Booth and his plot to kill the president consumed every front page. It was revealed that Booth had boasted to a confidant that he intended to go to Ford's Theatre, and to expect "very fine acting there tonight." At the time, the assassin's whereabouts were unknown, turning him into a demon intent on eluding justice at any cost. When one of his co-conspirators was arrested in Baltimore, a long letter Booth had written describing his plans was excerpted in newspapers throughout the nation, further inflaming an already frenzied public.

With Lincoln's death, Philadelphia's appearance and mood changed overnight. Gone were the brightly colored flags; in their place crepe and alpaca draperies hung from each building; houses of worship remained open around the clock; commerce ceased. The city that welcomed Lincoln's funeral cortege was awash in black, the silence beneath a brilliant blue sky complete.

At 4:30 p.m. April 22, the train bearing the president's body arrived at the rail depot at Broad and Washington streets. Thirty thousand mourners watched the train arrive; another 85,000 lined the route toward the State House where Lincoln's body was to lie in state; viewing was possible April 23 from six in the morning until midnight. Some 300,000 people congregated to pay their last respects. Caissons, batteries of artillery, detachments of cavalry, and infantry regiments moved through the streets; except for the sounds of the wheels, they were silent. The Drexel home at 1503 Walnut was along the route of the funeral procession. Emma argued against permitting the children to watch it; Lizzie was only nine, Katie not yet seven, and Louise still a toddler. Frank insisted that history taught vital lessons to everyone of any age, and that this was a day no American should ignore or forget. This time he won the argument. Together with their parents, the three girls gazed down from the upper windows. People of all conditions and races packed the roadway, or perched on rooftops or climbed lamp poles hoping for a better view. For the children, it was a nightmare vision: the tear-drenched faces contorted with emotion, the cortege noiseless save for the rolling wagons and tramping feet. Even voluble Lou didn't comment, or ask why everyone was crying.

When Lincoln's remains were escorted to the Kensington depot for the train's four a.m. departure, Beck's Philadelphia band played dirges as the cortege again proceeded in eerie silence; the crowd that followed the catafalque carried lighted torches; thousands of African Americans, unable to witness the earlier procession, marched among them. "The transition from jubilance to grief and woe was a shock more sudden than ever before befell a community or people," the *Philadelphia Inquirer* wrote, describing the president's death. A banner headline appeared above the newspaper's title: "The Nation Mourns Its Loss."

three

KATIE

WHILE THE CITY AND NATION ADJUSTED TO LINCOLN'S ASSASSINATION and emerged from the travails of the Civil War, bigotry increased rather than abated. The year 1865 marked the founding of the Ku Klux Klan in Tennessee; the same day that the Thirteenth Amendment outlawing slavery was adopted by Congress (December 6, 1865), Philadelphia announced that its nineteen streetcar companies would no longer permit black riders inside the carriages. All African American passengers, no matter their physical condition, were relegated to the platform; anyone daring to defy the rule was threatened with beatings, or worse. Few white citizens protested or even noticed the new rule; for the majority of the population in Philadelphia and the nation, racism was the norm.

The inequality of poverty if not of race was an issue Philadelphia's charitable organizations could and did address, however. In the Drexel household, Emma established a practical solution to the aftermath of war that had left widows and orphans unable to fend for themselves. Whether she felt she could accomplish more as a private individual, or whether her reclusive nature made her shy away from the role of church ladies' auxiliary member, the result was the same: she opened her home three afternoons a week in order to distribute rent money, medicine, and clothing to the city's poor.

"Never let the poor have cold feet," she told Katie and Lizzie when they were old enough to aid her charity work. The girls were in charge of making the applicants comfortable and conveying their needs to Emma, whose expensive gowns and refined air could make her appear unapproachable. Kate, always gregarious, talked easily to those who entered the house, smiling encouragement as she held their hands and cradled their babies. Walking among the beneficiaries of the Drexels' largesse, which was estimated at $20,000 annually, she delivered bundles of clean, folded clothes, or blankets, or coats and mittens when it was cold. Emma reminded her of her Scripture lessons as she carried out her tasks: "Thou shalt love the Lord thy God with all thy heart, and with all thy soul, and with all thy mind. This is the first and great commandment. And the second is like unto it. Thou shalt love thy neighbor as thyself." "For I was hungry, and ye gave me meat: I was thirsty, and ye gave me drink: I was a stranger and ye took me in: Naked and ye clothed me."

Pragmatic Katie, though, preferred the more direct: "Never let the poor have cold feet."

The scope of Emma's personal crusade reflected a changing role for women. During the Civil War, women had become single heads of households or had worked as medical nurses in field and recuperative hospitals. They'd successfully challenged the status quo, and were unwilling to relinquish their autonomy. An 1868 *Harper's Weekly* cartoon entitled "How it Would Be, if Some Ladies Had Their Own Way" depicted men as stay-at-home husbands, darning, sewing, and coping with squalling infants—contrasted with several chic women departing a theatre performance and lighting up cigarettes. In 1869, egalitarianism confronted the male-dominated medical profession when a group of students at the Women's Medical College, later part of Pennsylvania Hospital, took their seats in the amphitheater during a surgical clinic. After a naked male patient was partially exposed, catcalls and jeers rained down upon the women's bonneted heads. They were hounded from the room and into the street. When the same women graduated with medical degrees two years later, their ranks crossed gender lines as they joined other pioneering female doctors.

Those facts weren't lost on Emma. Women's suffrage may have been decades away, and the Drexel banking business the purview of men, but the house on Walnut Street was Emma's realm, and by extension, her growing daughters'.

Another strong female role model was Mary Bernice Cassidy, an Irishwoman with a soft, educated lilt to her voice, who was hired as the girls' governess. "Bern," as she would come to be called by her young charges, oversaw every aspect of their education. Schooled privately at home in an upper-story classroom with a sunny bay window, walls covered with pictures, a map rack, and well-stocked bookshelves, the Drexel sisters were tutored in reading, writing, history, mathematics, sciences, and languages. In addition to Miss Cassidy, Mademoiselle Clave was engaged to teach French, Professor Allen, Latin, and Mr. Cross, piano.

Bern insisted that learning structure and style was as vital a component in education as reading the classics, or developing musical proficiency. She expected her pupils to perfect a fluid technique that would serve them all their adult lives; and her curriculum became law in the third-floor classroom. It was Bern who decided that the tutorials should be followed by assignments in which the sisters wrote letters either to "Mamma," or to Louise when she was still too young for classwork. The compositions were intended to augment the learning process. Many of the letters to Emma were written in French, a language that caused Katie continual grief. Correspondence with Louise was easier.

Dear Louise,

I suppose you have often seen the moon shining in the heavens on a bright night and have wished that you could live in it, but I can tell you would not like it as much as you think... The sun does not go down in the evening, it stays up for two long weeks. Consequently, there are two weeks of daylight and two weeks of darkness. But in these dark times it would be illuminated on one of its sides by our Earth, which to the people of the moon (if there are any inhabitants) would look the same as the moon does to us, only thirteen times larger.

Creative writing was another facet of Miss Cassidy's curriculum, and one in which Katie excelled. Her pieces were full of humor, insight, and originality; she also had an excellent ear for dialogue and loved poking fun at social pretensions. *Nadal* depicted the European travels of "My Lady and my Lord Quinze Cent Trois de Rue Noix" and "their three delightful children," the eldest of whom considered herself "vastly important," and the youngest, Catherine, whom the twelve-year-old author described as "a frail, fair, delicate, little thing of twelve; with a slight and graceful figure; beautiful, diminutive feet and hands; and, in short, a very handsome child, lovely and attractive in the extreme." The story even had a tongue-in-cheek aside: "A friend has suggested to me that I should say something of the moral qualities of the peerless Catherine. Well I would; but as this friend will not tell me what *morals* are, and as I don't know exactly what they are, myself, I had better not venture on unsafe ground."

One of Kate's greatest joys during her early teen years was San Michel, the country house her father had purchased in then-bucolic Torresdale, fourteen miles from the city. It was a gracious home with tall windows set in a mansard roof, and a wide veranda dotted with chairs and tables that encouraged leisurely reading and writing. Jalousies kept the interior cool during the hottest days of the summer, and the sloping lawns led to flower gardens perfumed with phlox and roses. Nearby ran the Poquessing Creek, whose shimmering reflection could be glimpsed through the home's surrounding shade trees. For Kate, San Michel was a magical place. It was here that the constraints of town life vanished, as well as the era's stiff conventions. Noise and high spirits were the norm; there were stairways to roar up and down, cubbyholes to hide in, room upon room to dart through, stables and a barn to explore, and a hayloft to climb. And, of course, lessons with Miss Cassidy ceased while the family was in the country. Fond as the sisters were of Bern, they didn't miss memorizing multiplication tables or conjugating Latin verbs.

Emma underwent a startling transformation during visits to San Michel. Although her outward reserve and devotion to fashion remained intact, the moment she arrived she tossed aside the rigors of Victorian deportment as if ridding herself of her corset stays. Driving her own carriage—a liberty unheard of in the city—she took the girls on extended rides every summer afternoon. Often they covered sixteen miles a day with Emma urging the horses to greater and greater speeds. Those gallops along dusty rural lanes made an astonishing spectacle for the local farmers who stared in amazement and a good degree of disapproval as Emma and her brood flew past: the girls' bonnet ribbons and Emma's demi-train billowing backward in silken clouds. If Frank applauded her lack of circumspection, or winced every time the carriage returned, the horses steaming in their traces, and his wife and daughters' faces pink from exertion, he said nothing, preferring the role of passive paterfamilias, behavior that exacerbated Emma's edginess. She wanted him to be forceful; he preferred retreat.

If the sisters noticed their parents' discontent, they didn't question it. How and why adults behaved as they did weren't issues children pondered—even teenagers like Lizzie and Katie. It was understood that parents were mysterious and superior beings. Besides, their father was often away in town, and Mamma, except for those wild rides, was equally distant, preferring to remain in her room until lunchtime or later.

With scant parental supervision, and under the wing of an indulgent maid named Johanna, who'd been nicknamed "Boss" because she was the only person known to confront Emma, San Michel became a giant playhouse. Johanna never minded if "The Three," or "We Three" as they styled themselves, got dirty, as long as they were happy, and she argued with her mistress if she believed Emma was being too harsh. "Joe" thought her young charges could do no wrong; in turn, they loved her unreservedly, cheerfully teasing her and taking turns mimicking her thick brogue that was so different from Miss Cassidy's refined accent. Kate was especially good at copying Joe's speech and malapropisms; Johanna was too large-hearted to feel slighted. Instead, she was proud of being the center of the girls' attention.

This comfortable routine of life in the country and life in town, of Emma's charitable works, of daily prayers and Mass each Sunday, weekly visits with family members, and their father's punctuality when departing and returning from business was shattered by two painful events. One occurred when Kate was twelve; the other a year later. The first she overcame, the second she buried until much later in life.

In 1870, when Frank's mother Catherine Hookey Drexel died, her will left bequests to "all of my children living at the time of my death, excepting Mary L.B. Drexel (Louise), daughter of my son, Francis A. Drexel by his present wife, and excepting also any other child or children he may have had by her." In addition, she named Tony over Frank to act as her executor. Both actions stemmed from the old lady's displeasure with Emma. It was Frank who took the girls for their weekly Sunday afternoon visits to Grandmother Drexel while Emma stayed home, making excuses that her mother-in-law recognized as false. The rift between the women had created a tug of war of loyalties for Katie and Lizzie that dated to the earliest days of their father's remarriage, but, like their parents' sometimes moody silences, they considered the relationship normal. Louise, who was six when Grandmother Drexel died and unaware of the terms of her legacy, had experienced only polite coolness from her father's mother. It was Lizzie and Kate who felt spurned on behalf of their sister. The monetary bequest was unim-

portant; the sisters had everything they could possibly want. It was
the unfairness of the situation that hurt. They couldn't understand
how anyone could be unkind to a friendly little girl like Lou.

Far worse than the problem of Grandmother Drexel's bequest
was the discovery Katie made when she turned thirteen. Until
then she'd assumed that Emma was her birth mother. Hannah had
never been mentioned, although Lizzie had a vague recollection of
her; and everyone from the extended family of Langstroths and
Drexels to Miss Cassidy was aware of the situation. Kate had been
kept in the dark either purposely or from a kind of neglect, and the
lie—or misconception—once begun was difficult to terminate. In
Frank and Emma's defense, explaining the circumstances surrounding Hannah's death might have led a younger Katie to believe she
was responsible somehow, and that her birth had culminated in her
mother's demise. But given Emma's need to control her physical
and emotional environments as well as her underlying insecurities,
the omission appears intentional. Her gallops through the countryside near San Michel reveal a high-strung woman who kept her
passions in tight rein until she simply couldn't harness them any
longer; and she probably suspected her family's love and devotion
were as unreliable and turbulent as her own passions.

Kate learned the truth under the most ordinary of occurrences.
It was customary for the girls to spend part of Saturday at the senior Langstroths' home in Germantown, and each week Joe or
another maid—never Frank or Emma—escorted them. Kate
delighted in the excursions and the special children's playground
her grandmother had equipped for her and her sisters and cousins.
At thirteen, growing bored with dolls and wishing to spend more
time with the adults, she posed a simple question: Why were she
and Lizzie lucky enough to have *three* grandmothers to dote on
them when Louise had only *two*. As a result of this innocent query,
she was told about her father's first wife, Hannah Langstroth
Drexel.

The teen years are a volatile time in a girl's life; mother-daugh-
ter relationships can be tense at best. Here was a bond Kate had

assumed was maternal and loving; now it was ripped apart. Kate couldn't imagine how she'd ever be able to love Emma again.

If she'd been anything like her uncle Tony and aunt Ellen's daughters, or lived in the same permissive environment they did, she would have given voice to her dismay, making the home a stormy place full of hurt, recrimination, and tears. But she didn't. Despite her impulsive, impatient, and sometimes stubborn nature she said nothing. Neither did Emma or Frank after the initial explanation; and Kate's quiescence on the subject fooled them into believing she didn't care.

She did care, however, and deeply. Bitterly wounded, she retreated into herself. "We Three" ceased to exist while she made excuses and found solitary places in both the country and town houses where she brooded alone. She didn't even confide in Lizzie, and she'd been accustomed to share everything with her elder sister. A pattern of stoic self-reliance began.

Her fable "Wanted Gardeners" was written during this difficult time, its tone no longer playful but filled with sorrow and disillusionment. Although composed for one of Miss Cassidy's assignments in style and structure, it was a cry of anguish.

I have renounced my belief in fairies and hobgoblins this many a long year. All we old folks have, and I, of course, amongst the others. Merry Krisskringle with his six reindeers and sleigh full of toys. Goody Two Shoes, and poor little Cinderella were the first to die and live no longer to our childish imaginations; and then, kingdom upon kingdom fell. The Kingdoms of the Fair One with the Locks of Gold; of Rose Red, and Snow White; of Gracious and Percinet; the mysterious Kingdom of the Sleeping Beauty, and many others—all tumbled down, one day with a crash in the face of the practical realities of life, leaving behind only a heap of ruins to block forever the door of our childish credulity.

Imagine then, O Reader, my astonishment at what I am about to relate to you, and explain the following phenomenon, if you can.

Believe me, when I tell you that this morning, by wings unseen, I was carried, swifter than wind, through air and sky, nor stopped I until on the summit of a high and view-commanding mountain I found myself in the presence of a mighty palace build of gold and precious stones. I was filled with a desire of entering within—but in vain I tried each heavy door through which, as from a distance, faintly came melodious chorals most sweet and pleasant to the ear. Vain was it to peep inside the window-panes; for they appeared to be made of diamonds and sparkled with such marvelous brightness that mine eyes were unable to bear the refulgence of their reflected light. And now some unknown force seemed to drag me downwards, downwards, to the fertile valley below, over which the glittering castle looked from its high and frowning eminence. I ceased to move before a certain golden gate, on which I read these words "Garden for young Plants; enter."

As the story continued, the narrator encountered a desolate garden, its ruination all but complete:

Heliotrope and mignonette, violets and pensées struggled hopelessly through long and tangled weeds. The fig-trees and apple-trees, dwindled and bark-bound displayed nothing but brown and withered leaves. All through the long extent of garden did I wander miles and miles. A feeling of oppression and sadness stole over me. I cast my wearied eyes upon the ground, still walking on, and fell to musing. How was it that this garden remained desolate? How was it that these flowers ran wild and uncared for? The fertile soil and the young plants are indeed here, but where are the laborers?—I thought aloud, when to my surprise I found my queries answered by a pleasant voice, which seemed to come from someone near me.

Toward the conclusion, Kate's heroine noticed a small group of men and women working ineffectually to save the plantings. A mysterious voice then explained that the laborers were too few, and that the king dwelling in his distant castle grieved at the loss of each seedling and blossom. "O Stranger! When you again return to earth think often of the desolate garden, and of Him who asks for laborers. 'WANTED GARDENERS.'"

The passage can be viewed as prophetic, but it also reflected the centrality of worship to the family's life. Evening prayers were held in the home's private chapel; the rosary was recited daily; returning from work, their father customarily retreated for a time of meditation after which he played the organ. The practice of faith was a given; it was part of the fabric of existence, as it was in most homes of the period, whether Catholic, Protestant, or Jew. Kate, however, began to refashion her family's spiritual regimen into an intensely personal exercise. A duality in her nature was developing: the searching, meditative self who prayed fervently to God for guidance; and the fun-loving, teenage girl whom everyone believed was immune to doubt and sorrow.

She began keeping almost obsessive lists of perceived faults: *having impetuous ideas, want of calm and tranquility, not listening to others who have more experience*, although her outward persona remained effervescent, irrepressible, and vivacious. She was vain about the long, light-brown tresses that reached below her waist, took note of what her aunts and older cousins wore to cotillions and dinner parties, and judged which colors and fabrics were the most flattering and au courant. She begged Emma for clothes as beautiful as hers, but in the lonely privacy of her room castigated her own vanity.

On March 7, 1872, the tightly knit, domestic realm she shared with her immediate family expanded onto the greater world stage. The occasion was the wedding of her first cousin, Emilie, who married Edward Biddle in a sumptuous ceremony attended by President Ulysses S. Grant and his wife and daughter. Society pages were then unknown; it was considered the height of poor taste to trumpet personal information such as the names of bridesmaids, groomsmen, and guests, or the couple's respective lineages.

Reporters from the weekly *Sunday Morning Times*, which featured articles like "When May Diamonds Be Worn?" (answer: always) and had a regular column entitled "Balls and Parties," were kept at arm's length. The ceremony appeared as a mere squib in the March 8 *North American and United States Gazette*, the explanation being that the President was in town to attend the marriage of Anthony Drexel's daughter. That, of course, was enough. All of Philadelphia, as well as the nation, understood that if a United States president attended what was essentially a family affair, that family was among the country's elite.

To understand the change in the Drexels' status, it's necessary to step back to December 1864 when Tony, in partnership with his longtime friend George William Childs, purchased the struggling *Philadelphia Ledger*. At that time, the newspaper's editorial policy was strongly in favor of the Copperheads (who wanted a quick settlement with the Confederate states), which Childs, with Drexel as his financial backer, altered to one supporting Lincoln and the Unionists. The decision did more than rebuff the Northern "Peace Democrats," as the Copperheads were also known; it turned the *Ledger* into a profitable venture. Advertising rates rose; revenue increased. The newspaper, founded in 1836 as a "penny paper," cost twice that during the beginning of the Drexel-Childs era. The initial investment of $20,000 eventually generated profits of approximately $500,000 annually. By the time of his daughter's marriage, Tony's shrewd decision to enter the influential arena of publishing, as well as his guidance of the Drexel banking empire, elevated his standing and gave him entrée into the nation's political sphere. His acquaintance with Grant also began in 1864 when the general visited Philadelphia; Tony contributed to the purchase of a house intended for Grant's retirement following the war.

The advancement of the family's social stature allowed Emilie to break down the barriers dividing the *nouveau riches* from Philadelphia's old-money, old guard when she married Edward Biddle, a member of one of America's most prominent families. Urbane, handsome, a man-about-town who'd been schooled in

Europe, Edward was an avid sportsman and a considerable catch owing to his illustrious ancestry. But Anthony's eldest daughter had a fortune to recommend her, as did her sisters and brothers, who would also marry into the nation's aristocracy.

Although a grandson of the legendary Nicholas Biddle, the groom had little interest in financial affairs. Provided with employment at Drexel & Co., he aspired to a life of leisure, which Tony's wealth seemed to ensure: travel to fashionable resorts and frequent entertaining during the months the couple were "in town." Edward never adopted his father-in-law's rigorous work ethic, or abhorrence of idleness and waste. The differences in the two men eventually created a schism, and divided the couple's three sons after Emilie's early death.

On March 7, 1872, those future animosities were nowhere in evidence. Edward and Emilie made a glamorous couple: the twenty-year-old, fair-haired bride outfitted in a gown designed by Worth of Paris that was complemented by a necklace of pearls and diamonds while the groom with his equestrian's bearing was splendid in tailored black. Despite the journalistic silence surrounding the event, bystanders lined the streets on that Thursday morning, hoping for a glimpse of the president and his family, or the young couple, or other notable attendees. For them, it was as spectacular an occurrence as anything European royalty could boast.

For Kate and her sisters and cousins, the nuptials and their months of planning were equally enthralling. According to Victorian etiquette, they were considered too young to attend the ceremony and wedding banquet, but the preparations, the gifts—a grand piano from Frank and Emma, a silver tea set from George Childs, pearls from Mrs. Childs—the six bridesmaids in their white silk, point lace, and illusion, and the six groomsmen were the focus of endless conversations and conjecture. Emilie, who had once pranced about in outlandish costumes, waved spears, and recited poetry, was now the model for each girl's future: a cultivated woman whose family's position elevated her to the *haut monde*.

On the day itself, excitement reached a fever pitch. Emma wore a gown especially fashioned for the occasion, as did all the Drexel women. A progression of visitors came and went while "The Three" raced back and forth from the parlor to the kitchen, pantry and laundry describing everything they saw and heard. When the carriages pulled away, the girls were left daydreaming about their own wedding days. It was a given that the celebrations would be as splendid as their eldest cousin's and their bridal gowns as gorgeous. That night Kate summed up the event in her journal, then added a witty retelling of a conversation Emma overheard between the president's daughter and a young swain, underlining words that show Kate at her most superior and unforgiving self. In her estimation, Nellie Grant was shallow, silly, and dismissible while Kate was both clever and discriminating:

> President Grant, his wife and daughter, Nellie Grant, were at the wedding, along with everyone else you could think of who lives in Philadelphia. . . .
>
> Mamma heard Miss Nellie Grant say to a young gentleman "I like to read the newspapers, but I never read the deaths and marriages, I read the murders I do so love to read the murders, they are so interesting." The young man replied that he "liked to read the murders also, and the shipwrecks, they are so very exciting."

Grant's controversial 1870 "Peace Policy," the intent of which was to put "all the Indians upon reservations, where they will live in houses, and have schoolhouses and churches, and will be pursuing peaceful and self-sustaining avocations, and where they may be visited by the law-abiding white man with the same impunity that he now visits the civilized white settlements," probably wasn't among conversational topics at Emilie and Edward's wedding. Discussing politics was considered bad form on celebratory occasions, so the woes of Southern Reconstruction, and the Ku Klux Klan with its

"Midnight Riders" claiming to be ghosts of rebel soldiers killed in battle at Shiloh or Vicksburg, were politely avoided even though Drexel wealth had aided the Union cause. Besides, Grant's administration had begun focusing on international exchange and amity in the hopes of putting all memories of the Civil War behind it.

On March 7, 1872, the *North American and United States Gazette* made a brief reference to the Klan in a section entitled "By Telegraph and Rail": "Further Kuklux outrages are reported from North Carolina," but more ink was expended on the establishment of a women's gambling house in San Francisco: "the splendor of which is equal to that of an Arabian story," as well as to a formal reception the House of Representatives gave to the Japanese embassy.

The day following Emilie's wedding, the president met with members of the Centennial Commission to discuss an exposition scheduled to open in 1876. Drexel and Childs were eager proponents of the idea. Officially called the International Exhibition of Arts, Manufactures, and products of the Soil and Mine, the first major American World's Fair was to be built in the grandest possible scale. American prowess in manufacturing and engineering would be displayed in exhibition halls covering 285 acres of Fairmount Park.

During his State of the Union address in December 1871, the president had waxed euphoric when describing his vision of future world peace: "The year has been an eventful one in witnessing two great nations, speaking one language and having one lineage, settling by peaceful arbitration disputes of long standing and liable at any time to bring those nations into bloody and costly conflict. . . . I transmit herewith a copy of the treaty alluded to, which has been concluded since the adjournment of Congress with Her Britannic Majesty, and a copy of the protocols of the conferences of the commissioners by whom it was negotiated." The speech continued with the president's laudatory references to "His Majesty the King of Italy, the President of the Swiss Confederation, and His Majesty the Emperor of Brazil" as well as to "His Majesty the Emperor of Germany."

For Drexel & Co. these overtures were particularly welcome. Drexel, Harjes & Co. had been established in Paris in 1867; during the Franco-Prussian War of 1870, travelers carrying Drexel letters of credit had been temporarily stranded until quick action on the part of Anthony Drexel's French partners sent shipments of gold to Geneva and other European capitals in order to rescue clients from financial embarrassment.

An international impetus reflected itself not only in global entente but in Philadelphia's building boom during the 1870s. The synagogue of Congregation Rodeph Shalom designed by Frank Furness, the Masonic Temple designed by James K. Windrim, the University of Pennsylvania's College Hall designed by T. W. Richards all employed motifs that mingled French Norman bulk, English Gothic loftiness, and the Italian Renaissance's airy tracery. In the residences of the affluent, Gothic revival and Renaissance revival furniture—some crafted by German-born cabinetmaker Daniel Pabst in partnership with Frank Furness—banished to attic or auction the slim lines of earlier eras. Painters such as George Inness discovered the siren call of the Old World. Having an abbreviated tour of Italy in 1851–1852, he returned in 1872 for a four-year sojourn during which he painted landscapes for his wealthy American clients. For a family like Kate's, a Grand Tour of the Continent became obligatory.

In September 1874, Frank, Emma, and the three girls embarked on an eight-month journey, sailing aboard the Cunard Line *Scotia* in order to properly "finish" Lizzie and Katie's schooling in culture and the arts. Kate would turn sixteen in November, and Lizzie now styled herself a more mature "Lise" in anticipation of her debut into society. The lenient Joe was part of the group, but Miss Cassidy remained at home, with promises from "All Three" to write to her daily.

Bravado and a heightened sense of danger, drama, and romance bubbled through Kate's correspondence: "The crank of our engine broke on the tenth day of our voyage. Fortunately, however, we were able to mend it temporarily (that is to say it would work for one day and crack the next) or else, probably, if we had met with adverse winds, our respectable and esteemed names might have figured in the romantic account of a shipwrecked steamer and all the interesting horrors connected with the same."

With bright blue eyes and soft brown hair, she was growing up and gaining womanly beauty; and she, Lou, and Lise were off on an exhilarating adventure. The fact that the journey took twelve days and would go down in the *Scotia*'s annals as its longest North Atlantic passage to date added to its allure. Kate and her sisters were also granted unexpected freedom. While Frank and Emma remained in their staterooms until close to noon, or sat in the ship's library reading and writing, or reclined on deck chairs swaddled in plaid blankets, Joe took the role of chaperone, although she never reminded them to talk in ladylike tones, or fussed over etiquette and deportment. In fact, Joe sometimes encouraged their hoydenish ways. She didn't like pretensions any more than Kate did. "I have been having a really splendid time ever since we left New York and so far I have not been the *least* tired of sea life as we have a great many very agreeable passengers on board. There is a gentleman on board who astonished me greatly the other day by boldly asserting that Scott's Works are no longer enjoyed in Scotland. Now whether this young man considers himself a representative of North Britain, I know not; but I *do* know that he has not so much as scanned one of the Waverly novels, or any of Scott's Poetical Works."

By modern standards, this conversation sounds tame, but by the norms of 1874, Kate would have been considered quite the flirt. Young women of her station were instructed to treat gentlemen's attentions with artful reserve; it was expected that a marriage proposal would be refused the first, and even second and third times before being accepted. Often the reply was written rather than delivered verbally; if the woman intended to accept eventually, she would have found an encouraging phrase or two.

Kate, however, was behaving as "boldly" as her literary admirer. Reading between the lines, the exchanges—and there were numerous ones—would have raised eyebrows among the other girls' mothers and chaperones: Katie, unchaperoned, on deck or in the grand salon reading Sir Walter Scott. A young man approaches, asks if he may join her and noticing the book title, makes a sally about Scott's current popularity, which begins a lively, teasing exchange until Kate trumps him with one of her infectious smiles and demands to know what he thinks of *Ivanhoe* or *Waverly* or *Marmion*. If Emma had been present, she would have intervened, and the conversation would have turned stilted and dull, but Kate had only Johanna to stop her, or Lise to send warning signals her younger sister avoided.

Docking in Liverpool, the family hurried into London where they spent only one day on account of the ship's tardiness—they subsequently returned in May when Kate enjoyed "a jolly row on the Thames." Then they were off to Paris by way of Dover and Calais. "We arrived at the Hotel Meurice, in the evening of the sixth of October, & tired from our day's travel, we were soon dreaming about the wonderful city, which we were to see on the morrow. . . . I must say that I greatly prefer Notre Dame" to Westminster Abbey, which the family visited during their single day in London.

> It is that long sweep of aisle, extending around the whole church, even behind the central altar; the dim religious light thrown by those glorious old stained glass windows; & the tens and twenties of unexpected chapels, which make these European churches so attractive to us Americans, after our own stiffly planned places of worship. We next went to the sacristy to see the relics, which have been presented to the church at

various times by celebrated personages. No doubt the treasures may have been very elegant, but unfortunately we got into the midst of a regular crowd; & consequently could only hear "C'est beau, c'est splendide" ejaculated by a "Monsieur explication"— a nervous, quick old Frenchman. . . . He may have had a screw loose; but anyhow he was a very rich specimen of oddity.

Our second day in Paris was spent in racing everywhere to get hats for Lise and myself, but such was the disagreeableness of the shopkeepers that we had the greatest difficulty in getting them.

So much for the Parisians. On the return visit to Paris the following February, after seeing the rest of the Continent, Kate's feisty tone regarding the milliners, dressmakers, and cobblers the Drexel women encountered was no more forgiving: "They don't know any more than an inanimate object does about the meaning of the word punctuality." Impatience was, and remained, her bête noire.

In defense of her testiness, it's important to recall that she was being groomed to manage a large staff, and, presumably, more than one home where guests would be entertained at dinners that had upward of twenty separate offerings (not including desserts and ices) and where a ball supper might have sixty dishes. Organizing such events required precision and a gimlet eye for detail. Negligence and lassitude had no place in a well-run household, and Kate was following her stepmother's lead in punctiliousness. An exacting mistress, Emma kept a journal devoted expressly to the maintenance of her two residences: farming methods, improvements in crops, flower planting, livestock, trees, and so on, as well as a detailed list of those who labored for her—about whom she vented much spleen. "Life is discipline and nothing more," she wrote of those she believed incompetent or indifferent. The same entry concluded with an aside intended as a warning to herself: "The discipline that hangs about us day and night and never leaves us but in sleep, and even then it may possibly inflame our fancy into a nightmare."

Given Emma's power over of the domestic purse strings as well as her private charitable contributions, it's interesting that Kate's letters and diary entries make scant reference to the family's public financial concerns, the Drexel, Harjes & Co. office in Paris, or business acquaintances in other European capitals. Here was another division of gender duties in which the young women were schooled during this "finishing" year. Men were intended to cleave to the world of affairs; women's jurisdiction was confined to the household. One of their duties was to bring culture into the home, although the distaff side was cautioned not to speak too learnedly on any subject; the adage being that women should shine, but not *too* brightly. Nor should money matters be discussed in public. Being stylishly accoutered was a means of revealing taste and distinction. No Grand Tour could be accomplished without purchasing the latest fashions, or crating up artwork to be shipped home. While Frank made the rounds of his fellow financiers and other professional colleagues, his wife and daughters took in the sights and shopped.

Quitting Paris, they left for Switzerland in order to avoid the onset of winter. As the train wound its way through France, Kate and her sisters chatted with fellow travelers. As on the ocean voyage, the rules of etiquette were ignored. The buzz of foreign languages added to Kate's feeling of leaping into the marvelous unknown, and there was no disapproving chaperone to keep her volatile nature in check. She was a young woman in a hurry, rushing along the train passageways or into the saloon cars, voluble, ebullient, in the thrall of all that was new. "Of course there were people from all parts of the world in the [railway] 'carriage' Americans, English, Russians, Brazilians. . . . I talked to Mlle. the Russian, who spoke English very well . . . and succeeded in finding out that all but the most ignorant Russians speak at least two languages. That French is spoken altogether in Society in Russia, that the Churches are never heated even in the coldest days, that her Pa had been governor of Siberia."

In response to her companion's revelation about her father, doubtless a competitive Kate parried by informing *Mlle.* that the

President of the United States had been a guest at her cousin's wedding, and that *her* father and uncle were famous the world over as financiers—boastful talk that Miss Cassidy would have proscribed if she'd been present.

Reaching the Alpine observatory at Kulm, Kate reverted to childish pranks despite the fact that she prided herself on wearing the latest adult fashion: velvet traveling dress, fur-lined cape, and bonnet trimmed with aigret. After recording her disenchantment with the fabled view of the Matterhorn and surrounding glaciers, she added: "I enjoyed myself, however, immensely in chewing, sucking, & stuffing myself full of the icicles that were hanging all around the Kulm observatory, & in eating snow." What Emma made of this spectacle is unrecorded.

Beside the letters home, Kate kept handmade journals into which she inserted leaves, flowers (although she admitted she felt like a thief when plucking them, and grew red in the face), tourist postcards, menus, as well as a steady stream of observations of her experiences in Germany, Austria, Switzerland, Italy, and France. From Interlaken, after a ride across the Wengern Alps at the end of October she wrote: "[Our] cavalcade started in grand array . . . waterproofs for riding skirts, shawls and cabas strapped on horses' backs. . . . Behold us on the summit of the Wengern in a cold rain, the avalanches thundering in our ears and every peak of the Bernese Oberland frowning down upon us from its awful height with towering menace."

Then it was south into Italy toward Florence, where the sisters spent hours in the Uffizi and Pitti Palace, and in San Marco, where the former monks' cells were decorated with frescoes by Fra Angelico. Kate was enchanted. It wasn't the religiosity of Florence that engaged her imagination: the Duomo, with its august dome designed by Brunelleschi, or Giotto's Campanile, or Santa Maria Novella, or the Basilica di San Lorenzo, which had been the Medici family's parish church. No, it was the sheer joy of looking at beautiful pictures. The fact that nearly all had biblical themes was of less importance to her than their transcendent loveliness.

"Paintings," she declared of this immersion into the city's artistic heritage, "have opened up to us a new world of pleasure."

The novice art historian who penned those lofty lines had a good laugh with Lise over two young Englishmen who happened into the Drexels' private railway compartment after leaving Florence for Naples and who strove mightily to impress. Again, flirtation is the subtext. Kate and Lise could have simply opened their books, or strolled the train's corridors, or pretended to doze. Instead, Kate encouraged the young men. "They really tried to make themselves agreeable, but constant talk and extreme amiability is very tiresome, for both parties, if extended over an entire day. . . The scenery in Wales, particularly on the summit of Snowdon is 'jolly beautiful.' They are very fond of balls they are so 'awfully jolly,' etc., etc., etc."

Finally, in Rome on January 1, 1875, her tongue-in-cheek remarks slammed into her rigorous efforts at self-improvement. The year prior, when the family's Grand Tour was already in the planning stages, she had vowed to become a better person.

January 1, 1874
RESOLVED that during the year 1874 to overcome
IMPURITY
PRIDE and VANITY
To speak French
Attention to Prayers
Attention to Studies
Also:
Read a life of the saint or some other good book such as The Monks of the West every three months. Novels of the day, etc. every once in a while. [a rule disregarded when it came to the novels of Sir Walter Scott]
Try to go to confession less as if you were going to an execution.
During the day & if prefer when clock strikes offer up all yr actions to God.

One year later in Rome, on New Year's Day 1875, she made no reference to those resolutions. Instead, she wrote: "Have only got a glimpse of Prince Humbert and the Princess Margaret, but have not seen his Majesty at all. Accounts differ about the Prince. One party says he's a model soldier who retires at eight, and others that he has all the vices of his Pa exaggerated."

Ardent, impassioned, impulsive, her contradictory feelings were heightened by the family's sojourn. In mimicking the worldly Continental wit and arched asides she learned from the family's European acquaintances, Kate was aiming for what she believed was a sophisticated ideal. However, she was also beset by her religious strivings, her yearning to be purer and better, to be worthy of God's love. Those seesawing emotions must have been painful indeed. Tellingly, she kept her inner struggles private.

A cautionary tale then in circulation throughout the capitals of Europe described a certain princess who had been summoned to court with her three daughters, because the queen intended to choose one of them to marry one of her younger sons. Obediently, mother and daughters made their appearance, driving up to the palace gates in their coach. The moment all four had descended, the queen approached the second daughter, and announced, "I choose her." Startled, the mother asked the reason for the sudden decision. Her Highness' reply was succinct: "I watched your young ladies get out of their carriage. The eldest trod on her dress and nearly ripped it. The youngest leaped from the coach to the ground. The second, lifting her dress in front of her, descended with grace and dignity rather than awkwardness or haste. She is well suited to be queen should the situation present itself. The eldest sister is too unrefined, the youngest too rash." This story may or may not have been apocryphal, but it made the rounds of salons, dressmakers' waiting rooms, and the tables d'hôte frequented by travelers with marriageable daughters. Whether Kate wanted to conform to its moral or not, the implications were clear.

In her depiction of the family's private audience with Pope Pius IX, her missive to Bern aims for sophisticated wit, describing how always irrepressible Louise exchanged a white silk calotte with the Holy Father, who was amused by her temerity. The only other

description of the day is a rather sheepish portrait of Johanna pros-
trating herself before the startled pontiff. It's as though the fifteen-
year-old who resolved to overcome impurity, pride, and vanity had
ceased to exist. A subsequent audience in 1887 with Pope Leo XIII
would transform Kate's life, but for the present she was trying with
all her might to mold herself into a young lady lauded for her élan,
and style, like her cousin Emilie.

four

A YOUNG LADY
OF PHILADELPHIA

THE YEAR 1876 MARKED THE NATION'S CENTENNIAL. CELEBRATIONS were held throughout the United States, but in Philadelphia, the city in which the republic had been born, those festivities took on epic proportions. The International Exhibition of Arts, Manufacturers, and Products of the Soil and Mine opened in May and spread across Fairmount Park, comprising two hundred buildings with a fence three miles long. It was an exposition built on superlatives. The Main Building—the largest in the world—covered twenty-one and a half acres; the building's central avenue measured 120 feet in width and 1,832 feet in length. Machinery Hall was fourteen acres in size; in the place of honor was the huge Corliss steam engine that provided power to drive the fair's eight hundred additional engines. Forty feet high, weighing two hundred tons and generating 2,500 horsepower, the Corliss was considered the exhibition's most spectacular invention, although Alexander

Graham Bell's new telephone was a close rival, and Thomas Alva Edison's Quadruplex Telegraph astonished, as did George Pullman's Pullman Palace Car, which was outfitted as sumptuously as a royal residence. Horticultural Hall was a Moorish-inspired fantasy in glass. The Art Gallery, also known as Memorial Hall, was built in the Beaux Arts style and was equally impressive owing to its glass and steel dome. Works by artists celebrated throughout the world were on display, statuary mingling with paintings, the gilded frames mounted from floor to ceiling.

The Women's Pavilion became the focal point for issues of women's rights. Having been denied permission to exhibit in the Main Building, Mrs. Elizabeth Duane Gillespie and her committee created their own space. A popular display highlighted Miss Emma Allison tending a steam engine while dressed in formal clothing. The engine powered the printing press that published *The New Century for Women*. Miss Allison insisted that her task was no less dangerous or tiring than working over a kitchen stove, though she never would have toiled in a hot kitchen attired in a frilled gown.

Blending the sciences and arts, the Centennial Exhibition introduced the United States as a pioneer in technology and industry. Bertholdi's Liberty Torch was on display—a fundraising scheme to provide capital to build the iconic statue. Prof. Franz Reuleaux, a mechanical engineer and lecturer at the Berlin Royal Technical Society who chaired the German Empire's panel of judges at the exhibition, was greatly impressed by what he witnessed, and later posited that the strength of a modern industrial society required strong bonds between craftsmen, industrial workers, and engineers, and that educational reform was a necessity. His book published in 1877, *Letters from Philadelphia* (*Briefe aus Philadelphia*), urged his countrymen to model technologies on an American ideal that combined efficiency and quality. (In 1941, Adolf Hitler would refer to the mechanical advancements Reuleaux saw on display in Philadelphia in 1876 as the instigation for German production superiority.)

In order for visitors to appreciate the size and scope of the exposition, a narrow gauge railroad looped through the grounds, and rolling chairs with attendants were available. The House of Public Comfort advertised separate parlors for ladies and gentlemen, retiring rooms, and a barbershop. Restaurants representing the cuisines of contributing nations beckoned; the Great American Restaurant was surrounded by an eight-and-a-half-acre garden; the George's Hill Restaurant bill of fare proclaimed "all modern languages are spoken." The opening-day crowd that crushed through the gates was described as the greatest throng yet assembled in North America. Invited guests heard an orchestra playing the national anthems of sixteen countries, Richard Wagner's commissioned "Centennial Inauguration March," and a one-thousand-voice chorus singing Handel's "Hallelujah" Chorus. By the time the Centennial Exhibition closed, more than eight million visitors had marveled at its ingenuity and beauty.

On the eve of this grand adventure in national and civic pride, George W. Childs and his wife hosted a reception for more than six hundred guests in their mansion; the evening's honorees were the emperor and empress of Brazil. The next day, President Grant and Emperor Dom Pedro II turned the valves that started up the Corliss engine and officially began the festivities. During the latter's reign, in 1871 an emancipation law was put into effect in Brazil; from that time forward every child born to slave parents was free. For the Philadelphians fortunate enough to meet him, the emperor represented sage leadership, the fabled wealth of Brazil, and the mystique of the Amazon, a place shrouded in legend and romance.

———————

Kate began keeping a hebdomadary diary, to record her experiences during the Centennial year. The suggestion had been Miss Cassidy's, but Kate, with her keen gift for observation, leapt at the notion. "Heb," as she referred to the journal, became a running monologue about life in the Drexel household and the city. She made the booklet herself, as she would later versions, adding sketches or inserting keepsakes, so the formal-sounding tome became as quirky and personal as any teenager's scrapbook.

Page one opened on New Year's Eve, 1875, with the family and city aquiver with anticipation:

> I am happy to say that our New Year's Eve commenced in the most patriotic manner, or if not in the most patriotic manner, at least with the most patriotic feelings.—Louise decorated herself with five penny flags and danced violently before the dining room door. Lise and I rushed around the house lighting gas for our illumination, whilst Hance was conducted to the balcony to drape our enormous "Stars and Stripes" over the balustrade. . . . I never felt more indignant than when I saw about three fourths of the houses on Walnut Street in total darkness, notwithstanding the express orders of the mayor that every citizen should illuminate and drape his house on the evening of the 31st of December. Chestnut Street, however, presented a more lively appearance. Nearly every building was brilliantly lit up; flags were waving in all directions; the store windows were draped with red, white, and blue goods; the street was thronged with people; a calcium light poured down its effulgence on the Chestnut Street Theatre covered with the flags of all the nations.

Lise's debut into society, her "first entertainment," received less attention. The life-altering event occurred twelve days later at home, as was customary, and consisted of a formal dinner for twenty-five adult members of the extended Drexel family. The debutante ball that subsequently became popular was considered vulgar at the time; a young lady's social sphere was circumscribed and her friendships with both sexes dictated by her parents. Given George Childs's reception for the emperor and empress of Brazil, though, Lise's celebration was remarkably constrained. The occasion may not have been intended as an opportunity to introduce a marriageable young woman to a potential spouse, but the lack of fun and frolic was conspicuous even by 1876 standards.

Excluded from the party because they were still considered children, and then sent to bed prior to the guests' arrival, which added insult to injury, Kate and Louise had to satisfy themselves with scaring around the house while it was being decorated, with green smilax vines draping the chandeliers, a profusion of hothouse flowers filling the public rooms, and the endless and varied *friandises*, all of which Kate recorded in her Heb, as she did a postmortem on the party the following day. Emma was in high dudgeon; she insisted the evening had been a failure, and declared it was nothing like the success she'd expected. Lise, diplomatic and deferential, didn't comment on the dull atmosphere, or the scrutiny she'd been forced to endure. Instead, she assumed a polite, submissive persona as if she were trying to become more worthy, more loveable, more like Emma's ideal of a devout, dignified lady. Kate took note: "conversation did not become general; the guests were inclined to be stiff." She wasn't about to allow the same mistakes to be made at her own debut.

If Lise never dared poke fun at her elders, Kate was too full of life not to. "Miss A. Antello seemed to consider herself a figurehead and stalked around in her black velvet dress without speaking a word to anybody." And she didn't exempt herself from her barbs, especially a near debacle that occurred on the Centennial's opening day. Although still officially a girl, Kate was asked to attend the ceremony with her aunt Mary Drexel Lankenau and uncle John. By rights, Lise should have gone in Kate's stead, but the eldest sister remained at home with Emma, while Kate, without a backward glance, reveled in the coveted invitation.

Good gracious! What a scramble there was to get me dressed before nine o'clock that I might join Uncle John Lankenau's party going to the Centennial Opening. I was in full time, however, and on arriving saw our punctual and fussy Uncle descending the stairs just preparing for a regular onslaught. . . . He was accompanied by the German Ambassador, a middle-sized bilious-looking man with light mustachios who was dressed on this occasion in an appallingly grand uniform of dark blue cloth trimmed with gold lace. Uncle John immediately introduced him as Baron Shibilibiloi, or some such unpronounceable name, and simultaneously off went the three cornered hat and a most reverential bow ensued. This kind of treatment went rather hard at first, being always considered a mere child at home, but I believe I acted my part of young lady admirably.

A diplomatic tussle ensued. Kate couldn't make up her mind about how to exit the house. She hung back in deference to her elders while the baron also stood aside to permit a lady—albeit one not yet introduced to society—to pass first. It was an awkward situation, both of them bowing and indicating the other should proceed. What could Kate do but press forward? Her face scarlet, she darted for the door, but once through was confronted with her uncle's carriage; and the entire miserable tug-of-war over who took precedence started again. She even swore under her breath. Swore! The disastrous story she'd heard in Europe about the princess and the three sisters' confrontation on the coach's steps had left an indelible mark. Anything but this blundering ceremony! And with the German ambassador! She, Kate Drexel, was about to become a laughingstock throughout all of Bavaria. Maybe even the European continent.

The incident, although resolved after more backing and filling and bowing, left her mortified. Her flushed cheeks worsened the situation—by then her ears were red, too—and came close to ruining the day she'd looked forward to with such enthusiasm. It took a while for her to regain her composure and enjoy the company of her uncle and aunt and the baron with the unpronounceable name. When the carriage arrived at the exposition, she still felt chagrined and self-conscious, but she forced a smile and straightened her spine and joined the crowd surging forward to take their seats for the festivities. The Emperor and Empress of Brazil, President Grant, several regiments of soldiers and the diplomatic corps arrived in appropriate pomp and majesty with the orchestra playing the national anthem of each country represented.

After the notables processed in, though, an uncomfortable hush fell on the gathering. Kate tried to determine what was happening and whether she should continue to stand or sit. No one nearby seemed certain what to do. Several people began fidgeting; Kate, remembering her recent humiliation, simply clasped her hands, bowed her head and prayed she'd get it right this time. "A silence ensued and something evidently was going on. In looking at the program it appeared that Bishop Sidney was repeating or mumbling the Centennial prayer. Not a sound reached our ear, but as I afterward heard, 'It was no small loss.'"

The rules of behavior were strict at 1503 Walnut Street, but caution was thrown to the winds during Lise and Kate's summer visits to Drexel and Biddle relatives at the New Jersey seaside. Frank joined them briefly when work permitted, but Emma's absence on the excursions was noticeable, and was remarked upon by her in-laws though they never shared their unfavorable opinions with her stepdaughters. "To outsiders I do not wear well," Emma explained, "because their first impression of me is agreeable, then further intercourse is a disappointment." Because she mentioned this rationale only to her immediate family, her in-laws firmly believed it was snobbishness rather than insecurity that kept her away; while Emma remained at home after dispatching her daughters and their wardrobe trunks on extended sojourns, the two factions grew more and more distant and aloof. The aunts began to seriously consider their roles as matchmakers for their nieces, as it was clear that Emma had no intention of taking on the all-important task and making certain her stepdaughters met eligible gentlemen.

After Kate made her debut in January 1879, an event that was just as torturous and forgettable as Lise's, the two now marriageable women were whisked away to Cape May or to Asbury Park, where Emilie and Edward Biddle kept a "beautiful seaside plantation." Several weeks each year they visited Seacliff Villa in Long Branch, where Aunt Ellen and Uncle Anthony and their cousins resided. There the young people burst in and out of doors all day long, or lounged on the broad chair-dotted veranda. Daily activities kept the family in continual motion; there were phaeton rides, horseback and sailing excursions, a houseful of dogs ready for a romp on the beach, crabbing expeditions, swimming parties, "hops" enthusiastically attended by both sexes and only lightly chaperoned, and horse races at Monmouth Park, where Kate declared the "best horses in America run," and of course the daily companionship of their voluble male and female cousins and their equally gregarious friends. Mornings were a free-for-all. While the adults remained at home, Kate and her cousins were dressed in their bathing costumes and plunging into the waves by 11 a.m. It was a chance to show off figures otherwise concealed, and they shouted and splashed and drew as much attention to themselves as possible.

Even dinner at Aunt Ellen and Uncle Tony's was a boisterous affair. In a shocking break with tradition, Ellen permitted the butler to ladle out the food rather than wait for her family and guests to serve themselves while he proffered the soup tureen or tray of boiled or roasted meats. Lise stiffly described this iconoclastic behavior in a letter to Emma, but Kate was in her element. She felt that taming her tongue or confining her emotions was tantamount to wearing a corset all day and all night, too. And she'd become an unabashed flirt. She fussed about which clothes looked the most becoming, and how to best style her hair. Hours were spent changing from one costume to the next, because a morning dress trimmed in violet satin would never do for tea or dinner. The results of her preening in front of a mirror, which she shared with her sister and cousins who drifted in and out of the room, she pronounced "stunning."

Recognizing how independent and free-spirited his middle child had grown, Frank felt called upon to admonish: "I hope you are careful not to get into deep water either with the Beaux or the surf." And: "Don't let that blue-shirted Englishman steal your hearts." Kate ignored the warnings. Lise did, too. At one point, the two sisters and their female cousins collectively fell in love with the fifth Maryland regiment, and Kate made her vexations known when a visit didn't include a number of lively new male acquaintances.

A flurry of engagements and marriages of the Drexel cousins took place in 1879–1881, but there were no serious suitors for Lise and Kate. Lise, who turned twenty-six in August 1881, was on the cusp of becoming an old maid. For her and her aunts and uncles, the situation seemed dire. Despite the continual intermingling of the sexes during their summer holidays, and a good deal of encouragement, Emma, in distant San Michel, acted as a kind of weight on her stepdaughters' hearts. She wrote them letters that were laden with self-pity, or posted querulous replies when their responses didn't meet her standards: "Audi filiae, never send me a badly or hurried postal. If you wish to write, take time to do so, if you cannot find time in a short visit refrain from pen and ink altogether rather than to disgrace yourselves by such a trashy slip as reached me this A.M. and left me very indignant." "Papa will be with you before this reaches you tomorrow. . . . Do your utmost to make his time pass agreeably, as a little brightening up will benefit him, for I sometimes fear that unconsciously to himself he finds home slow and his household a bore. At least his depressed manner might often bear that interpretation."

These weren't the only occasions when Emma tried to elicit her stepdaughters' aid in manipulating their father's emotions, or portrayed herself as helpless, long-suffering, and misunderstood. Hypersensitive and riddled with anxieties, she made frequent visits to her elder sister Madame Louise Bouvier, RSCJ (Religieuses du Sacré Coeur de Jésus, or Society of the Sacred Heart), a religious at the convent and school known as Eden Hall, but nothing bolstered her self-esteem or made her happy. Finding herself seriously ill in 1879, Emma kept the fact secret and underwent a bizarre home operation for what turned out to be breast cancer. Despite all medical advice, she didn't inform Frank of her intentions, hoping that by private, silent suffering her trim, attractive body would be as beautiful as it had been before, and that her husband would never learn about the disfiguring surgery. His reaction was despair. When he questioned the unwise choice, she responded that she didn't want to worry him or the girls. A new medical prognosis was sought, but Emma, never robust to begin with, grew weaker despite constant care. Lise, Kate, and Louise reacted to the emergency by spending additional time closeted with her in her bedroom and sitting room, cutting themselves off from their cousins and friends. Frank, always a homebody, was happy to have his daughters nearby and away from the temptations offered by beaux and overly demonstrative Englishmen.

Emma's condition worsened; and Frank decided on Sharon Springs, New York, for their annual autumn pilgrimage in 1882 so his wife could take "the cure." Having visited the White Mountains the year prior in 1881, and Colorado in 1880, he hoped that the popular spa fifty miles west of Albany would restore Emma's health. President Grant had stayed at Sharon Springs; so did Oscar Wilde, who staged a reading at the Pavilion Hotel on August 11, 1882. Eventually Saratoga Springs would outshine Sharon, but at the time of the Drexels' sojourn, it was a prominent retreat for the social set: the invalids among the guests gathering at the Magnesium Temple where they sipped glasses of murky, foul-smelling brown water and bathed in the sulfur, magnesium, and chalybeate mineral springs.

Despite the restorative waters at Sharon Springs, Emma grew weaker. Back home, she no longer left her bed, and doctors were in and out of the house every day trying but failing to alleviate her pain, which had become intense. Frank and his daughters' daily routine gave way to continual worry; meals were either overlooked or eaten in silence while the four waited for summonses from the sickroom. Once there, however, they could only look on in helpless pity. Often the patient didn't recognize her family. After months of suffering, Emma Bouvier Drexel died on January 29, 1883.

Immediately following the funeral, when the last guest had left the home on Walnut Street, Frank retreated to his room to pound away dirges on the organ; he remained there for hours. Kate and Lise, who had nursed their stepmother through her protracted illness, were overwhelmed by a sense of powerlessness. They couldn't alleviate their father's sorrow; they weren't even asked to share in it, and they'd been useless when trying to help Emma. Nothing they'd done or said had mattered in the least. Year after year, they'd told her how much they loved her, but had she ever truly believed them? Or had every one of those giddy seaside excursions wounded her beyond bearing? Full of questions that could never be answered, Kate, Lise, and Louise barely spoke to one another. Although the *Public Ledger* published an obituary on February 2, 1883, praising Emma's work among the poor, it seemed to Kate that the beneficiaries of her stepmother's aid had been more devoted to her than her own family. For two hours, following the funeral, hundreds of recipients of Emma's aid had lined up outside the home waiting to express their condolences. Genuine grief had streaked every face.

———

Hoping to escape the depressing atmosphere at home, Frank arranged to take his daughters to Europe again. This time, no milliners were called in to create new wardrobes, no pink silk with garlands of roses, no filigreed hair combs or bejeweled pins. Corseted and bustled though the sisters were, they were dressed in mourning.

The somber group sailed in October 1883 and didn't embark for home until April 1884. As she'd done previously, Kate kept up a stream of letters and journal entries, attempting but not succeeding in imparting a tone of cheer with her descriptions of visits to Brussels, Antwerp, Amsterdam, The Hague, Cologne, Nüremberg, Venice, Nice, Marseilles, Lourdes, and London. The pace was hectic; at each stop, happiness and peace eluded them; and they rushed on to the next city on the itinerary. When they spent a week at the Château du Puy near the village of Perpezac in south-

ern France, all pretense of pleasure had worn away. As Kate
described it: "Six long, long, long days and six dark, cheerless, cold
evenings made more gloomy by melancholy whist."

Walking with Louise at the end of their visit, Frank bent to pick
up a small stick and throw it out of the road. When his daughter
asked why, the answer was terse: he wanted nothing whatsoever to
hinder the family's departure the following day.

Returned to Philadelphia, they found the house as depressing as
when they'd left it. Frank didn't resume his work at Drexel & Co,
but Tony provided another job for him, sending him and Lise, Kate
and Louise west on the Great Northern line aboard the Pullman
Private Palace Car *Yellowstone*. Drexel & Co. had ties to the
Pennsylvania Railroad, and Tony needed to ascertain whether the
bonds for the new Northern Pacific Railroad made a good investment. Drexel employees Joseph Shoemaker and George Thomas
accompanied the party. The private railway carriage was supplied
by legendary railway magnate James Jerome Hill.

Despite the luxuries their rolling home provided—burnished
wood veneers, floral-patterned carpeting, damask curtains, and
chandeliers—the journey wasn't without danger. Thieves regularly
patrolled the rail lines, especially when they learned that wealthy
Eastern bankers in Private Palace Cars were aboard. When the
Yellowstone was sidetracked in Bismarck, North Dakota, so the family could attend religious services, their journey was delayed by
twelve hours, and the desperadoes who awaited them in Gardiner,
Montana, were outmaneuvered.

In such close quarters Kate gained insight into the world of
finance. She wasn't asked her opinion, but she listened. J. J. Hill's
success lay not merely in building rail lines but in creating communities along them: a continuous symbiosis of supply and demand.
For her, the expanses of the western states were no longer abstract
ideals of beauty that she had admired in Albert Bierstadt's landscapes of Yosemite and the Sierra Nevadas displayed at the
Pennsylvania Academy of the Fine Arts in Philadelphia, they were
real people with real problems, ramshackle huts, and tiny commu-

nities that housed Hill's underpaid and mistreated laborers. She had hours and hours to ponder the chasm between rich and poor, and then to dine on mock turtle soup and wonder why she'd been provided with so much and others with nothing at all.

Back in Torresdale and San Michel on October 5, the family returned to Philadelphia for the winter season. They were still in mourning, so there was no thought of social engagements, and Lou's debut into society was postponed indefinitely.

When Frank took a chill during a February 1 walk with Louise to Drexel & Co. at 32 South Third Street, no one took particular notice. He maintained his usual routine, but a cold soon developed into pleurisy, and he was put to bed under doctor's orders. Kate and Lise assumed roles as nurses; they were assured by both their father and his physician that he'd soon be in the peak of health again. No one was the least bit worried.

On Sunday, February 15, he felt well enough to sit up and read. Having dressed, he sat in his favorite chair, a wingback covered in faded damask that Emma had never been able to persuade him to forsake. Kate sat near him, chatting quietly or allowing him to read. It was a relief to see him improving both in body and spirit.

With her eyes half on her own book, she watched him remove his spectacles and place them atop a page to save the spot. He began to rise, then slumped backward in his chair. Leaping to her feet, she called to him, but he made no response. He didn't seem to hear her. In horror, she moved close, whispering "Papa . . . Papa . . ." then watched his eyes grow confused. He no longer recognized her.

She raced from the room, tearing outside in her thin dress and pelting through Rittenhouse Square to St. Patrick's Church to get a priest to come attend her father. The men assembled there regarded her in stunned silence as she screamed that her father was dying, which finally galvanized a member of the group into action.

Running back home without waiting for the priest to accompany her, she bolted up the steps to her father's room where she found that one of the servants had had the presence of mind to hail a cab and find a priest at St. John's. But Frank had died before last rites could be administered.

The will he'd created after the conclusion of their European journey the prior spring left an estate valued at $15.5 million, one of the largest then recorded in the nation. Kate was now an heiress of unparalleled wealth, but the legacy was the farthest thing from her mind. Instead her thoughts churned round and round, a spiral of internal damnation. While she'd rushed headlong into the streets, her dying father had been placed upon his bed. Had he asked for her? Spoken at all? Regained consciousness? None of the servants seemed able or willing to answer her questions. In her mind, their silence further condemned her. Had someone heard him speak her name? Or had he been alone when he breathed his last?

All Kate could do was stare and stare at her father's lifeless body. She was too enervated to pray.

five

AN HEIRESS

Her father's death dealt a critical blow to Kate's physical and mental health. Ardent and empathetic, she was unable to withstand the shock. Everything lost meaning for her, everything seemed hopeless; there were days when it was difficult to clamber out of bed. When she spoke, her words were few and perfunctory. Mostly she cried or stared into space, inconsolable and mute.

Aunt Ellen and Uncle Tony tried to help, opening Runnemeade, their country retreat in Lansdowne, to provide the sisters with a neutral space in which to grieve in solitude while Tony, George Childs, and their uncle John Lankenau, who served as executors of Frank's will, attended to the business of managing and dispersing the estate. Runnemeade, though charming, couldn't help but bring to mind happier days when the sisters' sole problems were the choices of daily entertainments and attractive attire. Then, too, their cousin Emilie, whose wedding had seemed so glorious when they were in their teens and who had became a mother of three little boys, had died after an unexpected illness, which was then called "heart affection," on January 21, 1883, another reminder of heartache and sorrow.

Drifting about in their mourning clothes and often in abject silence, they quit their uncle and aunt's home and returned to the house on Walnut Street. By then the normally docile Lise had taken charge; Kate, who had always been the most assertive of the three, merely followed her older sister's lead, but with an inertia that frightened her siblings. It was Lise who fixed upon a possible antidote to Kate's persistent apathy. The sisters would follow their father's example of philanthropy and establish a trade school to provide orphans with employable skills. The system was a new one; orphanage residents customarily aged out of the institutions, finding whatever labor they could or being reduced to penury and the poorhouse. The new school was to be called St. Francis de Sales' Industrial School in honor of their father's patron saint. It would occupy two hundred acres of land in Eddington, north of Philadelphia near Cornwells Heights. Kate agreed to the proposal, though her participation in discussions regarding the purchase and funding of the property and buildings was tenuous at best. She wanted her father back rather than a school.

Francis Anthony Drexel's will provided that from his net residuary estate—about $15.5 million—one-tenth was to be dispersed immediately to the twenty-seven institutions he had designated as beneficiaries, including the Cathedral of St. Peter and St. Paul, Conferences of St. Vincent de Paul of the Archdiocese of Philadelphia, St. Joseph's Church (on Willings Alley), Sisters of St. Francis, Philadelphia Theological Seminary of St. Charles Borromeo, Roman Catholic Society of St. Joseph for Educating and Maintaining Poor Orphan Children, Little Sisters of the Poor, Sisters of Mercy, St. Vincent's Orphan Asylum, LaSalle College, Lankenau Hospital, St. Catherine's Female Orphan Asylum, St. Anne's Widows' Asylum, and the Institute of Ladies of the Sacred Heart of Philadelphia. Nine-tenths of the estate—about $14 million or in today's markets $328 million—was designated as the trust estate, whose annual net income was to be divided equally

among the three daughters. There were strictures to this disbursement: if a sister died without leaving heirs, the surviving sisters
received her income; if all died without issue, the trust estate
would be divided between the institutions to whom he had
bequeathed the original one-tenth of his estate.

In future years, Frank's precautions against perceived fortune
hunters siphoning off his daughters' legacy would create problems
for the institutions Katharine founded, but at the time, his stipula-
tions seemed prudent. Kate, Lise, and Louise were bright, attractive, and cultivated, but they'd led unusually sheltered existences,
and their exposure to the opposite sex had been more restricted
than customary. When they were left unsupervised by parents,
Frank had surmised that it was only a matter of time before suitors
came calling. He didn't want his daughters to wed unhappily as his
niece Emilie had. Nor did he want them allying themselves to
young men who only cared about their wealth. To his mind, his
brother Tony's offspring offered an object lesson in shrewd estate
planning.

While Lise devoted herself to establishing the St. Francis de
Sales' Industrial School, Kate's inner anguish increased, and the
eldest in desperation decided the three should take another journey to Europe. Conferring with their uncle Tony, a departure in
July 1886 was scheduled, a time when the seas would be calm and
the long, sunny days would provide plenty of opportunities for revi-
talizing rambles on deck. Although one of the stated purposes of
the trip was to visit industrial schools and use them as models, the
true motive was to restore Kate's mental and physical health.

From a twenty-first-century perspective, she was probably suffering from clinical depression, but at the time such diagnoses were
unknown. Melancholia was the closest physicians came to naming
the problem, and even that was spoken in hushed tones as if the
patient's lack of inner fortitude were the cause of her or his distress.
Healthful living, peaceable pastimes, and changes of scenery were
recommended as cures, as well as patent medicines such as Dr. E.
C. West's Nerve and Brain Treatment and Carter's Little Nerve

Pills which promised to treat "hysteria and nervous neuralgia." Most of the remedies then manufactured for nervous disorders were opiate-based. Addiction was a frequent result, but, like the core problem, this consequence was regarded as an embarrassing secret that families hid.

Accompanied by Johanna and Martin, who acted as valet and general factotum, the sisters sailed aboard Cunard Line's S.S. *Umbria* July 31, 1886. On July 29, Uncle Tony wrote them an anxious letter. Although he had built homes for his offspring, and relished having them near enough for boisterous family dinners, it was atypical for him to pen fatherly epistles on personal matters. His focus on health and happiness was advice aimed at nursing a convalescent.

My dear Children,

I send these few lines to bid you goodbye, and to beg of you to follow my advice in these particulars.

Don't travel too much in one day. I think six hours ought to be the outside limit. Don't travel at night.

You must not go to any Northern Country in the Winter;— remember the days are short, the skies gray and dark and the weather generally bad. Try to spend the Winter where there is sunshine and warmth, where you can be in the fresh air.

I don't want you to go to Egypt for various reasons. In Rome avoid being out about sunset as that is the danger time and while there always eat a hearty breakfast and lunch, never have empty stomachs. I think this very important, drink good wine at meals. Avoid staying too long in damp, cold churches; going from the warm sunshine into a cold church is often dangerous without you have warm coverings to put on while in the church. Your man can always carry a lot of wraps with him so as to have them ready for use.

Don't let exorbitant bills or any of the cheating you will meet with worry you. This is one of the expenses of traveling.

Avoid any place where there is suspicion of cholera or any other disease. Naples is unhealthy on account of bad drainage.

Sorrento is much the best place to stay if you want to go to Naples.

You must not go to the Holy Land or any similar long journey out of the way of railways.

In case of need telegraph Drexel, Paris, that is the telegraph address. I have no doubt Mr. Harjes would come at once if it would be necessary. If you want advice or aid in any strange place where you have no acquaintances or friends send for the banker indicated on the letter of credit. If you should require a doctor—if the hotel you are stopping at is a first class one apply to the manager for the best doctor in town. I would give a homeopathic doctor the preference if there is one in the town.

Now goodbye. May God have you in His holy keeping and bring you back in good health to

Your loving uncle,

A. J. Drexel

The subtext of the letter raises questions: Wasn't Kate eating? Was she continuing to berate herself for being absent when her father died, and therefore spending too much time alone with her despairing thoughts? Her uncle was adamant about her need of sun and warmth rather than winter's long nights and brief daylight hours—now recognized as another cause of depression. And what of the reference to wine consumption? Was that a hint that she was self-treating her symptoms with morphia-laced elixirs rather than drinking wine, which was then considered a more healthful and natural remedy for melancholia? And his concern about "staying too long in damp, cold churches": did he feel she was following her stepmother's example and praying obsessively, and therefore not getting enough exercise? Tony walked to his office at Drexel & Co., a daily round-trip journey of more than sixty city blocks. His sons were avid sportsmen, his daughters equally steeped in the theory that physical exertion was healthful. Even his religious views had a vigorous dimension. A vestryman, he carried his energy with him into service of his parish; he was a doer rather than a ruminator, and had little use for the emotion of regret. Finally, there were the emergency contacts; doubtless everyone on the list had been forewarned to expect his nieces' pleas for aid—all of which suggest that he anticipated the worst.

Did the sisters obey their uncle's advice? At first, yes. Reaching the Hotel de la Promenade in Bad Langenschwalbach in Germany, Kate was prescribed a five-week *kur* of daily mud baths and dosages of Weinbrunner spring water. While she remained at the spa, her sisters strolled the countryside; when they ventured out together, Kate was bundled into a coach while her siblings either rode donkeys or walked. During their time in Langenschwalbach, Kate gained eight pounds, a feat heralded in letters home. Lizzie, who had decided to revert to her childhood nickname, confided in Miss Cassidy on a regular basis: "Our stay has certainly benefited Kate; her face has fattened, her color is better—but the main trouble still remains, along with delicate digestion. We had hoped for a more decided cure."

Whatever Kate's "main trouble" was continued to be unmentioned and unmentionable, and Lizzie's tone, despite the effort at a positive slant, was rife with disappointment. She was thirty-one, and ill equipped to nurse her sister back to emotional stability and health. In addition, she was attempting long-distance oversight of the family's town and country houses, something she'd never been trained to do.

Leaving Langenschwalbach, the party journeyed through Germany and Switzerland with Lizzie posting consciously chatty missives home while Kate spent her hours writing desolate descriptions of the terrain in her journal:

> Sept. 30th At Handeck commences the Grimsel Pass, a dark and drear place. . . . The valley becomes narrower and bleaker and wilder. It looks as if it were just cooling after the fires of which geologists speak had left the earth. The whole pass is most somber and no relief to the eye, nothing but precipices, boulders, crevasses. . . . The torrent dashes over the stones which oppose its downward course, directed by God's great law of gravity. It is opposed by the boulders, knocked by them into

foam; but still it dashes on, on to the valleys which it fertilizes, and into the thronged cities whose population receives its life from its broad calm waters. Thus the will must be opposed, broken . . .

Oct. 2nd Saturday . . . Four in hand over the Gotthard [Pass] . . . the pass becomes a hopeless abyss, we look down into a gorge, shut around by masses of granite, thousands of feet high. There appears no escape from the abyss. An opening appears, the corner is rounded & still another & another dark shadowy abyss opens to view. Inferno. Farther on Purgatorio.

This was the same lethal defile her grandfather had traversed as a boy, a fact Kate obviously didn't know. If she'd realized that the austere old man who was more taskmaster than doting grandparent had preceded her, what would have been her reaction? Would she have shed tears over his frightened, solitary state? Or would her view into that "hopeless abyss" have found comfort in imagining that, like Francis Martin Drexel, she would also prevail?

While she was visiting the Falls of Staubbach and Schmadribach in Switzerland, her experiences turned mystical, but as if she didn't trust these nascent revelations or considered them too morose to share, she relegated them to her notebook pages. "Houses look so small and man an atom in the great creation. Immutable mountains, man's life the whole span—like the passing of a cloud over the unchanging mountains. Human affairs immeasurably small. . . . I felt as if I was standing at the Day of Judgment. How have you passed your life? How tiny the years of man appear in the face of the mountains. Man so small! *Behold the Handmaid of the Lord.* The Blessed Virgin realized her smallness. Why did a creator require a handmaid?"

By November, the sisters, Johanna, and Martin had traveled through Italy and down through the south of France. Their speed increased. Often they spent only one night in a hotel—this, at a time when "traveling light" meant four trunks rather than ten. Their haste could be interpreted as a flight from reality, or from the demons Kate was attempting to outpace. The truth was happier.

"All Three" had begun enjoying the adventure. If they acted
younger than their years, regaling each other on near disastrous
scrapes, and giggling over impossibly proper matrons they met at
various stops along the way, it was because their upbringing had
kept them in an adolescent state. No one had ever treated them as
women who were responsible members of their community. Little
wonder they behaved like schoolgirls out on an illicit spree. For
Kate, the burden of sorrow was starting to lift; for Lizzie, years of
quiescent duty began slipping away; Lou, who needed no encouragement, grew ever more exuberant.

Uncle Tony heartily disapproved of their haphazard itinerary:

Philadelphia, Nov. 8/86
My dear Children,
    I have just received Louise's letter from Nimes. I don't won-
der you exhausted the ruins there in a couple of hours. I don't
take much stock in any kind of ruins. I think I could have
"done" those at Nimes in a quarter of an hour.
    I am afraid you are traveling too fast from the way you write
you propose "doing" Spain.

He might as well have saved the ink, for by this time his
nieces—with ineffectual protests from Johanna and Martin—were
pelting along through Europe, and having as many escapades per
day as possible. Trying to reach Gibraltar in mid-December, they
piled atop a public omnibus whose coachman whipped the bony
horses until the vehicle was careening downward through the
mountains toward the sea. Marbella was their destination, from
whence they intended to hire a boat to take them to the famous
rock. Night fell; the wrong road was taken; the coach banged into
boulders and straddled holes so deeply carved in the roadway that
the passengers had to descend so the omnibus could be eased
across.

At one point the party nearly tumbled off an embankment.
Shrieking, the travelers leapt to safety, then walked over a bridge
under construction. Sensibly, the sisters determined to quit the

dangerous vehicle, which by then had been righted and the protesting horses returned to their traces. But when it crossed the creaking, half-built bridge, they climbed aboard again; and the driver, to show his gratitude, offered them swigs from his bottle of cognac. They declined. The remainder of the night, such as it was, was spent in a dirty posada that Louise declared "impregnated with rancid oil." Despite missing Marbella, which the driver had purposely avoided, Louise and Martin tried to find a sailing vessel the next morning. None being available, they hired guides, and continued by horseback, crossing fjords and nearly losing Martin and Johanna when their mounts attempted to roll them in the water. The currents were so swift anything toppling into the stream was lost. When they ascended into the Sierra Nevada, Lou giddily described their progress as "jumping from boulder to boulder."

By the time the party wound its way back down to the ocean again, it was dark night. Crossing the sands under a moonless sky, they found the gates to Gibraltar locked until morning and the nearby posada full. The inn where they lodged was a wretched place, their room having been occupied by three men who'd been playing cards, drinking, and smoking and who were ejected in favor of the wealthy newcomers. The Drexel sisters asked for clean sheets, but made no further complaints. Each was having the time of her life.

Arriving in Gibraltar, they discovered that a steamer, the *Vérité*, was departing immediately for Tangiers. Nothing ventured, nothing gained. They engaged a small harbor vessel to carry them to the steamer, and leapt aboard. Once alongside the ship, though, they realized the waters were too rough to allow them to scale the *Vérité*'s flimsy rope ladder. The long black skirts of their mourning garb provided a dose of reality, and the proposed trip to North Africa was abandoned.

Had Uncle Tony known, he would have been aghast at his nieces' recklessness. If Egypt was forbidden, how much more perilous was North Africa to three naïve, ill-guarded heiresses? Fortunately, his nieces never informed him.

Christmas momentarily dampened the sisters' high spirits. It didn't help that they were so far from home, visiting Valencia after whirlwind stops in Cordova and Alcazar. Trying to stave off a sense of rootlessness, they spent Christmas Eve attempting without success to purchase the perfect gift for one another from street-side stalls where their hectic pace betrayed their feelings of dislocation. Then their flight continued, taking them through Barcelona, Estramadura, Andalusia, La Mancha, Catalonia, and finally to Marseilles. Uncle Tony could barely control his frustration with their devil-may-care attitudes:

> My dear Children:
> I have no doubt the absence of restraint has its charms, as you say, but I think it dearly purchased at the expense of dirt and want of proper food and comfort. I have felt anxious all the time you have been in Spain fearing one of you might have taken ill, in which case you might have fallen into the hands of a Spanish doctor. I must confess having a prejudice against the practice of medicine in Spain, coming from my reading so often Gil Blas.

Again, his warning fell on deaf ears. From Marseilles, they moved on to Rome, where their Aunt Ellen and cousin Sallie (Sarah) Drexel Fell and her husband, John, awaited. The sisters were finally, to their uncle's immense relief, joining sensible folk who dressed for dinner each evening and who visited acceptable landmarks in an orderly fashion. Or so he believed.

Kate, though markedly improved, still suffered rapid mood swings. On January 23 she wrote Miss Cassidy that she and her sisters were all "prayer-dry":

> First we heard Mass at Sant'Andrea, assisted at a marriage and a funeral; second, we have visited the entire seven Basilicas (six Our Fathers and ditto Hail Marys) in each; third, we rushed up the Scala Santa on our knees, winning the race by five minutes in advance of the numerous peasants and blind orphans performing the same devotion; thirdly, we have visited San

Pietro in Vincoli and seen his true chains; fourthly, we caught a Benediction at St. Stephens; fifthly, we knelt in the Church of St. Labre.

Cryptically, she then alluded to a "COUNT PILA," capitalizing his name and adding "be still palpitating heart!" then, as an afterthought, mentioned that their private audience with Pope Leo XIII hadn't yet been scheduled. What was the cynicism of her tone masking? The audience, when it did take place on January 27, was a pivotal point in her life.

A myth has sprung up around the occasion, the tale being that when Kate asked the pontiff for missionaries to send to the Native Americans—which she did—his supposed response was "Why not, my child, yourself become a missionary?" There's no corroboration to the story; Kate's journals made no reference to the exchange. Nor did she report becoming violently ill afterward, although she was. Her sisters were well aware of the situation, however, and feared her mysterious ailment had returned.

Brushing aside their worries, she treated the remainder of the journey as the stuff of comedy. At least, that was the façade she chose. Her letters home painted tongue-in-cheek portraits of *couturières* and corset-makers whom the Drexel sisters patronized while staying at the Hôtel Normandie in Paris in early March, or encounters with Aunt Ellen and the Fell relatives who also descended upon the French capital, or a jovial dinner with Mr. and Mrs. Harjes, or a drive in a rented livery in the Bois de Boulogne, which was crowded with "all Paris." Kate was determined to keep her tone humorous and her private struggles private, or perhaps she was trying to avoid a wrenching inner dialogue. Her only serious moments occurred during tours of the industrial schools: Mettray, near Tours, which was prior to their sojourn at the Hôtel Normandie, and in the environs of Paris the Horticultural and Agricultural School operated by the Christian Brothers at Igney, and an orphanage under construction at Fleury.

For the mystics of the world, the impetus toward religious vocation is easy to comprehend if impossible to emulate. Catherine of

Siena had her first vision of Christ while still a young child; Joan of Arc's came a bit later in life but was every bit as real and present; the visions of John of the Cross, and of Teresa of Avila were irrefutable. Kate Drexel, however, had been raised to be a pragmatist; she was the daughter, niece, and granddaughter of men of affairs. Her maternal and paternal great-grandfathers had been merchants who viewed life through the prism of plus and minus columns; investments of time and capital were weighed, and decisions based on the practical rather than a spiritual ideal.

Whether Pope Leo XIII gave her the advice ascribed to him, or whether she intuited the suggestion—or even believed she heard it—the private audience resulted in a shift in her thinking and behavior. Fighting against the weight of heredity, she was, as John of the Cross had written, entering her own "dark night of the soul," her *noche oscura del alma*.

Her quest wasn't as unexpected as it seems. A crucial figure since childhood had been Father James O'Connor, a priest who regularly visited the household in Torresdale. Born in Queenstown, Ireland, on September 10, 1823, he immigrated to America at the age of fifteen, was educated at the St. Charles Borromeo Seminary in Philadelphia, and was ordained in Rome in 1848. In 1876, he became the first bishop of Omaha. When he left the Philadelphia area and moved west, he and Kate began a correspondence that lasted until his death in 1890. Customarily she wrote him a long, affectionate letter every week, and sometimes more often.

His responses were equally expansive. His first missives to "dear Katie" or "My dear child" colorfully described the *desperadoes* drawn to the region on account of the newly discovered gold seams, as well as the vigilantes and "road agents" he encountered during his travels. In turn, she included parodies of nursery rhymes, or wrote about family excursions to Lake George or the White Mountains, or the new electric lights in John Wanamaker's store, or the latest fashions, theater evenings, or lyrics from Gilbert and Sullivan's operetta *H.M.S. Pinafore* that she declared was "all the rage." At one point, she asked whether Keats's "Endymion" was political; he answered by suggesting she read Metternich's memoirs. Their relationship, easy and intimate, was more like that enjoyed by close older and younger relatives than a spiritual advisor and his charge. Kate shared every experience with him; he repeatedly urged her to reveal those same thoughts to her father and Emma. Kate disregarded the advice.

When she made her debut, he penned a stanza of a poem he'd learned in boyhood, then mused that in future he hoped he wouldn't be forced to address her as "my dear Contessa, or my dear Marchesa, or even my dear Principessa. God protect you from that fate that would involve such a title." In June 1882, he scolded her for being "venturesome to rashness," and like her uncle Tony fretted repeatedly about her health, especially following her father's death when even his compassionate counsel couldn't console her. From then on, every letter from him mentioned this abiding concern.

It was to Bishop O'Connor that she revealed the various phases of her soul-searching, starting when he was still the family's parish priest. His answers were candid and wise. Though convinced that she'd ultimately succumb to family tradition by marrying and following her stepmother's example of charity, he never treated her as a child, in love with the image of religiosity, but as someone laboring with genuine spiritual dilemmas. The "interior trials" she shared with O'Connor were examined with gravity and empathy.

In addition to her Heb, Kate created miniature notebooks, entitled "Strictly Private—The Holy Ghost Speaking to My Soul," in which she made observations and rules to govern her inner life. Not even her sisters were allowed a glimpse of these writings, which proves how disquieting she found them.

Choose a secret place to thyself; love to dwell with thyself alone.

Reflect much on the relative emptiness of earthly things.

Try not to be so scrupulous. [This was in response of O'Connor's suggestion that her "predominant passion" was "scrupulosity."]

Love is essentially a sacrifice. Oh, how little love of God there is in the world. How many of us make a sacrifice to God?

Tellingly, the reverse of the page contained a recipe for "Blanc Mange Chocolate." The sometime ascetic loved to eat, referring to herself in her correspondence with O'Connor not as a gourmet but as a gourmand, and occasionally as an out-and-out glutton.

As early as May 1883, four months after Emma's death and without informing her family, Kate had begun considering a religious vocation. It would be a mistake to assume the decision was in reaction to her stepmother's illness and the nearly incapacitating grief that caused Francis to cede his position at Drexel & Co. There was no passive sorrow in her deliberations. At twenty-five, she was a woman of action. True to her methodical nature, she wrote down the pros and cons in parallel columns, matching them up against one another. She was unstinting in exposing what she perceived as personal impediments, and she knew herself very well.

My Reasons for Entering Religion

1. Jesus Christ has given His life for me. It is but just that I should give Him mine. Now in religions we offer ourselves to God in a direct manner, whereas in the married state natural motives prompt us to sacrifice self.

2. We were created to love God. In religious life we return Our Lord love for love by a constant voluntary sacrifice of our feelings, our inclinations, our appetites. Against all of which nature powerfully rebels but it is by conquering the flesh that the soul lives.

3. I know in truth that the love of the most perfect creature is vain in comparison with Divine Love.

4. When all shadows shall have passed away I shall rejoice if I have given in life an entire heart to God.

5. In the religious life our Last End is kept continually before the mind.

6. A higher place in Heaven is reserved for all eternity.

7. The attainment of perfection should be our chief employment in life. Our Lord has laid a price upon its acquirement

when He says, "If thou wilt be perfect go sell what thou hast and give to the poor and thou shalt have treasure in Heaven and come follow Me. . . . He that followeth Me walketh not in darkness." How can I doubt that these words are true wisdom, and if true wisdom why not act upon them?

My Objections to Entering Religion
1. How could I bear separation from my family? I who have never been away from home for more than two weeks. At the end of one week I have invariably felt "homesick."
2. I hate community life. I should think it maddening to come in constant contact with many different *old maidish* dispositions. I hate never to be alone.
3. I fear that I should murmur at the commands of my Superior and return a proud spirit to her reproofs.
4. Superiors are frequently selected on account of their holiness, *not* for ability. I should hate to owe submission to a woman whom I felt to be stupid, and whose orders showed a thorough want of judgment.
5. In the religious life how can spiritual dryness be endured?
6. I do not know how I could bear the privations and poverty of the religious life. I have never been deprived of luxuries. When with very slight variety the same things are exacted of me day in and day out, year in and year out. I fear weariness, disgust and a want of *final* perseverance which might lead me to leave the convent. And what then!

Despite the negativity of her self-evaluation, she felt impelled to move toward the next step of becoming a religious. On May 21, 1883, she sought out Bishop O'Connor's advice and included her analysis. There was a caveat.

Prior to Emma's death, a suitor had appeared. O'Connor was aware of the couple's growing intimacy, although her sisters and father were not, which was another instance of Kate's preferring to confide in the bishop rather than her family. Shortly after her stepmother's demise, the situation changed and the man proposed.

The timing was odd. Households in mourning during the late nineteenth century were expected to be melancholy places that followed established bereavement etiquette, which suggests that the suitor felt emboldened by a sudden dearth of parental restraints. Perhaps Frank absented himself from family gatherings during this period, leaving his daughters to receive visitors or not. The young man had to have appeared at the house regularly, been included in family luncheons or dinners, and been in Kate's company when outdoors. How she managed to keep Lise and Lou in the dark is a mystery because they were together almost constantly. It's hard to believe they didn't notice Kate's agitation, either when in her admirer's presence or after she'd rejected him and decided to remain "an old maid." But they didn't.

Kate was on her own, trying to plan her future. Her father's counsel also failed her. She wanted answers, not platitudes. Again, she turned to O'Connor: "Please do not feel obliged, dear Father, to answer me for months, if it is not convenient to you to do so soon. I am in no hurry about the response. I think it clearly my vocation at present, to remain an old maid. My reasons for desiring a speedy decision to my vocation have now been removed. The gentleman who was paying me attention has proposed, and I have refused the offered heart. I have every reason to believe that it was not a very ardent one. *No one* (not even my sisters) knows of this little affair except Papa, who gave me my free choice, saying that he desired but my happiness."

Although Bishop O'Connor took her appeal seriously, he felt that the life of a religious was too rigorous for someone of her temperament and upbringing.

Omaha, Nebraska, May 26, 1883

Most of the reasons you give, in your paper, for and against your entering the states considered are impersonal, that is abstract and general. These are very well as far as they go, in settling one's vocation, but additional and personal reasons are necessary to decide it . . .

In the religious state, a young lady becomes the mystic "sposa Christi." She gives her heart to Him, and to Him alone. If she loves others it is in Him, and for Him she does so . . .

You give positive personal reasons for not embracing the religious state. The first—the difficulty you would find in separation from your family, does not merit much consideration, as that would have to be overcome, in any case. The second—your dislike for Community life is a very serious one, and if it continues to weigh with you, you should give up all thought of religion . . .

The same must be said of the "the privations and poverty," and the monotony of the religious life, to which you allude. If you do not feel within you the courage, with God's help, to bear them, for the sake of Him to whom they lead, go no further in your examination.

He was more pointed in a subsequent communication:

Omaha, August 5, 1883

What most makes me hesitate to say that you have a vocation to religion, is the fear that you might not have the strength to endure the sacrifices it calls for. From your home, from your table, to the cell and refectory of a nun, would be a very great change indeed. And what makes me hesitate, in this matter, should cause you to do the same . . .

You are in doubt in regard to a matter of the very gravest importance to yourself individually. It is a doubt that, usually, takes time to solve. Don't be in a hurry. Think, pray, wait, and all will turn out for your peace and happiness.

He also suggested that Kate test herself by eating "convent rations," and dressing in "unbecoming colors," which she did.

In 1884, during the European tour the sisters made with their father, her correspondence with O'Connor followed the same theme: her questing heart attempting to make sense of her dueling nature. A letter dated January 27 vacillated between self-discovery, confusion, hesitation, and doubt. "Please instruct me, dear father" was her ongoing cry.

European travel brings vividly before the mind how cities have risen and fallen, and risen and fallen; and the same of empires and nations. And the billions and billions who lived their common every day life in these nations and kingdoms where are they? The ashes of the Kings and mighty of this earth are mingled with the dust of the meanest slave. The handsome sculptured sepulchres, the exquisitely finished Etruscan vases, the tombs of Egyptian mummies are exposed in museums, the dust of the great which these sepulchres and vases were intended to preserve are scattered to the winds. . . . How long will the sun and moon, and stars continue to give forth light . . . ?

I hope that God may place me in a state of life where I can best know Him, love Him and serve Him for Whom alone I am created. I am ambitious, I desire to become the disciple of our Lord Jesus Christ. What am I to do now what am I to do in the future?

Added to this was an analysis of her relationship with Emma. It was the first time Kate publicly acknowledged Emma's reclusive nature, and how it had impacted her choices: "She [Emma] never prevented our entering into society, in fact, encouraged it, provided us with the means of going into the world abundantly, so that our friends marveled at the variety, and elegance of our toilets. We loved her dearly, as well we might and our family union was complete in every respect. Yet we found that if we gave our lives or even a part of them to the world we could not be in *entire accord* with her, for she was not 'of the world.' It was because we appreciated close intimacy with her that we left others for her."

Then Kate veered toward her wish to enter a convent, as well as her recognition that if she were "under the rule of a cranky superioress" she wouldn't like it a bit. O'Connor denied her request: "For the present be content with the role of life I've given you." And there the matter rested, at least for a while.

But then came her father's death, and her tortured reaction. Kate again appealed to Bishop O'Connor, writing him from Long Branch, New Jersey, in August 1885 while her cousins disported themselves at the seaside resort, and her aunt Ellen and uncle Tony tried to distract her with pleasurable activities, brisk walks on the beach, wholesome meals, and early bedtimes.

> I presume He wishes me to be where I can first save my own soul, secondly, to do as much good as He intends with the means Dear Papa has left me. If Our Lord wishes me to go to a convent, I should be an idiot did I not obey the call. If amongst the temptations of the world, it is His will that I should steer my course to Heaven, fiat. It is His strong grace alone which could enable me to keep out of sin in that ocean. I confess the ocean of the world is full of dangers for me, and the route to God very indirect . . .

> To tell the truth, it appears to me that God calls me to the religious life. But when is it prudent for me to obey the call? Next week? This Fall? This Winter? In what religious order? Please tell me, dear Father, what I should do.

O'Connor's response was firm:

Omaha, August 29, 1885

> The conclusion to which I have come in your case is, that your vocation is not to enter a religious order. The only order to which I could have thought of recommending you, as I more than once told you, is the Sacred Heart; but you have not the health necessary to enable you to discharge the duties that would devolve on you as a member of the society . . .

> But, although God does not will you to a religious order, He has, I am persuaded, a special mission for you in the world. . . . Living as you do, and as you will continue to live, you will benefit not only Christ's poor, but by your example, the rich of this world also, who after all, are the poorest of the poor.

That final piece of advice contained a modicum of hope. Kate clung to it, determined to find her "special mission."

During this period of spiritual and emotional crisis, and before the 1886–1887 escapade in Europe, two priests seeking financial aid for the struggling Indian missions arrived at the Drexel house on Walnut Street. It's probable that the visit was inspired by Bishop O'Connor in an effort to help Kate find her secular calling, but he remained mum about his involvement.

One of the priests was Bishop Martin Marty, vicar apostolic of northern Minnesota, the other Rev. Joseph A. Stephan, director of the Bureau of Catholic Indian Missions. By happenstance, Kate received them; and the information they shared took hold of her imagination. They were eloquent in describing the privations facing the indigenous peoples, the need for increased education, as well as the human suffering caused by Ulysses S. Grant's disastrous "Peace Policy" which moved entire tribes away from their ancestral homelands and into reservations. Miners attracted to the the gold-rich Black Hills of the Dakota Territory had violated the Fort Laramie Treaty of 1868 by trespassing on tribal lands and, worse, abusing the earth the Lakota considered sacred. The 1876 Battle of the Little Bighorn in eastern Montana Territory had been one of the outcomes of the failed policy.

By 1886, controversy still swirled around the conflict during which Lakota Sioux, Northern Cheyenne, and Arapaho convened by Sitting Bull had destroyed General George Armstrong Custer's forces. Rather than retreating, however, the mining interests in the Black Hills were thriving, and the general's widow, Elizabeth Bacon Custer, was busy touring the country promoting her memoir *Boots and Saddles, or Life in Dakota with General Custer*, which had been published in 1885 by Harper & Brothers and painted a glowing portrait of her husband and his military career. She hoped the book would redeem his reputation. From the enthusiastic reception she met during her speaking engagements, she had reason to believe it would. For her and many other settlers intent on taming the West, the "Indian Wars" were far from finished.

Bishop Marty and Rev. Stephan made their case, including a plea for new schools and teachers for the Indians. Kate pledged monetary support for the missionaries' work in the form of a check for $3,000.

Her quest for a greater purpose for her life coincided with the Social Gospel movement, which came to define a late nineteenth-century ideal: that to serve God meant to serve those created in God's image. In 1886, Walter Rauschenbusch, a founding member of the movement, was called to become pastor of the Second German Baptist Church in New York City. He would have an illustrious career and publish widely read books on the Social Gospel theory, among them *Christianity and the Social Crisis* (1907), which the *New York American* deemed "the most illuminating religious book of the century," *For God and the People: Prayers of the Social Awakening* (1910), *Christianizing the Social Order* (1912), *The Social Principles of Jesus* (1916), and *A Theology for the Social Gospel* (1918). At the time, though, Rauschenbusch was a recently graduated seminarian—he was born October 4, 1861—appalled by the abject misery of the impoverished within his parish and the neighboring streets of the city's Hell's Kitchen area. As he wrote in *A Theology for the Social Gospel*:

> The saint of the future will need not only a theocentric mysticism which enables him to realize God, but an anthropocentric mysticism which enables him to realize his fellow-men in God. The more we approach pure Christianity, the more will Christianity signify a man who loves mankind with a religious passion and excludes none. The feeling which Jesus had when he said, "I am the hungry, the naked, the lonely," will be in the emotional consciousness of all holy men in coming days. The sense of solidarity is one of the distinctive marks of the true followers of Jesus.

Washington Gladden, who was born in 1836, was another Social Gospel visionary and a Congregational minister. He is popularly remembered as the librettist of the 1879 hymn that began:

"O Master, let me walk with thee / In lowly paths of service free." Among his published works were *Applied Christianity* (1886), *Burning Questions* (1891), *Social Salvation* (1901), and *Christianity and Socialism* (1905). He believed that the uneven distribution of wealth was an evil that needed to be addressed on a governmental and personal level. When Kate was supplying monies to fund schools for Native Americans, Gladden served as pastor of the First Congregational Church in Columbus, Ohio. In 1886, in Cleveland, he used his increasing fame and oratorical skills to intervene on behalf of the laborers during a rail strike.

Jane Addams, who was born in 1860 and became the first American woman to win the Nobel Peace Prize, was also a social reformer determined to improve the lives of the oppressed. Hull House in Chicago, founded in 1889, became the model of American settlement houses and was inspired by her 1883 visit to London where she witnessed the near starvation rations of the poor. Seeing a man bid for and win a rotten cabbage at a Saturday night sale of decaying produce—legally, the vegetables and fruits couldn't be sold on Sundays—and then consume it on the spot, she never forgot the memory of hungry hands thrust upward toward the auctioneer, beseeching him for any type of food no matter how putrid. "Myriads of hands," she wrote, "empty, pathetic, nerveless and work-worn, showing white in the uncertain light of the street, and clutching for food that was already unfit to eat." Toynbee Hall in London's East End was the forefront of the settlement house movement that encouraged a communal approach to addressing societal injustice; it inspired the founding of Hull House. For Addams, her work among Chicago's immigrants was a form of secular religion.

Addams, Gladden, and Rauschenbusch came from Protestant backgrounds; their radical theology was much discussed among all creeds when Kate and her sisters journeyed west to visit the Indian missions in September 1887. Traveling by train to Omaha, they and Bishop O'Connor continued the trek by wagon and horseback into the southern Dakota Territory. Lizzie and Louise, who had

brought their own saddles from Torresdale, started the trip by posting themselves as outriders for the party and treating the excursion
as a lark as they galloped through grasslands that were rife with
antelope, bison, and deer. Eagles soared overhead; the skies were
infinitely blue, the horizon limitless. Hours would pass without the
group encountering another human being, although they spotted a
few sod houses at a distance, tiny things that looked uninhabitable
and that were so huddled into the earth it was nearly impossible to
imagine families dwelling within them. For all the raw beauty of
the landscape, the jagged buttes and the sand-colored mountains
striated by wind and time, the journey was a tough slog; the road
no more than a dirt track; sustenance and water only what the
group carried with them.

Their first stop was the as yet unfinished St. Francis Mission
serving the Lakota Tribe on the Rosebud Indian reservation. For
the Sisters of St. Francis who were struggling to build the school,
the visit was an unwelcome surprise, but they did their best to
cease work and be cordial. The Lakota were as startled as the nuns.
Women in red and yellow face paint, men accoutered in a combi-
nation of native and European garb, and semi-clad children surrounded the Philadelphia ladies who weren't attired for the western plains but wore riding costumes better suited to English saddles
and manicured hacking paths: skirts with moderate bustles, tight-
fitted bodices, veiled hats, dainty jewelry, and kidskin gloves. The
three sisters bore no resemblance to the hard-pressed nuns or the
other white women living in the Black Hills, one being the infamous Calamity Jane, who had been born Martha Jane Cannary in
1852 and whose reputation as a crack shot and sometime prostitute
made her one of the region's most notorious females.

That night Kate and her sisters were given a sleeping space in
the uncompleted school's first floor; when they awoke, they saw
faces crammed together at the unglazed windows, staring at the
Easterners in wonderment. Later in the day an ox was slaughtered
for a feast honoring the visitors. The Lakota ate it raw. When a
native dance was arranged for the guests, Kate was shocked to find

the men wearing nothing but bells tied around their knees and feathers festooning their long hair. She'd never seen a naked man.

The tour of mission schools continued, the group covering thirty to sixty miles each day through swirling dust and swarms of insects while the buckboard jounced over washed-out trails. Louise and Lizzie's horses repeatedly shied under the unfamiliar English saddles. Their hosts informed them that in winter blizzards engulfed the plains; summers customarily brought drought, parched soil, and windstorms black with desiccated earth. The white men and few white women who had established the gold-rush shanty towns of Deadwood and Lead expected these privations, but for Kate and her sisters, the tour turned into a trial. There were times when they questioned their wisdom in leaving home.

At Pine Ridge Reservation, they met the august Lakota Sioux Red Cloud and exchanged gifts with him: a bridle for the chief, a fringed shawl for his wife. Red Cloud stood six feet tall; his manner and tone were commanding. A seasoned leader, he had first journeyed to the nation's capital in June 1870 in the company of Little Bear, Spotted Tail, and other tribal chiefs. There he excoriated government policy toward the indigenous peoples:

> I come from where the sun sets. You were raised on chairs. I want to sit where the sun sets. The Great Spirit has raised me in this way: He has raised me naked. I run no opposition to the Great Father who sits in the White House. I don't want to fight. I have offered my prayer to the Great Father so that I might come here safe and well. What I have to say to you and to these men and to my Great Father is this:—Look at me: I was raised where the sun rises, and now I come from where he sets. The nation which has the bow and arrow—the red man—and the whites were raised together on this land. Whose voice was first heard on this land? It was the red people who used the bow.
>
> The Great Father may be good and kind, but I can't see it. I am good and kind to the white people, and have given my lands, and I have now come from where the sun sets to see you. The

Great Father has sent his people out there and left me nothing but an Island. Our nation is melting away like the snow on the side of the hills where the sun is warm, while your people are like the blades of grass in spring, when summer is coming . . .

The white people have sprinkled blood on the blades of grass about the line of Fort Fetterman. Tell the Great Father to remove that fort, that we will be peaceable and that there will be no more trouble. I have got two mountains in that country, Black Hill and Big Horn; I want no roads there. There have been stakes driven in that country, and I want them removed. I have told these things three times, and now I have come here to tell them for the fourth time. . . . I was born at the forks of the Platte; my father and mother told me that the lands there belonged to me. From the North and the West, the red nation has come to the Great Father's house. We are the last of the Ogallalas; we have come to know the facts from the Great Father why the promises made to us have not been kept . . .

The Great Spirit has raised you to read and write, and has put papers before you, but he has not raised me in that style. The men whom the President sends us are soldiers, and all have no sense and no heart. I know it today. What has been done in my country I did not ask. The whites are going through my country and killing game and it is the Great Father's fault.

Born in 1819 when his tribes' ancestral lands held no interest for white settlement, Red Cloud had much to criticize. He had participated in signing the Fort Laramie Treaty in 1868; at that time he announced that his great-grandfather had told him the whites were the Ogallalas' friends. The treaty, like numerous others, was hardly worth the paper on which it was written. Government agents robbed the peoples they were sent to aid; protests against those depredations were met with swift and lethal reprisals, "the kill and burn policy" described in a *Philadelphia Inquirer* article recounting Red Cloud's 1870 speech.

During that initial visit, a gala dinner for the tribal chiefs and their wives was held at the White House June 7, and was attended by members of the cabinet, their wives, foreign ministers and their wives, as well as Mrs. Grant and Nellie Grant. Amid all the pomp and ceremony, Red Cloud told President Grant that he would "quit the war path and go to farming . . . if you will always treat me like this and let me live in as big a house." His words were met with laughter.

How did this justifiably aggrieved but pragmatic tribal leader feel when confronted with the Eastern belles? Could he have hoped they intended to do good rather than harm? Or were they viewed as mere curiosity seekers privately scoffing at the Lakotas' simple, savage ways? The aftermath of the massacre at Wounded Knee in 1890 would reveal Red Cloud's recognition of the importance of Kate's work, but for the time being the visitors were treated with wary courtesy.

Leaving Pine Ridge, Kate and her sisters ventured toward the Canadian border at present-day Belcourt, North Dakota, to visit the Indian mission at Turtle Mountain where they found about two-hundred full-blooded Chippewa and five times that many of mixed race, who were considered the lowest of the low and treated as outcasts by both races. By then the territory's early winter was approaching, the grasslands turning a brittle brown, the raked hills dun-colored and sere. The days grew cold, the nights in the log and mud cabins colder.

Finally it was a train to St. Paul and a real hotel with feather beds, baths, hot water, and dinner served on china plates, and thence to Chicago where they boarded their connection to New York City. They reached Torresdale on October 16, 1887. The worn saddles were hung in the stables. As Louise succinctly put it: "Pennsylvania's beauties doubly appreciated after a dose of prairie."

Kate thought otherwise. Despite the hardships of the journey, she'd become convinced that building schools for indigenous peoples, or Drexel Indian Schools, as they were popularly named, was her calling. She pledged $30,000 for the construction and staffing of educational facilities, and planned to make a repeat visit in autumn 1888, this time to the Chippewa tribes along southern

Lake Superior and up into the White Earth and Red Lake reservations in present-day Minnesota.

As yet, though, she held herself back, acting the patronizing role of a Lady Bountiful. Not until her return east from her second western sojourn did her inner quest resurface.

six

RENOUNCING MILLIONS

FOLLOWING THE 1887 AND 1888 JOURNEYS WEST, KATE THREW herself into the work of helping empower Native Americans. She felt inspired by these people who had managed to maintain tenacity and hope in the face of abuse; their courage impelled her to action. Bishop O'Connor had further discouraged her wish to enter religious life by stating unequivocally in June 1887, "You, my child, have not the strength, the constitution necessary to perform the duties of an active order, and the confinement of a contemplative order would break you down in no time." Although the words stung, she determined to prove him wrong about her stamina, and embarked on a project that was daring in its scope and vision.

She began by hiring architects to design schools for the Lakota, Chippewa, Crow, Cheyenne, Arapaho, and Blackfeet tribes in the Dakota Territory, for the Coeur d'Alene and Nez Perce in Idaho, the Cherokee, Comanche, and Osage of the Indian Territory, and the Pueblo in New Mexico. When completed, the institutions were to be deeded to the Catholic Indian Bureau. A government contract was drawn up stipulating that one hundred dollars would be paid yearly to teach each pupil. Having come to know and respect the indigenous people she'd met on her journeys, Kate resolved to overcome decades of cruelty and neglect by providing the means of achieving a basic education. When it became apparent—and it soon did—that building schools was one issue and staffing them another, she became a whirlwind of activity, contacting religious institutions she believed could send teachers to carry out the work. She was as persuasive as she was resolute; there were few who could refuse this determined heiress whose wealth and family connections gave her something akin to celebrity status.

Her uncle Tony helped her manage the financial part of her mission, though she'd begun proving herself adept at fulfilling that role herself. Among her generation of Drexels, it was Kate who developed into the most fiscally astute, and the most precise about business and organizational matters. Tony's sons John, Anthony Jr., and George, though nominally employed at Drexel & Co. had little interest in professional affairs. They were rich and socially prominent; they saw no reason why they shouldn't enjoy the fruits of their father's and grandfather's labors. Following the senior Anthony's death on June 30, 1893, George and Anthony Jr. would give up all pretense of working, and instead commission palatial steam yachts in which to wander the globe, entertaining royalty and touring the coast of Africa and bagging big game. Their yachts and winter and summer homes, as well as those belonging to their siblings, were emblematic of Gilded Age excess; and their father, although glad to provide them with the advantages he'd once been denied, grieved over their immoderation and utter disregard of the principles by which he'd guided his life. It's no wonder he relished Kate's company, as she did his.

In 1888, Drexel & Co. moved into its new home at 428 Chestnut Street, which was contiguous to the building that had housed Nicholas Biddle's Second Bank of the United States. With a glistening, white marble façade and classical lines, the eleven-story structure was fitted out with elevators and broad corridors enabling easy access to its 398 rooms: a prototype of a modern office building. The use of natural light enhanced a feeling of spaciousness; mosaic floors added grandeur and depth. A rooftop viewing pavilion towered above the neighboring edifices, offering sights of the city's historic monuments clustered nearby: the State House (now Independence Hall), Carpenters' Hall, the First Bank of the United States, and the Merchants' Exchange on Third Street. When the Philadelphia Stock Exchange moved to the Drexel Building, its luster as a place of fiduciary eminence became unparalleled in the city. Kate was a frequent visitor as she managed the disbursement of her trust income for the "Drexel schools."

Her uncle had also embarked upon a major educational undertaking in 1888. Six years prior, he'd begun contributing financially to the New Century Guild of Working Women, an organization designed to address the needs of self-supporting women. Eliza Sproat Turner, an author and committed social reformer, had founded the guild, recognizing that large numbers of women were entering the workforce but had no support services to help them find better or more stable employment. Turner had been instrumental in establishing the Pennsylvania Woman Suffrage Association in 1869, and in 1875 published the suffrage tract "Four Quite New Reasons Why You Should Want Your Wife to Vote." During the Centennial Exposition of 1876 she had edited and written articles for the *New Century for Women*, a newspaper distributed at the Women's Pavilion. By 1886, Turner's New Century Guild offered self-improvement and career-enhancement classes to hundreds of women. The building contained a clubhouse, dining room, and a library staffed with a full-time librarian.

The focus on women's rights was given a ghoulish sense of immediacy that same year due to the Whitechapel murders in London during autumn 1888. Although the notorious "Ripper" was an ocean removed from the United States, the savage misogyny of the crimes served as a reminder on both sides of the Atlantic that no woman was immune to violence. British feminist Florence Fenwick Miller expressed the communal outrage in a letter to the editor of the *London Daily News*: "Yet week by week and month by month women are kicked, beaten, jumped on till they are crushed, chopped, stabbed, seamed with vitriol . . . and this sort of outrage, if the woman dies, is called 'manslaughter'; if she lives, it is a 'common assault.' Common indeed!"

Reformers in Britain and America agreed that the murders demanded engagement with suffragist tenets. Systemic change was necessary if women were to rise above their demeaned status and be considered coequal with men. The New Century Guild represented that new paradigm for empowering women in Philadelphia.

Inspired by the work of Eliza Sproat Turner, and with advice from his wife Ellen and doubtless from Kate, too, Anthony began plans to create an industrial college for young women. He purchased the former Louella estate in Wayne for its home, then decided to expand his approach, and founded a school for both men and women. The institution would provide young men and women with skills and practical knowledge to improve their earning potential and enhance their lives. Not wanting to establish merely a vocational school, Anthony believed it was important that the students develop an appreciation of the arts, in design and execution as well as for aesthetic value. He hired the firm of Wilson Brothers and Co., the Drexel building architects, to create a space at once stately but accessible, imposing yet grounded in reality. With a footprint measuring 200 feet by 200 feet, and four stories high, it would be able to accommodate up to 2,500 pupils. Art collected from his European travels would grace the halls.

When the Drexel Institute of Art, Science and Industry, now Drexel University, was formally dedicated on December 17, 1891, the Honorable Chauncey M. Depew, an attorney, former member of the New York State Assembly, as well as its Secretary of State, and a future U.S. senator representing New York (1899–1911), stressed one of the institute's basic precepts: socioeconomic equality in the workplace for men and women.

One of the chief glories of the new education is the advantages it gives to women. . . . It is still the reproach of our times

that women receive less pay than men for the same work equally well done. But chivalry is an emotion, not a habit, and sentiment is left at the shop door in the business world. . . . The
Drexel Institute . . . is a practical and beneficent illustration of
the Divine injunction, "Thou shalt love thy neighbor as thyself." . . . It is a noble recognition of the needs of the youth of
both sexes by placing before them the weapons and the armor
for the battle of life and training them in their uses. It will nur-
ture and instruct a better and broader womanhood, a braver and
more intelligent manhood.

The progressive ideals represented in the Drexel Institute of Art,
Science and Industry were still several years from reaching fruition
when Kate underwent another intense experience of religious call.
Although she was busy building and staffing schools for indigenous
peoples, the meditative side of her nature rebelled against that part
of her that was pragmatic and driven. She was at war within herself, believing God wished her to withdraw from the world, while
also recognizing her gifts for organization and leadership. If an
inner balance could have been struck, all might have been well,
but the extremes were too great: quiescence and a desire for monas-
ticism on the one hand, dynamism and action on the other.

Agonizing over these seemingly irreconcilable facets of her persona, she wrote to Bishop O'Connor in November 1888, although
she anticipated that his response would be the same as it had been
before: Remain as you are; the work you're doing is saving lives in
the present time and for generations to come. Or worse: Remain as
you are in order to provide a positive example for those in your
social sphere. What he didn't appear to recognize was her compelling need to feel at one with God, a sensation of the emptying
out of self in order to make room for the divine, rather than engaging her mind, soul, and body in specific tasks.

Her former struggles seemed insignificant to what she was now
facing. It was no longer *I, Katharine, choose this*, but God who was
guiding her, who was urging her to a life of contemplation and
prayer. As important as her schools were, she felt like the rich

young man in Matthew's gospel who couldn't part with his wealth. Kate was ready to do just that, but she recognized how alone she was in her aspiration. No one, not even Bishop O'Connor agreed with her.

> Do not, Reverend Father, I beseech you say, "What is to become of your work?" What is to become of it when I shall give it all to Our Lord? Will Our Lord at the day of Judgment condemn me for approaching as near Him as possible by following Him, and then leaving my yearly income to be distributed among the Missions, or for the Missions in some way that I am sure could be devised if only Our Lord will free me from all responsibility save that of giving myself to Him. . . . I am afraid to receive your answer to this note. It appears to me, Reverend Father, that I am not obliged to submit my judgment to yours, as I have been doing for two years, for I feel so sad in doing it, because the world cannot give me peace, so restless because my heart is not rested in God.

Added to Kate's inner turmoil was another—albeit happier—emotional adjustment. Louise was engaged to be married to Edward De Veaux Morrell, a twenty-five-year-old attorney and colonel in the Pennsylvania National Guard, a man whom the New York *Times* called "uncommonly handsome." Rumors among the larger family claimed that Morrell had originally courted Kate following Emma's death. If true, the engagement could have precipitated the impassioned appeal to Bishop O'Connor, but the gossip was never proven. Kate maintained warm relations with both Morrell and Walter George Smith, who became Lizzie's husband in January 1890, and about whom rumors of a prior attachment to Kate also circulated. What is known is that matchmaking plans for her were under way, and that she was expected to choose a fiancé with all appropriate speed.

As much as she loved her sisters and her uncles and aunts, the life they modeled for her was becoming increasingly abhorrent. She dreaded being confined to an existence centered on worldly pleasures: opulent houses, cotillions, and opera evenings, weekly rounds of dressmakers' and milliners' establishments, and daily social calls made and received. Despite O'Connor's repeated appeals that she remain in her position as philanthropist, and that she was "doing more for God, for yourself and for others than you could do in religion" and his concerns about her "woman's heart and affections," his counsel, though well-meaning, couldn't expunge her fears. She envisioned herself imprisoned within a public persona of a wealthy matron dabbling in charitable deeds.

From her earliest years, she'd been taught that God listened to every prayer and was an active participant in each human life. For her, God wasn't an abstract ideal, but a genuine presence in all endeavors, joys, and sorrows. Her faith crisis wasn't that she'd begun doubting her faith, but that she was unable to act on it.

At long last, Bishop O'Connor withdrew his opposition, writing her on November 30, 1888, and suggesting three religious orders for her to consider: the Sacred Heart, the Sisters of Mercy, and the Ursulines of Brown County, Ohio.

Kate disagreed, informing him in no uncertain terms that she had no interest in entering one of those orders. Instead she desired one that served the peoples she'd been helping to educate. "I want a missionary order for Indians and Colored people."

O'Connor demurred, listing additional orders for her to consider. He worried that her health wouldn't withstand a rigorous ministry. There was also a note of snobbery. He pointed out that Kate might be uncomfortable unless surrounded by "ladies" of her social class.

Discussion over her future continued in this private manner, but then came Louise's marriage on January 17, 1889, and Kate's plans were interrupted as she was thrust into the weeks and months of parties leading to the nuptials, giving advice on the couple's wedding trip—which entailed a journey through the southern states and Mexico, with a subsequent sojourn in Europe—as well as the purchase of a trousseau and bridal dress, and the organization of the festivities. Throughout this period, she never told her sisters about her own expectations.

The wedding of Louise Bouvier Drexel and Edward De Veaux Morrell was the social event of the new year. The Most Rev. P.F. Ryan D.D., archbishop of Philadelphia celebrated the marriage ceremony in the Basilica Cathedral of Saints Peter and Paul, which was nearly smothered in hothouse flowers, many of which had been grown in greenhouses on the Torresdale estate. Bishop O'Connor traveled east to celebrate the Pontifical Mass. Kate was one of four bridesmaids, their gowns described by reporters who crowded the exterior steps for a view of the first Drexel heiress to wed. Uncle Tony gave away the bride. Harrison W. Biddle served as Edward Morrell's best man. In addition to the two hundred family members and close friends, four hundred of Philadelphia's most elite residents were present. According to the *New York Times* of January 18, 1889: "No wedding that has occurred in Philadelphia has equaled this in widespread interest. The prominence of the bride's family and its close identification with Philadelphia, the great wealth of the three heiresses, of whom the bride to-day was the first to form a romantic attachment, the many benevolent gifts of the Drexel family, the great popularity of the bridegroom in the most fashionable society—these and many other considerations invested the wedding ceremony with a peculiar and far reaching interest."

Kate, in her *directoire* coat, her petticoats of *mousselin de soie* empaneled with Valenciennes lace, smiled and smiled while hiding an inner anxiety. She was happy for Lou, who was as joyous as any bride could hope to be, but worried about how the greater family would react when she informed them of her decision to enter a convent. Rightly, she surmised that the news would be unwelcome.

Maintaining her secret, less than a month later she again appealed to Bishop O'Connor. She had a new plan she needed him to endorse. In it, she proposed to set aside trust income to continue her school efforts, and then endow a newly created organization, the Bureau for Colored and Indian Missions, which she intended to base in Washington, D.C. When the bureau and its programs were fully operational—which she meant to happen quickly—

she'd be able to leave the work to others. She wanted O'Connor's advice on establishing policy: the number of paid staff, and how monies might best be distributed.

By this time expanding her focus to include educational facilities for African Americans was very much on her mind, and she had a deadline for putting her programs in place. On May 5, the house on Walnut Street was to be closed in anticipation of another European trip; the two unmarried sisters were to accompany Louise and her husband and Uncle Tony, who was scheduled for one of his annual "cures" at the hot-springs spas in Karlsbad. Kate had ostensibly agreed to the journey, but she was determined to quit her secular life beforehand:

> I confess that I am very anxious to know whether I can settle all temporal matters, so as to go into a Novitiate this Spring—May 5th—when we close our home, and go abroad. I dread to go with the European party. . . . I dread to expose my vocation to the test of more world.
>
> How would it do to enter a Novitiate on May 5th and leave my income to Lise and Louise, making them trustees for the application of my income in developing the rough plans we have formed. . . ?

O'Connor's response was unexpected. He suggested that instead of creating a separate, charitable entity, she use her vast reservoir of funds to open her own religious order: "You have the means to make such an establishment. Your social position will draw to it subjects and friends without number. God has put in your heart a great love for the Indian and the Negroes. He was given you a taste and capacity for the sort of business which such a foundation would bring with it."

Astonished by this turn of events, Kate wrote back opposing the plan. Strongly. It wasn't that she was afraid of work, rather that she felt inadequate to the task O'Connor proposed. "The responsibility of such a call almost crushes me," she explained, but O'Connor wasn't dissuaded.

Omaha, Nebraska, February 28, 1889

I was never so quietly sure of any vocation, not even my own, as I am of yours. If you do not establish the order in question, you will allow to pass an opportunity of doing immense service to the Church, which may not occur again. . . .

An order established for the Negroes and the Indians will make a much more direct and economical use of your money than an Indian Bureau could.

Even as a foundress you will have your faults, but God, not you, will do the work. He often makes use of very weak instruments. The question is not, will you be all that you should be, but does God will that you be His instrument.

Adding impetus to the argument, he traveled to Chicago and put the matter to Archbishop Ireland, who announced, "Why, it is just the thing we needed. It is a great, an indispensable work. Miss Drexel is just the person to do it, and if she does not undertake it, it will remain undone."

What could Kate do? She felt outmaneuvered, and more lost than before. O'Connor had at first rejected her application for a religious life; now he was forcing one upon her, but one she intuited might be based on a pragmatic rather than a spiritual decision. Yes, she recognized how great was the need for the order he proposed, but why should the responsibility fall on her shoulders? What if she were to fail? She was only one inexperienced person, after all. Or, equally frightening, what if she became wholly consumed with concrete matters, with facts and figures rather than with the infinite and holy?

Engrossed in those dilemmas, she foresaw a future in which she spent her hours not in prayer but in tallying ledger accounts, fretting about organizational matters, and negotiating construction costs and wondering what had become of promised supplies. God seemed nowhere in the equation. In fact, the opposite was true, and she felt that O'Connor was purposely engaging those attributes she was most ashamed of: her attention to detail, her single-mindedness, and the "scrupulosity" about which he'd formerly chided her.

Bottling up growing feelings of dread, she maintained an appearance of calm while she and Lizzie accustomed themselves to the lack of Louise's sunny presence. Missives home in which the new bride described the sites she and Edward enjoyed on their honeymoon increased the sense of loss to "All Three." Kate knew that if she were to act upon her call, Lizzie's loneliness would be extreme. The secret became all but unbearable.

Aching for answers, she prayed, her body taut with confusion. If Bishop O'Connor was correct, and founding her own order was God's vision for her, could she possibly refuse? The answer at first, was a beleaguered "no," then a hesitant "no," then silence as she pondered the awful ramifications of saying "yes." Had she been wrong about the gifts God provided for her? Was her intentionality, her natural ability to lead and inspire others to follow, designated for enterprise instead of a cloistered existence? Was the pragmatic descendant of financiers and merchants meant to be a Martha, bustling about taking care of Jesus and his disciples, rather than a Mary, sitting pensively at the rabbi's feet? Was she denying God the very nature He'd given her?

"Be still then, and know that I am God." The words from Psalm 46 had particular resonance for a woman who yearned to be "still" but rarely was, and who hungered to "know" God and God's divine plan, but found herself fighting what O'Connor and Ireland insisted was her life's mission. Could they be correct? Was she mistaken about her previous assumptions? And finally: if she did follow Bishop O'Connor's advice, was she capable of reconciling the dualities of her personality? Could she be a woman of daring and innovation while also finding respite in prayerful meditation?

At length, she succumbed to what she believed must be divine counsel, though she continued to feel painful reservations about her aptitude and inner strength. That initial step taken, she told Lizzie of her decision to enter the Sisters of Mercy, her first step along the path. Traveling under their mother's maiden name of Langstroth, the two sisters visited the convent to make certain it was the correct home for Kate. She was wise to take this precaution, because when her decision became public, newspapers in Philadelphia and New York made headlines of the story, and reporters encamped outside of the Mother House in Pittsburgh, hoping for an interview or even a glimpse of the heiress turned postulant.

Before that exploratory journey, Kate screwed up her courage and told her uncle Tony. He said she was making the mistake of her life, then tried to convince her to remain as she was: a wealthy woman controlling her choice of charities. Kate remained unshakable. She loved, admired, and respected her uncle, and had always welcomed his advice, but she knew he was wrong.

When Louise returned home and established her own home at 1826 S. Rittenhouse Square, there was nothing to delay Kate's decision.

On May 7, she Lizzie, Louise, and Edward attended Mass. Bern was there too, as were Kate's personal maid and a few servants who had been with the family since the sisters' earliest days. At the conclusion of the service and amid copious tears from everyone but Kate, the groups parted company: Kate and her sisters traveling to Pittsburgh where she said her farewells to them and to life as she'd known it.

As anticipated, journalists leapt at the sensational tale of an heiress who willingly walked away from a fortune. Headlines blazed across newspapers in Philadelphia and New York. The report in the *Public Ledger* May 8, 1889, ran:

RENOUNCING MILLIONS
Miss Drexel, so well known as the most attractive of the sisters of her branch of the family and one of the greatest heiresses in America, will henceforth be "dead to the world," and the circles of Walnut Street, where she has been so familiar, will know her no more. . . .

Something more than a local interest is attached to this act of the lady from the fact that she is one of the three sisters who inherit a fortune of about $17,000,000, which is said to have increased to about $21,000,000 since their father's death. The fortune is invested not only in real estate all over Philadelphia and in securities and bonds of various organizations and industries in and out of Philadelphia, but in the great banking house of which her father was a member.

The following day, as planned, Louise and Edward, Lizzie and Uncle Tony sailed for Europe. Kate's ties to home and hearth were severed. The pampered ease of her youth, the frivolous adventures she'd shared with her sisters, and the small and large joys, triumphs and sorrows she'd experienced, would henceforth be replaced with poverty, chastity, and obedience. She could only pray she had the inner fortitude to cleave to those rules.

Francis A. Drexel, Katharine's father.

Hannah Langstroth Drexel, Katharine's birth mother.

Emma Bouvier Drexel, Katharine's stepmother.

Katharine Mary Drexel at age seven.

Elizabeth Drexel Smith, Katharine's older sister.

Louise Drexel Morrell, Katharine's younger sister.

Anthony J. Drexel, Katharine's uncle.

Bishop James O'Connor.

Katharine, Elizabeth, and Louise Drexel visiting the Red Lake Indian Reservation with Bishop O'Connor in 1888. Following a previous trip, Katharine had pledged $30,000 to begin construction of schools for indigenous peoples.

Katharine photographed by F. Guntekunst in 1888.

Sister M. Katharine photographed by F. Guntekunst at the time of her First Profession of Vows, February 1891.

Mother Katharine on the steps of Sacred Heart School, Port Arthur, Texas. Mother Katharine traveled about half of each year visiting her missions.

Mother Katharine being helped aboard the boat St. Thomas in Lake Charles, Louisiana, on a visit to remote parts of the state.

Mother Katharine visiting a Hopi farm in Arizona in 1927.

Mother Katharine, right, and Mother M. Mercedes O'Connor, left with Navajos.

Mother Katharine pinning a button on Doris Wiltz during an alumni celebration at Xavier Normal School. Doris's mother was a graduate of Xavier's first class in 1917.

A cadet greeting Louise Drexel Morrell and Mother Katharine at the St. Emma Military and Industrial Academy (Belmead) June 1923 graduation ceremony.

Louise Drexel Morrell and Mother Katharine on the grounds of St. Francis and St. Emma schools in Virginia. The large dog is the supposedly ferocious Mardo.

A formal portrait of Mother Katharine later in life.

Part of the crowd in Rome on October 1, 2000, the day Mother Katharine was canonized, photographed by Sr. Elizabeth Collins, Sisters of the Blessed Sacrament. The banner honoring Saint Katharine is at the upper left.

seven

SISTER M. KATHARINE

REACTION AMONG KATE'S AUNTS, UNCLES, AND COUSINS TO HER
decision to become a postulant in the Order of the Sisters of Mercy
was mixed at best. Tony had already expressed his opinion, but he
shared a strong bond with her and had resigned himself to her
choice. His children, however, and the other third-generation
Drexels found themselves perplexed and even threatened by their
cousin's self-abnegation; what she was undertaking cast into high
relief their self-indulgent lifestyles. Rather than embrace her
courage they began carping that she was overly ascetic and more
than a little odd. If she was determined to establish schools in
inhospitable places, why didn't she simply use her wealth to build
and staff them instead of donning a proverbial hairshirt like John
the Baptist and wandering off into the wilderness to subsist on a
diet of locusts and wild honey? Prophetic voices are discomfiting to
confront, especially among friends and family; to their way of
thinking, the newly styled "Sister M. Katharine" was still just ordinary Katie about whom everyone had an amusing childhood story

to share. Yes, she'd taken a name in religion: M. (for Mary) Katharine, but it was similar to her birth name of Catherine Mary, so wasn't she the same person she'd been before this drastic step? Wasn't she the girl who'd flirted and danced during summer holidays, and been vain about her new dresses and long hair, who'd loved to joke and tease and skewer all pretensions? How had she unaccountably become so serious and severe? True, she still had the same smile and ready laugh, but was the behavior genuine, or was she feigning camaraderie while secretly decrying their hedonism? These were mysteries they couldn't fathom, and they felt judged and unequal to Kate's high-minded ideals.

Although Lizzie and Louise assured their relatives that their sister's time as a postulant would be a bit less rigorous than the other young women undergoing the same process, the differences appeared inconsequential to their Protestant cousins: additional hours for Kate to read and reflect; the ability to continue her correspondence with various mission schools; an orange every morning before breakfast; permission to change her garments twice a week; permission to have a bath every morning, as well as occasional visits to a countryside convent where she could exercise in the fresh air of the garden. For her relatives, accustomed to reading whenever they wished, or dashing off notes or invitations, or changing their gowns four or more times daily in order to meet their numerous social commitments, such boons seemed laughable. To say nothing of the gift of the daily orange. The Drexels, Lankenaus, Pauls, Fells, and Biddles habitually consumed "simple" family dinners comprised of at least five courses such as salmon *à la Genovèse* and chicken *vol-au-vent* and roast fillet of veal and ducklings and asparagus and other seasonal vegetables, as well as desserts of blancmange and lemon tartlets and charlotte *à la vanille*. Here was Sister Katharine trading in all the bounty with which she'd been raised for the opportunity to have a single citrus fruit each morning. Who wouldn't find the image absurd? For some of her cousins, disbelief at her decision turned into derision.

Kate gave no thought to her detractors at home. She had more immediate problems, as she was still grappling with her conflicting sense of vocation: the meditative person she ached to be, and the role of leader Bishop O'Connor was urging upon her. "Ye cannot serve God and mammon" (Matthew 6:24) had special resonance, because her understanding of mammon was interwoven with all things financial and worldly, whereas life with God was a surrendering of earthly desires. How could she reconcile serving God while dealing on a daily basis with mammon's creations? The question seemed impossible to resolve. Then, too, were her feelings of inadequacy. She was comfortable with and comforted by menial convent duties, and was frightened of assuming responsibility like Mother Sebastian, Superior General of the order, or Mother Inez, the Mistress of Novices, let alone becoming foundress of a new order. At the same time, she was struggling to become submissive to her superiors—deferential behavior with which she'd had little experience beyond her childhood relationship with her stepmother. For Kate, the leap from heiress to postulant that she had believed would bring her peace instead intensified her fears.

On May 12, 1889, five days after entering the convent in Pittsburgh, she turned to Bishop O'Connor, beseeching him for help in addressing her qualms:

> The undertaking you propose, Reverend Father, seems enormous, and I shall freely acknowledge that my heart goes down in sorrow when I think of it. To be the head of a new order!
>
> All these dismal thoughts are not generous to Our Lord, and in chapel and meditation I am striving to overcome this selfishness and self seeking, and to look upon the future life you propose for me with cheerfulness, since you say it is the will of Our Lord. But are you sure it is God's will for me to establish a new order. . . ?
>
> Eternity will be too short for me to regret not doing the will of my Creator and my God, to whom I wish every part of my being and life to be as a instrument for fulfilling His Divine will.

Please tell me, Reverend Father, what your wishes are with regard to me. Do you wish me to think constantly of my own individual sanctification irrespective of your future plan, leaving that to God and to you and those you appoint? Then when I shall have obtained the religious spirit you will tell me what you wish me to do? Or on the contrary, do you wish me to learn the religious spirit, continually bearing in mind that I am learning it not only for myself, but for the order you are establishing?

Even in this letter, she couldn't bring herself to refer to the future order as one *she* and not O'Connor was founding.

His reply on May 16, 1889, was blunt. Kate must have found it wounding and unhelpful: "If you expect an angel to be sent to enlighten you in regard to this matter, you may be looking for a little too much." This harsh assessment was softened by his recognition of her struggles, but he provided none of the absolutes she sought. "The work will be God's work," he added, which was precisely what she doubted.

In the absence of angelic intervention, Kate busied herself learning the practicalities of mission life: medical services and teaching. Her sole experience with educating children had been a summer Sunday school she and her sisters maintained when they stayed in Torresdale. Having never been required to teach the basics of arithmetic, spelling, and punctuation, she discovered she lacked simple pedagogical skills. She was also a failure as a disciplinarian. During one particularly boisterous classroom experience, when she attempted to reprimand a young boy who blared out ear-piercing screeches on a tin whistle, the class erupted in a communal jeer of "You don't know how to teach. I'll teach you." The chant and ensuing free-for-all was mortifying. Added to her chagrin was the ease with which a more experienced teacher quelled the riot, and then tamped out a fire illicitly kindled in the cold hearth. Although popular novels like *Jane Eyre* and *Daniel Deronda* depicted once-wealthy young women forced into service roles as governesses, romantic endings rescued them from the classroom grind. Kate had no such outcome in mind. In the wake of this initial debacle, she tried to affect an authoritative glare, which was how the other sisters kept order, but her high spirits doomed the effort. She was already famed in the convent for her mirth and wit.

In the meantime O'Connor gave her further advice: "In regard to your funds, allow me to remind you that for some years, your community [the proposed order] will have no regular revenue. It would, then be only prudent to begin now, to lay aside, say fifty thousand dollars a year as a fund for its support."

This was precisely the kind of fiscal bargaining Kate was trying to avoid. Naturally, her wealth was crucial in aiding Native Americans and African Americans, but she believed that a separate entity to disburse the necessary funds was preferable to maintaining personal control. She couldn't reconcile taking vows of "poverty, chastity and devotion" with acting like a banker's daughter. Instead, she felt that her fortune should be dedicated immediately, rather than being eked out in yearly sums. Recalling the gospel verses "Lay up not for yourselves treasures upon earth, . . . For where your treasure is, there will your heart be also." Kate knew where her heart lay; now it was a matter of persuading others that her methods regarding her earthly treasures were correct. On October 28, 1889, ten days before she was received as a novice, she explained her thoughts to Bishop O'Connor. She had no intention of following anyone's rules: "If I thought that you were my ecclesiastical superior and that Holy Church binds me to obedience, then with all my heart and soul and mind, I shall obey you in all that the Church demands, and renounce now and forever my opinion and judgment."

A private rail car was engaged to carry the Drexels, Lankenaus, Pauls, Morrells, Fells, Bouviers—all names synonymous with Philadelphia's social elite—west to Pittsburgh for the service marking Kate's novitiate in the Sisters of Mercy on November 7, 1889.

When the family next saw her, she would be adorned as a bride of Christ in a creamy white satin wedding gown and bedecked with diamond rings and a diamond necklace. Eight young girls clad in white satin and veils would accompany her down the chapel aisle. Bishop O'Connor's failing health kept him in Omaha, but the panoply of attending clergy presiding over the ceremony was impressive: Archbishop Ryan of Philadelphia, presiding; Bishop Phelan of Pittsburgh; Bishop Brondel of Helena, Montana; and Bishop Glorieux of Boise City, Idaho Territory.

The occasion was intended to be a joyous one, but most of the family members who filled the railway carriage felt less than elated despite their festive attire: the women sporting Medici cuffs, Chantilly and Marquise laces, and hats surmounted by bows embroidered with jet beads. If this were a earthly wedding like Louise's, rather than a spiritual undertaking, there would be champagne punch and toasts, a noisy gala meal enjoyed by many friends and with much family conviviality, following which the newly married couple would make their escape and then begin an extended sojourn to exotic climes. Instead, after the convent ceremony Sister M. Katharine would be stripped of her bridal white and return to them dressed in coarse, funereal black.

All but Lizzie and Louise experienced dismay, if not covert hostility toward the event. Many were certain Kate was making an egregious error, and that her rebellious streak had inspired an act she'd regret. None of the naysayers discussed their misgivings in front of Kate's sisters, but the trip had the brittle artifice of polite rather than candid conversation. Yes, they anticipated a sumptuous breakfast banquet after the service, and understood that Chef Albert Mengou of the Duquesne Hotel had been specially commissioned to provide it, which meant none in the party would need to forsake *casserolettes de terrapin* or *bleu points en coquilles* or filet mignon, and yes, they knew the tables would be fittingly decorated with exotic flowers. But no amount of attractive display or fine comestibles could alleviate the family's consternation. Like Bishop O'Connor during his earliest critiques of Kate's vocation, most of the travelers believed she would fare better in her philanthropic activities by remaining among her peers.

The journey home was another matter. All agreed that although they remained unconvinced that Kate's choice was correct, she had seemed truly happy, that convent life suited her, that the ceremony was splendid, the sermon delivered by Bishop Phelan eloquent, the choir in fine voice, the archbishop's invocation "What God has commenced in you may He perfect" was a marvelous moment, and that her vision of educating the nation's poorest and most forgotten people might, just might, be attainable after all.

Although hesitation remained, it now seemed possible to allow Kate to go her own way while her worldly cousins trod other paths. Adding to their communal relief came wonderful news from Lizzie. The eldest sister, who by then had purchased San Michel as her residence, revealed that she and Walter George Smith, an attorney with a patrician background, were engaged and planned a country wedding in early January 1890. She'd kept the matter secret so as not to overshadow her sister's reception as a novice; only Kate and Louise knew.

The announcement was greeted with ecstatic exclamations. For the aunts and uncles, their niece's choice of Walter Smith as a husband was reassuring; for her cousins, it reaffirmed the fitness of their own lives. Now Lise would be ensconced in an estate replete with ample grounds, gardens, and stables, and occupying herself with the pleasures and duties appropriate to their class.

When January 7, the wedding date, arrived, the *New York Times* account bore the headline "A Brilliant Wedding." A special train transported the guests from Philadelphia to the Torresdale station, requiring every available local cab and several hastily conscripted stagecoaches to carry the group to the church and thence to San Michel for the nuptial banquet. Uncle Tony gave the bride away. Archbishop Ryan performed the ceremony; among the assisting priests was Father Stephan of the Indian Bureau. Lise wore a gown of white brocaded silk trimmed in satin and point lace, with high, puffed sleeves that set off her v-shaped bodice. A diamond neck-lace and diamond pendant complemented the diamond cornet in her hair. Despite a cold, persistent rain that made the countryside look bleak and desolate, and turned the dirt roads heavy with mire, which created problems for the horses and carriage wheels attempting to traverse them, the quiet elder sister was happier than she'd ever believed possible. And looked far happier, too, the two hundred guests concurred. Lou, who was attired in blue velvet with a hat trimmed with gray ostrich feathers, couldn't stop beaming.

———————

While her sisters embraced married life and devoted themselves to new roles as matrons among their social set, Kate's solitary strug-gles continued. She remained uncertain that she had the manage-rial abilities to found and preside over a teaching order. None of her internal battles were shared with her siblings, so the exchanges between them became lopsided: her sisters sending cheerful news to "dear Kitten" in which Lise and Walter described embarking on their European tour, and Louise and Ned recounted entertain-ments in their home on Rittenhouse Square or their evenings at the opera and other cultural events.

An unforeseen division developed. Much as the three loved one another and believed each understood and supported the others' life choices, their daily realities grew increasingly disparate. Nothing in Lise's or Louise's experiences enabled them to empathize with her, or even communicate in a meaningful fashion. For her part, Kate continued warm and tender, but she had as lit-tle ken of their domestic affairs as they did of her hours of service and agonized prayer.

Her sole confidant was Bishop O'Connor, but even he grew impatient with her litany of self-doubt. In a letter dated November 7, 1889, the day of her reception, he rebuked her in no uncertain terms. He had been seriously ill for two weeks, and therefore unable to journey to Pittsburgh, but the stringent tone cannot be attributed to his physical state:

It is your propensity to re-open fundamental questions already settled with the greatest care and deliberation. A habit of mind of this kind is fatal to important and lasting results in every kind of conduct. Surely, if anything had been settled in regard to your affairs, it was that you would found a new order. I shall not here recapitulate the reasons that ultimately decided you to do so, but simply refer you to my letters and conversations with you on this subject. But, lo! and behold! In your last [letter], you treat the matter as still an open question. . . !

Nevertheless, unless you feel a strong desire to found the new order, do not attempt to do so, for you would not go through with it. Even enthusiasm is necessary in such an enterprise. . . .

Almost everything else was considered and settled, at our last interview at the Mercy Hospital. Yet, you have allowed the weighty reasons then considered to be lost sight of in view of vague apprehensions that have entered your mind.

What was Kate's reaction to this angry, impatient tone? The one person she had relied upon for so many years was not only berating her, but trivializing her manifold worries as "vague apprehensions." His admonishment must have hurt, because from this time onward her behavior changed and she ceased confiding her fears in him.

Here was another turning point in her life. She had been sheltered from earliest childhood, and her family's fortune had cushioned her from the reality that any chosen action produced consequences—some of which could be dire. O'Connor's scolding, difficult though it was to accept, made her confront that fact. She recognized that not only had she agreed to his proposal, she had instigated it. Now, there was no choice but to begin, or to turn and run, which wasn't an option. Kate had too much of her grandfather Francis Martin Drexel in her psyche to retreat.

Using her considerable strength of will, she summoned up her courage and proceeded as she had promised she would. She no longer discussed personal issues with O'Connor; instead, she detailed the practicalities of her future endeavors: applicants for her new order, or a preferable location, or else chatted amicably about her sisters and their husbands' lives. The intimacy of vulnerability was gone.

———

The announcement that Sister M. Katharine planned to create a new order was deferred until she became a novice. Less than two months later, she learned that Bishop O'Connor was terminally ill. He died May 27, 1890, without being able to witness the results of his years of counsel to his "dear child." A sense of foreboding haunted her, and she became convinced that the bishop's death proved that founding a new order was futile, or worse, that it had been an act of vanity on her part. Archbishop Ryan, whom she knew well, offered his assistance, visiting Pittsburgh after officiating at O'Connor's Requiem Mass in Omaha, but Kate was immobilized by sorrow. Sequestering herself in prayer, she sought answers that did not come. Every prior weakness and failure rose up to rebuke her. She couldn't imagine how her mission would succeed.

Her practical side persevered, though; if she couldn't fully trust she was the appointed visionary Bishop O'Connor had believed her to be, at least she could behave as though she did. Accustomed to and comforted by the routine of praying, she understood that sometimes habit was enough. Perhaps, too, this period of self-doubt was part of a discernment process through which God was challenging her to new heights of vigor and motivation.

Then came the frightening news that Lise had become so ill in Florence during her honeymoon that last rites were administered. Improved after a dangerous six-week period of uncertainty, the patient remained weak enough to require nursing care for the rest of the journey and voyage home. She was pregnant. Walter hovered at her side in a state of perpetual apprehension while Lise wrote valiant notes to her sisters, gushing over her husband's devotion while assuring them that his trepidations were misplaced. Although she believed she would recover and enjoy a healthy delivery, her husband feared for her and the baby's well being.

Unable to help her elder sister, and now bereft of James O'Connor, Kate continued to go through the motions of establishing her motherhouse, choosing for its location sixty acres of land on a Pennsylvania hilltop overlooking the Delaware River in what today is Bensalem. At the time, the area was known by its older name, Andalusia, so called because the financier Nicholas Biddle had maintained his Greek-revival villa Andalusia there. Torresdale was nearby. Sister M. Katharine, though no longer the once-mischievous member of "All Three," would be near to her sisters. But before plans could be completed or a cornerstone laid, tragedy struck.

Lise and Walter had returned from Europe September 7, 1890. Although still weak, she seemed to be on the mend, and she wrote Kate about a gala dinner party with Walter's family their first night home, and a subsequent dinner with Uncle Tony, Uncle John Lankenau, and George Childs. She and her husband were "settling down" and anticipating a "quiet and peaceable life." She was very much in love, and busy preparing the home for her baby's arrival, ordering a layette and overseeing changes in the household staff. She confessed that she "very seldom [had] time to say my prayers," and added a half-joking: "I draw on your reserve stock." Lise, always so good and dutiful, so selfless and kind, was ecstatic over her impending motherhood. Walter, she declared, would be a stellar father.

On September 25, she and Miss Cassidy decided to walk to the site of Kate's future convent. It was a longer hike than Lise should have risked, and she collapsed after returning to San Michel. Dr. Wymer, the local physician, was called in and remained at the house all night, but Lise's condition worsened. Early the following morning, Dr. Theophilus Parvin and Dr. Jacob M. DaCosta arrived; they decided to perform an emergency caesarean section. Lise was now unconscious owing to puerperal convulsions. It was almost certain she would not survive, but the operation was the only hope for saving the baby.

Parvin and DaCosta's ministrations failed. Lizzie died on Friday evening, September 26; her child was stillborn. Uncle Tony and his sons, Tony Jr. and George were present at her deathbed, as were Archbishop Ryan and Father Vandegritt, the Smiths' priest. Kate arrived too late from Pittsburgh; Louise and Ned were at sea, homeward bound following a European sojourn where they'd briefly joined the newlyweds. Kate was left to face her sister's death alone, and to comfort Walter as best she could.

This time her grief didn't implicate her as it had after her father's demise. She didn't confront the private demons that had demanded to know why she had run to fetch a priest rather than remain with her parent. Instead, she tried to focus on the blessings her elder sister's company had always provided: their earliest years together when Lizzie had understood the dismal loss of their birth mother, and she had not. Then childhood, schoolroom mornings, clambering through San Michel when their father first purchased it, summer rambles in the countryside and down to the Poquessing Creek, fireside games in winter, the cheery smell of the kitchen, the homely, starchy scent of the laundry room, innumerable con-versations shared, and laughter, too.

In Kate's mind's eye she could picture her older sister becoming taller and more mature, a young lady of poise and grace who liked to remain a bit in the shadows, reserved while her younger siblings said or did whatever they wished and whenever they chose. How carefree they'd been, gossiping on the upper piazzas at their aunts and uncles' seashore homes, drying each other's hair, flirting, dash-ing in and out of the waves, and always, always laughing.

Then came Emma's death, followed too soon by their father's, and almost immediately thereafter the time when Kate had broken down emotionally, and Lise had been forced to take charge. How long ago that harum-scarum trip through Europe seemed. Reconstructing their escapades, Kate recognized how worried Lizzie must have been. And how frightened. She wasn't intended for weighty responsibilities. She never had the feisty nature of her next-youngest sibling.

And now she was gone. Maternal, nurturing, empathetic Lise would never be surrounded by children, nor would her quiet sup-port envelop and sustain her husband and sisters.

Autumn's leaves drifted over the lawns at San Michel and onto the wide veranda. Kate sat in one of the familiar wicker-work chairs and watched them fall. When she wept it wasn't simply because she missed her sister, though she did; it was for Lise's lost earthly joys, and for Walter and their baby.

A message she had sent Bishop O'Connor in June 1888 seemed particularly poignant, because its focus had been on how she, Kate, could act as matchmaker to her sisters—Lou, at that particular moment—by pushing them out into society instead of allowing them to be isolated in the seclusion of San Michel. She remembered making the bishop promise to keep her plans a secret, and that she'd also had the temerity to demand whether finding her siblings husbands wasn't a more "sacred" goal than working among the indigenous peoples. Concluding her letter, she had reproved him for destroying her letters to him, and joked that they might have been needed for her canonization. What an imperious, punctilious person she'd been. What presumption. What nonsense. Sister M. Katharine was only Katie Drexel, after all.

Remembering, it seemed impossible that she wouldn't always yearn for her older sister's reassuring presence. And always mourn over the mother Lise might have been.

eight

HERE AM I; SEND ME

In the year that king Uzziah died I saw also the Lord sitting upon a throne, high and lifted up, and his train filled the temple. Above it stood the seraphims: each one had six wings; with twain he covered his face, and with twain he covered his feet, and with twain he did fly.

And one cried unto another, and said, Holy, holy, holy is the Lord of hosts: the whole earth is full of his glory.

And the posts of the door moved at the voice of him that cried, and the house was filled with smoke.

Then said I, Woe is me! for I am undone; because I am a man of unclean lips, and I dwell in the midst of a people of unclean lips: for mine eyes have seen the King, the Lord of hosts.

Then flew one of the seraphims unto me, having a live coal in his hand, which he had taken with the tongs from off the altar: And he laid it upon my mouth, and said, Lo, this hath touched thy lips; and thine iniquity is taken away, and thy sin purged.

Also I heard the voice of the Lord, saying, Whom shall I send, and who will go for us? Then said I, Here am I; send me.

Isaiah 6: 1-6

GRIEVING FOR LIZZIE, KATE OPTED FOR ACTION OVER DESPAIR. SHE understood how wholeheartedly her sister had supported her vocation, and how much she'd believed in Kate's mission and the future of her religious order. Continuing on that path was a means of giving homage, and of recognizing God's presence in every occurrence, no matter how calamitous.

Convinced that God had work for her that couldn't wait, she reapplied herself to the foundation of the Sisters of the Blessed Sacrament. By December 19, 1890, when the *Philadelphia Inquirer* ran a front-page story entitled "Kate Drexel's Big Projects," she had met with the Secretary of the Interior in Washington to discuss her intention of establishing schools for Native Americans as well as African Americans. She had twelve novices ready to help her, and in February 1891 she expected to take her vows of "poverty, chastity and obedience," giving over her entire fortune of close to $8 million to the order. The Sisters of the Blessed Sacrament would then be among the world's wealthiest religious orders: rich, powerful, and led by a woman.

That same February, the Women's National Council of the United States was held in Washington at Albaugh's Opera House. Among the topics for the week-long conference were women in the church. Four women pastors participated: Caroline J. Bartlett, Ida A. Hiltin, Anna H. Smith, and Anna Garlin Spencer, the first woman ordained as a minister in the state of Rhode Island. Additional issues addressed at the Council were charities and philanthropies, education, and the political status of women. Speakers included prominent suffragists Clara Barton, Susan B. Anthony, Elizabeth Cady Stanton, and Julia Ward Howe. The number of would-be attendees was so great that many were turned away. The convention concluded with the singing of the *Battle Hymn of the Republic*, which had been composed as a poem by Howe. The *Philadelphia Inquirer* entitled its initial article on the council "Great Week for Women." Kate, though focused on her singular mission, wasn't immune to the changing political climate of the time. Throughout the nation, women were arming themselves to fight for gender equality; and though mainstream religious denominations were controlled by men, the wealth of Kate's new order and the tenacity of its founder gave it authority.

The style of the motherhouse and novitiate in Andalusia, present-day Bensalem, was to be Spanish Mission, a reminder of the people the order was to serve, as well as of the journey west with Frank in 1884. Kate enlisted Louise's husband, Ned Morrell, and her uncle Tony to provide hands-on advice about architectural plans and construction, roles they enthusiastically accepted. It soon became clear that the buildings wouldn't be ready to occupy when Kate made her profession on February 12, 1891. Archbishop Ryan suggested she remain in Pittsburgh, where her young community could grow without dealing with the problems of bricks and mortar, pipe fittings, and foundation walls. He also proposed that she consider renting a house near St. Peter Claver on 12th and Lombard streets in Philadelphia, an African American congregation and school she was supporting.

As she considered her options, fearsome news came from the Pine Ridge Reservation. The Lakota and other tribes appeared to be on the verge of waging a large-scale war against the whites. The prior June during a council at Pine Ridge, Red Cloud had publicly decried the treaty of 1868, calling it nothing but "sugar paper" and that the decades-old promise of government funds for their lands had been no better than "sugar talk." An old man now, he was tired of the whites' history of duplicity, of the appointed Indian agents' thieving treachery, of the lie that the myriad prospectors and railroad men encroaching on native lands wanted peace when he could see that they plainly did not. The railroad was especially contentious, although Red Cloud had no means of understanding how powerful the moneyed interests were that promoted it, or how insignificant his peoples' protests were.

Beginning in 1870 with his first visit to the capital, to his second attempt to reach accord with those in Washington in 1872, to his third visit in 1885 when he'd exposed the corrupt behavior of Indian Agent McGillicuddy, he had tried to act as liaison between his tribal brethren and the land-hungry, rapacious whites. His patience was at an end. The younger men of the tribes were equally impatient with their elders' conciliatory attitudes. They felt the time for action was long since past. Into this leadership vacuum, Short Bull, whom journalists called a "so-called prophet or Messiah" danced—literally. He created the "ghost dance," urging the participants to dress in their finest garments, and, fully armed, spin themselves into a state of frenzy. In that altered condition, they believed that their spirits were no longer human but animal, especially bison, and therefore more powerful than any puny soldier, whether armed with a Gatling gun or not. Short Bull's incantations were intended for all the tribes: the Sioux to the west; the Cheyenne to the north; the Arapahoe in the east; the Crow at the south:

> My father has shown me these things, therefore we must continue to dance. There may be soldiers surround you, but pay no attention to them, continue the dance. If the solders surround you four deep, those upon whom I put holy spirits will sing a song, which I have taught you, and some of them will drop dead. Then the rest will start to run, but their horses will sink into the earth. The riders will jump from their horses, but they will sink into the earth . . .
>
> Now you must know this, that all the solders and the race will be dead. There will be only 500 of them left living on the earth. . . . You must not be afraid of anything.

Short Bull's visionary words took hold of a subjugated people. There were explosions of ghost dancing on all the reservations, the ceremonies lasting up to four days during which the armed tribesmen neither ate nor drank. A few cautious white voices recommended letting the mania play itself out, but unnerved settlers, traders, and railroad workers began fleeing the region. There were reports of ranchers and prospectors attacked and killed. By early December 1890, a state of terror existed in the Dakotas. Daily dispatches made their way eastward by telegraph to be printed in every newspaper. In most cases the unnerving details appeared on page one. It was reported that ghost dances were held all night long, every night. No one knew when or where the situation would erupt, or whether "friendly Indians" would remain loyal to the United States government or turn into "hostiles." It was assumed that the "hostiles" would greatly outnumber the "friendlies."

Troops were readied, and the 7th Cavalry, which had been decimated in June 1876 at the Battle of Little Bighorn while under the leadership of George Armstrong Custer, was deployed to the Pine Ridge Agency. Gatling guns and Hotchkiss revolving cannons were wheeled into place on the hills above Wounded Knee Creek. The attempted arrest and subsequent murder of Sitting Bull on December 15 exacerbated the situation. Fearful that the charismatic leader would support the ghost dancers, native and white policemen attempted to bring him into custody, with disastrous results and casualties on both sides. The Lakota received the loss in silence, but this seeming quiescence was viewed with understandable alarm, especially among those intent on conquering the West.

On December 29, 1890, as a heavy snow began to fall, contentious but noncombative Lakotas were ordered to relinquish their weapons. When they didn't comply immediately, an order was given to a detachment of K and A troops to search the teepees on foot. Outraged, the Lakotas shot at the soldiers, which generated a violent volley of firepower from the Hotchkiss guns. Teepees ignited and native men, women, and children fell dead. The fight became a rout with the troopers prevailing. Then the Lakotas rallied, killing as many soldiers as they could until the superior force overwhelmed them.

By then the snow had turned into a blizzard; sleet whipped sideways, cutting exposed flesh; horses fell and broke their legs on the ice. Amidst the human and animal carnage, the bursts of gunpowder, and the blinding snow it was difficult to discern which side was which; cavalry sabers and war clubs alike sliced through the air. When the final shots echoed from the troopers and cavalrymen pursuing their prey into the creek and beyond toward the hills, the description of the battle that appeared in the *Philadelphia Inquirer* likened the devastated hollow in which the Lakotas had been encamped as a "sunken Vesuvius." Hundreds of Native Americans perished.

The ongoing blizzard didn't prevent a retaliatory attack on the nearby Catholic Mission the following day, or a mass gathering of Lakota on January 2, 1891. Three thousand men, women, and children were reported encamped in Pine Ridge, and on January 5 the number had increased to 4,000. Along the White River, houses belonging to settlers were torched. A larger battle was expected at any moment. Standing Rock, Rosebud, Cheyenne River, and Tongue River reservations were under tight government control.

On January 8, the bodies of dead government soldiers were found mutilated. On the 10th, the Oak Lake Reservation tribe was rumored to be "dancing." Nerves among the whites were stretched thin; outnumbered on these snow-laden prairies, their artillery wouldn't be able to protect them if the tribes rose up in a communal war. Those reading the reports within the comforts of their eastern homes couldn't believe the settlers and the commercial interests in the western territories were about to be annihilated, but it seemed possible.

During this anxious period, news of a very different sort grabbed the public's attention, serving as a balm to frightened railroad men and to all those with investments in the West. The nation was ready for good news rather than dire, and what better panacea than a celebrity marriage? Twenty-four-year-old Philadelphia socialite Ava Lowle Willing and New York's John Jacob Astor IV were to be wed in February, the ceremony certain to out-sparkle anything previously witnessed in either city. Conversations in drawing rooms and saloons alike focused on this hot topic. Who would be on the guest list? What would members of the famous "four hundred" wear? How would they react to staid Philadelphia? Was it true that the groom's father intended to give the couple a furnished mansion on Fifth Avenue? And that Mrs. Astor's gift was a quantity of diamonds? The same newspapers that detailed a running account of the engagement and future nuptials also devoted space to advertisements for the most fashionable furs: lynx, marten, French seal muffs, and monkey capes. The placards took more prominence than the ominous news that the Russian czar had suspended anti-Semitic laws. In fact, that report was given even less space than information on the Dempsey-Fitzsimmons boxing match in New Orleans.

While citizens safe in the nation's cities turned their attention elsewhere, the breastworks at Pine Ridge were extended. All-out war now appeared imminent.

For Sister M. Katharine this was a frightening period. She'd visited the home of Red Cloud and his wife, Woman-Without-a-Bow; she'd happily interacted with the Lakota of Pine Ridge and elsewhere; she understood and empathized with their plight, and had pledged herself to serve and uplift them. But sitting in distant Pittsburgh, she was powerless. She feared for the schools she'd begun funding, and wondered whether the teachers or students survived. Only toward the end of February did she receive word from Mother M. Kostka at the Holy Rosary Mission in Pine Ridge that Red Cloud himself had saved the mission from destruction while the government schools were being burned to the ground. According to her account, the chief had insisted that the "black-robes" be spared, and further made clear his intention to side with the whites and fight against his own people if the mission came to harm.

On February 12, 1891, when Kate made her final vows, the safety of those posted to Pine Ridge was unclear; it must have been hard to listen to Archbishop Ryan's sermon lauding her good works and her future order's focus when much of the Badlands remained in a perilous state.

The only family member present at the ceremony at the Mercy Chapel on Webster Street was Lizzie's widower, Walter George Smith. Flowers from her cousin George's wife, Mary, from Louise, and Walter made a lush counterpoint to the starkness of her habit. A simple Lenten reception meal of dry toast and black coffee followed. Sister M. Katharine had recently begun wearing spectacles. When she smiled the glass appeared to glint as brightly as her eyes.

Her cheeks were rosy with joy and health. She looked younger than her thirty years. She was where she had longed to be.

The front-page report in the *Philadelphia Inquirer* "Miss Drexel's Final Vows" that appeared February 13, 1891, created much speculative talk and gossip in Philadelphia, but Kate and her intentions to educate the nation's forgotten peoples disappeared from public consideration with the next piece of headline news: the Willing-Astor marriage on February 17.

Spectators crowded the street outside the Willing mansion at 511 South Broad; an equally large number thronged the railway station hoping to glimpse the famous "four hundred" as they descended from two private trains—one for those attending the wedding; the other for those invited to the reception only—and climbed into a waiting phalanx of carriages. The Bellevue Hotel was reported fully booked for the ushers and bridesmaids and their families; eighteen rooms of the Stratford Hotel were reserved for the Astors. The groom's gift of a diamond tiara was described as "unsurpassed," and the value of the gifts was estimated at $5 million. Louise and Ned Morrell's gift of a silver centerpiece four feet long was among those listed in the *Daily Evening Telegraph*; Mr. and Mrs. James Roosevelt also gave silver. It was no wonder that Edward Willing hired private detectives to safeguard the proceedings.

While the busy worlds of politics, commerce, and society continued to whirl around her, Mother Katharine, as she was now called, and her ten novices and three postulants settled into the quietude of San Michel. Lizzie's gentle memory hovered throughout the place, as did all of Kate's girlhood recollections. There wasn't a space on the property, from the attic to the cellar, to the barn, stables, garden, and orchard that didn't contain remnants of her happiest moments, and most difficult and impassioned, too. It was here that she had first made her discovery about God's call to her. It was here that her father had been at his most relaxed, walking among and admiring the numerous specimens of trees he'd brought to the property, and where her stepmother had reveled in tearing across the countryside.

Nearby the Motherhouse of the Sisters of the Blessed Sacrament continued to take shape on its hillside commanding a sweeping view of the distant Delaware River. An old elm spread its branches over one of the choicest spots on which to build, but tradition held that General George Washington and his staff had eaten their lunch under it during their march toward what would become the Battle of Trenton, so the tree was spared and the convent's location adapted to another site. The *Philadelphia Inquirer* called the project "costly," and it was. A main building and two wings formed a cloistered garden with a fountain; one wing had a chapel that could accommodate sixty Sisters; the other contained the archbishop's room and additional apartments; the main building housed the superior's office, a novitiate, a refectory, and a recreation room. Brown stone trimmed the rough-cut local stone; the roofing was Spanish tile; the bell had come from a mission in the Southwest. The total sum for the construction was $100,000. Lizzie's presence was here too, for the convent was named after her patron saint—St. Elizabeth's House.

Charles Marquedant Burns was the much-lauded architect. Specializing in ecclesiastic structures, especially Protestant Episcopal churches, his work locally could be viewed in the Church of the Redeemer in Bryn Mawr, Cavalry Protestant Episcopal Church in Conshohocken, and additions to the Church of the Savior in Philadelphia, whose new transepts and baptistery were gifts from Tony and Ellen Drexel. The George W. South Memorial Protestant Episcopal Church of the Advocate, which later became known as the Church of the Advocate and was the scene of the first ordination of women into the Episcopal Church in 1974, was also a Charles M. Burns design. A muscular form of Gothic revival as was most of his work, it was under way when he designed Katharine Drexel's motherhouse. Recommended by her uncle Tony, Burns was balding, dapper, and mustachioed. Born in 1838, he interrupted his education in 1862 to serve in the Civil War where he saw action in the naval battles of New Orleans and Mobile under the leadership of Admiral Farragut. In 1876, he studied painting and drawing with Thomas Eakins at the Pennsylvania Academy of the Fine Arts. Although courteous and urbane, Burns had a devil-may-care side to his personality, which proved useful on the day the cornerstone for St. Elizabeth's House was laid.

On July 16, 1891, Archbishop Ryan was to preside over the ceremony, which Katharine had decreed should be private and therefore free from journalists. However, an unnamed source insisted that a lighted stick of dynamite would be tossed into the middle of the service, maiming or killing as many people as possible. The cause for the purported attack was racial prejudice; the boarding pupils who would soon be housed in the Holy Providence School on the motherhouse grounds were African American. In years to come, members of Kate's order would often be called "Nigger Sisters" when working in the South. This was the beginning of the bigotry and vitriol that they faced—and of genuine danger.

Archbishop Ryan, Louise's husband, Edward Morrell, and Burns were informed of the threat. Kate was not. Plainclothes police officers were stationed on the grounds, while Burns created a subterfuge, placing broomsticks in wooden boxes, nailing them shut and affixing signs: HANDS OFF. DO NOT TOUCH. HIGH EXPLOSIVE. NITROGLYCERIN. A guard stood watch over the crates, and warnings were circulated that the slightest vibration would set off an explosion. Whether Burns's ploy prevented a tragedy, or whether the threat was hollow, the day proceeded as planned. Told what had happened, Kate later admitted, "Oh how audacious I was in those days."

Racism was a pernicious fact of life during this supposedly Gilded Age. In the South, it took the form of a holy war, with caped and hooded "knights" misinterpreting and misrepresenting scriptural passages to justify the actions of the Invisible Empire. In the North it could be every bit as virulent, if more insidious. Europe and the United States had promoted and would continue to promote "human zoos." Saartjie Baartman, the former South African slave and so-called "Hottentot Venus," was put on display in London and Paris from 1810 to 1815; nearly a century later Ota Benga, a Congolese Mbuti pygmy, also appeared before a gawking populace. In Baartman's case, she was turned into a freak show; Benga and other Africans were housed in what was genteelly referred to as an "anthropology exhibit" at the Louisiana Purchase Exposition in St. Louis, Missouri, in 1904; subsequently Benga appeared as the "missing link" in the monkey house at New York's Bronx Zoo. The Cincinnati Zoo exhibited one hundred Sioux in a "native village" for three months in 1896; and in 1889, the Paris World's Fair, in which the Eiffel Tower represented all that was modern and marvelous, put four hundred Africans on display in the "village nègre." This form of intolerance and cruelty didn't die during the early twentieth century. As late as 1958, the Brussels World's Fair exhibited a "Congolese Village," complete with living inhabitants. In the papal encyclical *Rerum Novarum* delivered May 15, 1891, by Pope Leo XIII concerning *The Rights and Duties of Capital and Labor*, and which sought to create a definitive approach to managing escalating labor problems and to support unionism and fair practices, the issue of workers' rights was addressed, and the chasm between wealth and abject poverty identified, but nowhere was there mention of racial equality.

In professing her vows and the vows of her order, Kate stated, "In the name of Our Lord and Savior Jesus Christ, and under the protection of His Immaculate Mother Ever Virgin, I Katharine Drexel, called in religion Sister Mary Katharine, this twelfth day of February do vow and promise to God for five years from this date, Poverty, Chastity and Obedience, and to be the Mother and Servant of the Indian and Negro Races, according to the Rules and Constitution of the Sisters of the Blessed Sacrament . . . nor shall

I undertake any work which may lead to the neglect and abandonment of the Indian and Colored Races."

Burning with zeal, in June prior to the laying of the convent's cornerstone, Katharine had journeyed to St. Stephen's Mission in Wyoming, a rough trip through arid and often treacherous terrain. St. Stephen's was the intended beginning of her Sisters' work among the tribal peoples, and Kate wanted to travel there and make arrangements for her life's mission to begin. Aside from the hardships of a trip through a mostly wild and sparsely inhabited terrain, the memory of the ghost dances and white reprisals lingered. Mother Katharine ignored the danger. Clothed in her habit, she and Sister Patrick and Maurice Burke, bishop of Cheyenne, jounced out across the empty expanses in "an old Stage Coach— the meanest I ever saw—a wagon covered with cheap white duck (not even canvas)—a two seated affair—one back, one front." With them was an irascible "Western specimen" who complained about being promised first-class arrangements and threatened to renege on his payment; there was also a bag of oats so large the passengers had little room for their feet. After hours of discomfort, a wheel of the miserable conveyance broke; as the driver had no rope with which to repair it, Kate supplied twine from one of the parcels she and Sister Patrick had brought.

Traversing the "tall broad backed barren hills" required two days and a night; there were no travelers' hostels, no ranchers' homes at which to stay. With infrequent changes of horses and almost inedible food, the wagon kept rolling, its human cargo sore-backed and bruised from continually bumping up and down on the wooden seats and banging against the coach's wood slats. Sleep was fitful or nonexistent. Kate, though, was in her element. Her letter to Mother Inez shows her reveling in a glorious adventure. The woman who'd charged recklessly through Europe with Lizzie and Lou was very much in evidence:

> Imagine besides during the journey a wind and rain storm; imagine the leaking white duck wagon roof; imagine on one occasion the Rt. Revd. Bishop holding to a white handkerchief

(red bordered) which was ingeniously fastened to an umbrella stick, the umbrella itself being punched through the tear in the roof and unfurled over the roof; imagine a wild cañon called Beaver over which we passed at 4 a.m. so steep in descent that travelers prefer to walk down the arid declivity rather than cling to the stage. How grand and expansive is the view one gets of the Rocky Mountains a fabulous number of miles off on the horizon beyond the vast, rolling prairie. . . . Three miles from the Mission we heard the pealing of the bell as a welcome to the Bishop. The carriage cannot drive to the other side of the Wind River on which the 160 acres of St. Stephens lies. We crossed the rapid current in a picturesque boat tied by pulley to a ferry rope. Father Scollen did the rowing, Father Pamken welcomed us to the shore. . . . We shook hands with William Shakespeare, the Indian interpreter, a fine, big 24 year-old graduate of Carlisle.

After so much anticipation, Kate found the mission's interior a shambles, and saw vermin in abundance in the beds and kitchen cupboards. Worse, the school, which she'd longed to see, was closed. Its students had taken ill in May, and classes had never resumed. The two priests were also ailing due to poorly cooked food; they were waiting to be replaced, but she questioned whether they would survive long enough for their replacements to arrive. The situation looked grim indeed.

Ever intrepid, Kate took heart from a goodly number of future pupils who arrived anticipating the school's reopening. The visit was brief, but left her more determined than ever. Leaving her hopeful students and their parents behind in order to recross the river and begin the brutal journey back to Cheyenne, she promised she'd be at St. Stephen's with teachers and fresh supplies in August.

Archbishop Ryan disagreed. The reason he gave was that she and her Sisters weren't ready, and he was correct in that assessment. Kate and her novices could scarcely care for themselves, let alone oversee the physical wants of their future students. He didn't mention the massacre at Wounded Knee, or the subsequent battles and raids, but to anyone dwelling on the East Coast the western territories remained volatile and potentially unsafe places.

Kate took the archbishop's decision hard. Despite her vow of obedience, her obduracy wasn't easily conquered, and the indefinite delay to her plans tested her. In her heart of hearts she realized that Ryan was right, but she didn't want to be told to sit quietly and wait; she never had. However, she forced herself not only to acquiesce but to accept that his judgment was for the greater good. She returned to San Michel, which had been renamed Nazareth, and her infant order determined that she and the others would learn the housekeeping, teaching, and mechanical skills they lacked.

One of the most noticeable problems was that none of the young women had ever learned how to cook. They'd grown up with staffs of varying sizes, and they lacked proficiency in simple tasks, such as how to heat stoves with coal. Anthracite was used in Philadelphia, but some of the novices hailed from Pittsburgh or from the enclave of the elite in nearby Sewickley, where bituminous coal was used. They didn't understand that firing anthracite was different because bituminous was softer and more easily lighted. No meal could be prepared if the cast-iron stove didn't maintain an even temperature. When one of the young postulants was assigned the duty of becoming cook for the day, she failed in every attempt to light the stove. The raw materials for the dinner had been delivered by one of Louise's servants, a man named James, who came to the rescue, calmly made the meal while suggesting the postulant busy herself by preparing toast. Summoned for supper, the other Sisters praised the supposed chef who accepted the accolades until someone proposed that her culinary skills should be used daily and that she become permanent cook. A tearful confession revealed the truth. Washing laundry was another challenge; so was cleaning. The Sisters may have been zealous about tending to the needs of others, but they couldn't help themselves.

Eventually they mastered the techniques they lacked, though the individual lessons contained a humorous element, at times making the women seem as immature as girls. Mother Katharine, who had decreed that physical exercise be part of the daily regimen, participated. Often she joined hands with her novices and ran down the long hill fronting San Michel. Ten or so abreast, their habits flying, their faces glowing with exuberance, they pelted along gaining speed and momentum with each stride as if playing a version of crack the whip. At one point they nearly crashed into a carriage bearing a visiting bishop from North Carolina. He wasn't amused by the ladies' lack of decorum. Kate remained polite and appropriately demure as she welcomed the unexpected prelate, but she held her ground. The young women in her charge required physical as well as spiritual challenges.

A frequent and welcome visitor and a person upon whom she relied was Father Joseph Stephan, one of the priests who had initially approached her and requested aid for the tribal missions. Six feet tall, imposing in height and girth, he had a white beard and white hair and a regimental bearing at odds with his priestly garb and sage counsel. Stephan could be shrewd and blunt, two characteristics invaluable when dealing with the policy makers in Washington who were aware of his devotion to the cause of uplifting the nation's indigenous peoples. Born in Gessingham, Germany, Stephan trained at a military academy intending to make that his career, but experienced a conversion nearly as dramatic as Paul's on the road to Damascus. As he was riding through a thunderstorm, a crack of lightning struck a tree nearby, electrocuting one of his companions as well as the horse on which the then-soldier was riding. Thrown but not killed, he discovered he was blind when he recovered consciousness. For three months the condition continued; there was scant hope he would see again. It was then that he began questioning whether he was called to serve God. Praying that his sight would be restored, he entered seminary following a seemingly miraculous healing, then learned that missionaries were needed and came to the United States. During the Civil War, he served as chaplain with the Ohio regiments in one of which the future president William McKinley was a major.

Stephan's advice and intermittent presence helped Katharine overlook the mundane tasks and concentrate on her order's goal while she and her Sisters waited for the archbishop's approval. Despite Stephan's support, an undercurrent of disapproval flowed through the local community. Most of the residents weren't Catholic, but had found it easy to accept the Drexel family's faith when they were affluent landowners. Now that the middle daughter was building a school for poor African Americans, the nearby farmers and laborers felt understandable envy. They resented the family's largesse being squandered on those they viewed as unworthy. A cobbler from the village of Andalusia called in to teach the Sisters how to repair their shoes complained, "Miss Drexel is spending too much money on these Colored people, and she can't afford to buy the good stuff she used to buy." There were no repeated threats of dynamiting the convent, but adverse sentiments lingered. Kate recognized the problem, but knew there was nothing she could do to ameliorate it.

Meanwhile she continued to work behind the scenes, writing letters and making in-person appeals urging that schools be built in the West, and pledging monetary support:

Oct. 17th, 1891

I have received a letter from Most Revd. Archbishop Gross endorsing your appeal for additional building for boys at Umatilla [Oregon]. The Sisters of the Blessed Sacrament will contribute five thousand for this building. . . . I groan in spirit every time I think of St. Stephen's Mission. On Oct. 1st not a single child in school. . . !

Jan. 14th, 1892

Have I yet thanked you for your kind letters from St. Stephen's & also I wish to say that unless I die before payments are due [per stipulation of her father's will], the Sisters of the Blessed Sacrament will give a sum not exceeding

for Church $3000

for Boys School $10,000

to be built at St. Stephen's Mission Wyoming . . .

April 3rd, 1894

Father Stephan inquired in Washington whether it would be possible to obtain a contract school for the interior of Alaska. The response was, "let your Church have the building erected & we shall see about the contract," perhaps even the promise was more encouraging. Father Stephan succeeded in having the promise written by, I believe, the Secretary of the Interior . . .

Father Stephan is to start 5 Missions before, I believe, July next. . . . One of the Missions is amongst the Navajos where there are 22,000 Indians. . . . The Navajos are an agricultural & pastoral people. They manufacture blankets from the wool of their sheep, some blankets being sold at $150 each. An industrial school, therefore where farming, blacksmithing, shoe-making, etc., could be taught.

To Louise, she declared she was "fat and well" and dashed off notes about learning to preserve pears and tomatoes. "In wild haste for mail" was her habitual closure, but then Kate was in a perpetual state of haste.

Her energy and passion could be difficult for her novices to emulate. Forty-one women entered the congregation prior to December 1892; nineteen quit before taking their final vows. Kate demanded a great deal of herself and failed to recognize that others might lack her indomitable spirit. Like her grandfather Drexel, once she'd set her sights on a goal, nothing would hamper or dissuade her. The characteristic was useful in leadership, but could make her intimidating, a woman on a mission with no time to waste on those who couldn't maintain the same pace. Unforgiving of her own failures, Kate was equally dismayed by others' weaknesses, and revealed her displeasure. She understood that she was schooling the women in her charge for hardships greater than mending their own clothes or preparing meals; she needed each member of the order to commit herself to enduring harsh terrains and primitive living conditions while gaining the confidence of a people who had no reason to trust a white face.

One of the schools Katharine had financed before entering the convent in Pittsburgh was St. Catherine's in Santa Fe, New Mexico. Built in 1887 to educate Pueblo boys (girls were added later) it started with promise, then went through a sputtering decline and eventually closed. In distant Philadelphia, Katharine could only send appeals to keep the school open. In 1894 she was able to act rather than wait on the sidelines. That February, eleven Sisters took their final vows; they were now ready to be sent out into the world.

On April 9, 1894, Katharine and Sister Mary Evangelista departed for Santa Fe to assess resuscitating the institution. Kate wrote daily letters to "My dear Ones," or "My dear Sisters," signing herself "From your Mother," or "your Mother." The warm tone conveyed a maternal bond rather than that of superior addressing members of her order; Kate had begun to view herself as a loving parent to the younger women in her charge. "The country—I think it is Ohio—we passed through this morning and last evening is beautiful. The cheerful rolling hills, watered by streams, seem to make it good pastureland for sheep. I have seen many flocks this morning and their wool looks thick and almost ready for shearing. They have such a comfortable look—some blinking in the sunshine and kneeling down—by the way is that the way they sleep? just as if enjoying too much the morning nap to rise with the others."

All bucolic reveries ended when the two women arrived in Santa Fe. Archbishop Chapelle met them at the railway depot, telling Kate "Thank God! My prayer is answered. You are coming to take St. Catherine's."

He had reason to rejoice. Without pupils and teachers, the facility was in serious disrepair. The women stayed a week, overseeing efforts to make the premises livable; all the mattresses needed to be remade; there were no sheets; the blankets were in ruins; cutlery and basic cooking equipment was gone. Kate was too busy to write the Sisters; Sister M. Evangelista described the scrubbing and rebuilding, and hours spent with a "heavy broom and lye." When they had accomplished all they could and left orders to complete the remainder of the repairs, they traveled to what Kate called the "grey sand hills" of Albuquerque where "the wind sends a fine sand against the face like the prick of a fine needle." Then it was home to dispatch the first four Sisters of the Blessed Sacrament to serve as teachers at St. Catherine's. Sister M. Evangelista would act as superior; with her were Sisters M. Gertrude, M. Sebastian, and M. deSales. They departed by train on June 13, 1894; five more were scheduled to leave a week later.

Katharine had had ample experience with travel; she had grown more prudent but was still fearless; she accepted and expected different customs and potentially hazardous situations. Her new Sisters weren't as confident. En route to Santa Fe, they were continuously fretting about losing their luggage, or being overcharged while transporting it from one train depot to another. When they reached Chicago the sight of blind men, women, and children being led in a procession appalled and frightened them, and the discomforts of the road produced numerous complaints about being dirty and not being able to launder their clothes. Enormous signs in Chicago warning travelers to BEWARE OF PICKPOCKETS; BEWARE OF SNEAK THIEVES; WATCH YOUR LUGGAGE added to their distress. They found the food unfamiliar, to say nothing of the upper berths that they tried to climb into while fully dressed and without the benefit of a ladder. When a porter produced the necessary apparatus and told them they didn't need to clamber up by standing on their valises, they were chagrined.

Arriving in Santa Fe, all but Sister—now Mother—Evangelista were equally perturbed. There were no curtains in the bedroom windows; the bathroom was a quarter of a mile distant from the building. They had believed themselves prepared for deprivation; they were not. As they attempted to settle in and make the place home, Katharine left on another journey on June 19 to start two more schools: this time in Virginia on property that had held antebellum plantations on the James River and been farmed by eight hundred slaves. St. Francis and St. Emma Industrial Schools would educate boys and girls, many of whom were descended from those same slaves. While she was gone, the next wave of teachers left the motherhouse in Torresdale for Arizona. Their timing couldn't have been worse, because they were swept up in the Pullman rail strike that crippled the country, sent stocks plummeting, and spread violence all along the railway lines. Five young nuns, the eldest of whom was twenty-four, were ill prepared to battle their way west and south.

The Pullman strike, which became the first nationwide workers' strike in the United States, had its roots in the financial panic of 1893. In response to the economic downturn, George Mortimer Pullman, whose company manufactured sleeper and luxury rail cars known as Pullman Palace Cars, cut his workers' wages—some by an estimated 28 percent, but maintained pre-1893 rents in his company-owned town of Pullman, Illinois, where all employees were forced to reside. Although billed as a model of laborer housing, the homes were poorly constructed; many had no plumbing. Negotiations to lower the rents to match the lower wages failed; on May 11, 1894, the manufactory closed after employees quit their jobs. Pullman refused to capitulate; the strikers grew increasingly desperate as days became weeks. Eugene V. Debs, who would help create the Social Democratic Party in 1897 and be nominated for the Nobel Peace Prize in 1924 and who vociferously opposed everyone and every organization that oppressed the poor, was then president of the newly formed American Railway Union. The ARU sided with the Pullman workers.

When the Pullman wildcat strike was joined by the ARU, Chicago, a hub of transcontinental travel, became a scene of abandoned cars and locomotives. On June 30, the General Managers' Association vowed to fight, declaring that all strikers would be replaced by new laborers—scabs, of course. William Pinkerton lent his weight to the proposal. All along the lines, violence ensued. Cars attempting to leave Chicago were mobbed by protesters; locomotives were uncoupled, and engineers and firemen beaten; Union stockyard freight was either derailed or sent back to the packing houses. Five thousand men in Cincinnati joined the strike, and the entire Gould Southwestern system went out. Trains to Santa Fe ceased operation. The nation came to a standstill; produce rotted; mail went undelivered; nothing moved. By July 5, federal troops, under orders from President Grover Cleveland, were in a state of readiness in Chicago, and prepared to shoot anyone interfering with the trains. Chaos ensued with mobs of people overturning rail cars and setting fires that raged through south Chicago. An estimated 700 railway cars were destroyed.

Throughout the nation, both the striking workers and management had supporters. Both sides were vilified; Debs and other union officials were arrested while management claimed that if the ARU hadn't entered the fray on behalf of the Pullman laborers, all would have been well, and Pullman's workers would have peacefully returned to the jobs. Debs objected, insisting that the charge was "wholly untrue," adding, "At the time they struck the employees were in arrears to the Pullman Company $70,000 for rent alone. Wages had been reduced, but rent and other expenses remained the same. At this rate it would have been a question of a short time only until the employees would have been hopelessly involved in debt, mortgaged soul and body to the Pullman Company."

While the fight raged on, and heated words as well as gunfire were exchanged, the five Sisters of the Blessed Sacrament had been continuing on their journey despite delays and constant feelings of peril. In size and bearing, the women made an unusual sight; in temperament they were equally dissimilar: Sister M. Mercedes was of middling height and plump; Sisters M. Inez and M. Gertrude were tall and thin, and when they walked had a stork-like bend to their knees; M. Sebastian was called "long and lanky"; Sisters M. Clare, M. Anthony, and M. Loretto were short and acknowledged themselves to be overly stout, though Sister Anthony won in that category. She also had the added distinction of being imprudent and a bit of a blabbermouth. Sister Sebastian loved to play pranks on the others. However, concealed by their street veils when in public and covered in their black habits it was impossible to recognize how young and out of their depth they were. The black clothing lent them a gravitas they didn't feel.

When the telegraph lines going east and west were cut, the five were physically and psychically stranded. After their train escaped Chicago, it was stopped at Dodge City, Kansas, and then at La Junta, Colorado, on July 4. Surrounding them were "rough types" whose "conversation" wasn't "at all what women should listen to." This was a shock. Growing up, the young women had admired and respected the religious they met, and had been inspired by their example to enter vocational training. But here there was no courtesy, no civility, no reverence. They were gawked at when they left their locked car to take meals while the train was sidetracked in La Junta. By then water was scarce, and they were forced to make do with only two glasses a day. Obviously keeping their habits tidy was out of the question. Maintaining their prayer life and daily devotions was a struggle.

When the train was finally allowed to proceed, it was manned by members of the United States Infantry, a soldier with a fixed bayonet sitting behind each window, a measure intended to reassure the passengers, but which frightened the sisters into silence.

Then came the twisting Raton Pass through the Sangre de Cristo Mountains separating Colorado from New Mexico and the Raton Tunnel. Rumors flew about that it had been mined with explosives. Fearing they were about to die, the five began praying fervently while the locomotive drew closer to the tunnel's entrance. They were convinced they were drawing their last breaths. Except for their murmured prayers and the continuous squeal of the iron wheels surging over the track, the train was silent. No whistle blew. If a locomotive could be stealthy, this one was.

Once through, however, a violent storm engulfed the train and caused the cars to crash through their trestles and stall in floodwaters that roiled across the tracks. Sister Anthony announced, "Well, it seems when the strikers didn't kill us, God Almighty him-

self seems bound to do it." Her sally released the sisters' tension,
but didn't dispel it. Sidetracked again, this time with three hundred fifty solders who pitched their tents along the lines, Anthony
stated that she couldn't stand "this sitting business any longer,"
then added, "I am certain we are riding to our deaths." Sister Inez
retorted that she thought the soldiers "most noble."

It was hardly an auspicious beginning to their ministry. Nor was
it made easier when the remainder of the journey was made
crammed into in an airless freight car. They arrived in Santa Fe at
twelve-thirty in the morning of July 8, 1894. Naturally, no one was
there to meet them at the depot. Straggling to the school, they
found their first days were filled with more hardships. The once-
vacant building still leaked like a sieve. Every night that it rained
the women dashed about with buckets, but the rain poured
through the roof and down their backs till they were all soaked to
the skin. On top of that, there were hailstones so huge they looked
artificial; they packed a wallop when they hit.

There was little time to deal with the vagaries of nature, however. They needed to learn Spanish, and quickly, if they were to
communicate easily with their pupils. Despite the Sisters' lack of
proficiency they drove by buckboard into the Tesuque Pueblo
where the roads, or what passed as roads, looked like gullies. Dogs
greeted them first, snarling and barking as if intent on driving away
the strangers, then came a welcome sight as children surrounded
the visitors. One elderly man caught Sister Anthony's attention;
she couldn't take her eyes off his headdress, which consisted of various lengths of strips of animal skins tying up his hair. "Well," she
whispered, "did anyone ever see such styles since God put them on
the face of the earth?" No one remarked that God had never been
in the fashion business; they were too overwhelmed by the outpouring of affection from the Tesuque Pueblo, and the work with
which they'd been entrusted.

They persevered despite a typhoid epidemic that killed thirty
from Cochiti Pueblo and sickened one of their pupils. He survived,
but it was a frightening time, and no one knew if the epidemic

would sweep through the entire school and infect teachers and students alike. The cultural differences were also acute; nightly, nine or ten of the older Pueblo men and women, their faces painted red and green, arrived at the school, expecting to be fed. They brought their horses, and considered provisions necessary for them too. This was an ancestral form of hospitality in a terrain that was rarely verdant. Although the women understood their guests were peaceable, their wild appearance combined with the recent memory of the tribal uprisings in the north following the massacre at Wounded Knee created an anxious tension that made them deviate from what they'd been taught to believe and what they felt viscerally. Sister Anthony was particularly prey to unfounded terrors, which made her the brunt of an elaborate practical joke staged by Sisters Sebastian, de Sales, and Gertrude who attired themselves from head to toe in native garb and pretended to be "three wild Apaches, as wild as wild can be." After Sister Anthony was summoned to confront the intruders, who appeared "very fierce," even though they refused to speak or explain why they'd come, she raced off to sound the alarm, yelling at the top of her lungs, "Oh, Sisters, Sisters, we will all be killed." When the ruse was revealed she stormed about, grousing that she hoped "a band of Apaches will come and break every window in the house."

All this time Katharine was bustling about, visiting her young teachers in Santa Fe briefly and chastising them for their immaturity and exhorting them to behave like the sensible women she'd supposed them to be, then journeying to Chicago to purchase additional furniture and carpeting for the school. Her letters show her negotiating better prices, and fretting about the quality of each article. At the same time, she fell into raptures over the magnificent scenery she passed, even quoting Byron's "Childe Harold's Pilgrimage" as she gazed out the train window in Kansas and compared it to the poet's: "Where the Day joins the past eternity."

> *The moon is up, and yet it is not night:*
> *Sunset divides the sky with her: a sea*
> *Of glory streams along the Alpine height*

Of blue Friuli's mountains; Heaven is free
From clouds, but of all colours seems to be,—
Melted to one vast Iris of the West,—
Where the Day joins the past Eternity,
While, on the other hand, meek Dian's crest
Floats through the azure air—an island of the blest!
(canto IV, stanza XXVII)

How much of the epic work she knew by heart isn't certain. Memorization had been part of her education, and reciting poetry in vogue during her youth. Her uncle Anthony had read her poems when she was a toddler, and her cousin Emilie had been adept at declaiming. The line from "Childe Harold's Pilgrimage" was an acknowledged favorite. In this instance, she added, "If we have died to self in life, and lived in God's Presence and near Him and with Him, and in union with Him in life, surely on that Day when Eternity shall commence to us, God's own beautiful light will glorify all our thoughts, words and actions because His Will and light will appear in them, and thus they will glorify Him forever and ever."

So, here was Mother Katharine, rushing from one part of the nation to another, the railway cars clattering through hamlets, farmland, and long expanses of uninhabited terrain while she considered Byron, a poet proud of his dalliances, and whose morality was the antithesis of hers. The image is a striking one: this very holy woman ruminating on the words of a man who was anything but a saint, and weaving them into her perception of a just and perfect existence.

It was Katharine's ability to be both in the world and separate from it that gave her power as a leader. She could appear humble, and she was, but she could be steely and commanding when necessary. By 1894, the motherhouse required a new laundry building; plans were executed, and she and a young Sister visited the plumbing firm that would be in charge of the construction. Kate was a stickler for detail, and determined that she and her order get their money's worth in any negotiation. Entering the office, the two women found a young man hunched over a desk, so busy writing he didn't bother to look up at the visitors. Katharine asked to see William R. Dougherty, the head of the company, but received no reply. She asked again, at which point the young man impatiently tossed a nickel across the desk; the coin bounced so hard it landed on the floor. She picked it up, and requested an interview with Dougherty again; this time she informed the young man of her identity, her demeanor assertive. He leapt up in dismay, his eyes darting toward his boss' closed door, and began babbling that the business was accustomed to having visits from so many "begging nuns" it was hard to get any work done. The apology lasted so long and was so convoluted that Katharine stopped him with a cool, "It's beautiful work these good religious are doing, *begging* for poor outcasts." Then she marched into Dougherty's office. When she left the premises, the young man was nowhere in sight.

By the close of 1894, the St. Emma Industrial School for African American boys was under construction in Rock Castle, Virginia; the building was funded by Louise. Katharine purchased the adjacent property in order to erect and staff a school for girls. In addition, St. John's School for boys had opened in Oklahoma— then called Indian Territory—and its companion facility for girls in Pawhuska, fifteen or so miles distant. St. Elizabeth's, named in memory of Lizzie, also educated Native American girls. At home in Torresdale, Holy Providence School served African American boys. However, there remained considerable tension within the neighboring community over the mission of Katharine's order.

nine

LISTENING AND ACTING

THE GILDED AGE WITH ALL ITS RIOTOUS EXCESS WAS IN FULL SWING while Katharine was struggling to fund her schools. The term, coined by Mark Twain in the novel of the same name, still conjures up images of wealth run rampant. Pleasure palaces built by the Vanderbilts, Astors, Rockefellers, and others competed in size, luxury, and the value of their artwork and opulence of their grounds. Biltmore, the Asheville, North Carolina, "little mountain escape" owned by George Washington Vanderbilt II, boasted 250 rooms; the Breakers in Newport, Rhode Island, the summer home of Cornelius Vanderbilt II, chairman and president of the New York Central Railroad system, had a dining room that would have been acceptable in Versailles; Lynnewood Hall, the Philadelphia-area estate of streetcar magnate Peter A. B. Widener, contained paintings by Rembrandt, Raphael, Velasquez, Botticelli, Turner, Constable, and Corot.

As the chasm between wealth and poverty grew, political viewpoints diverged. The presidential election of 1896 polarized the nation. Big money threw its heft behind William McKinley and his kingmaker Marcus Alonzo Hanna, whom political cartoonist Homer Davenport, who worked for William Randolph Hearst's *New York Journal*, depicted as a giant beside the candidate. Hanna was habitually shown wearing a checkered suit—each check being a dollar sign. Standard Oil, Carnegie, and the Duke Tobacco Company were early McKinley supporters.

McKinley's opponent was William Jennings Bryan, a populist, charismatic progressive, sometimes known as "the Boy Orator of the Platte." When Bryan concluded his famous speech at the Democratic National Convention in Chicago explaining why he supported a "free-silver" policy instead of the gold standard that he believed had caused the nation's economic woes, his words became a rallying cry for the working class: "We shall answer their demands for a gold standard by saying you shall not press down upon the brow of labour this crown of thorns, you shall not crucify mankind on a cross of gold."

Bryan, though a savvy political leader who took his message to the people by traveling 18,000 miles and delivering six hundred speeches in twenty-seven states, lost to McKinley. The Progressive Era had been established, however. With it came voices intent on criticizing the status quo.

Ida Bell Wells-Barnett was one of those voices. A fiery woman and gifted writer and public speaker, she co-founded *Free Speech and Headlight* in Memphis in 1889. *Southern Horrors: Lynch Law in All its Phases* was published in 1892. "Civilized America," she declared, was a fiction if men and women were readily lynched and/or burned alive.

Mary Church Terrell was another woman determined to attack racial injustice. The daughter of former slaves, she majored in classics at Oberlin College, from which she earned a master's degree. She was a teacher and principal and was appointed to the District of Columbia Board of Education in 1895, the first black woman to achieve the position. She pulled no punches when attacking the claim that Washington, D.C.—then known as "the Colored Man's Paradise"—was anything but.

Wells-Barnett and Terrell were educated, articulate women with public forums; even for them, parity was difficult to achieve. For the uneducated, the situation could be hopeless.

———————

By 1896, Katharine Drexel had begun plans for her first schools to educate African Americans. Her sister Louise and her husband, Edward Morrell, had purchased Belmead, a former plantation on the James River in Virginia; part of the land and Gothic-revival mansion house were to be transformed into an industrial and agricultural school for boys and named St. Emma after Louise's mother. From Louise, Katharine purchased land to build a nearby school for girls that would be both high school and normal school— teaching its students to become teachers themselves.

Edward de Veaux Morrell and Lizzie's widower, Walter George Smith, often acted as Katharine's advisors; at her behest, each carried out specific tasks for which their careers provided expertise. Smith, at one time the head of the American Bar Association, was a highly qualified lawyer who had connections with attorneys throughout the United States. He would become instrumental when Katharine purchased land in the deep South, where residents vehemently opposed opening schools for African Americans. Morrell, also a member of the bar, focused on politics. He believed in educating those for whom education was denied. From 1891 until 1894, he was a member of Philadelphia's Select Council. From 1900 to 1906 he was a member of the House of Representatives. He served as a colonel in the Third Regiment of the Pennsylvania National Guard and later became a brigadier general.

A speech Morrell delivered on the House floor in 1904 exemplifies his social justice ideals. Despite the requisite decorum among congressmen, his tone bristled with outrage when he attacked one of his colleagues—Thomas William Hardwick who later became Georgia's governor—declaring: "The gentleman from

Georgia alleges that 'of the more than a million and a half negro males of voting age' in the eleven States that once constituted the Southern confederacy 'three-fourths of a million can neither read nor write.' . . . I would ask him if he is proud of this record; if he experiences self-satisfaction in the reflection and the declaration that a majority of the negroes in the South can neither read nor write." The address was eloquent, his obvious anger contained only by his desire to win the battle over repeal of the Fourteenth and Fifteenth Amendments, and thereby strive to ensure equality among the races.

If it is true that, as a distinguished southern statesman has remarked, "A smart nigger is a bad nigger," we must change all our opinions of the value of an education. For such a conclusion would involve whites as deeply as blacks. If education tends to depravity, debauchery, and an increase of criminality, then we have too many schools, too many colleges, too many books, too many newspapers, and for that matter, too many educated Members of Congress.

It is not alone in the Southern States that the negro is unfairly treated in the enforcement of the law; it is also true that in the Northern States courts and juries are often his enemies, always ready to exaggerate his faults and ignore his virtues.

The negro, especially the ambitious and aspiring negro, is treated very much as the Jew is treated by the ignorant peasantry of Russia. Everywhere prejudice tracks him and defeats him; everywhere he is more or less looked upon as necessarily inferior . . .

Governor Vardeman, of Mississippi, made a crusade through the North in opposition to negro education. Here is a choice sample of his refined classic style:

"I am opposed to the nigger's voting, it matters not what his advertised moral and mental qualifications may be. I am just as much opposed to Booker Washington, with all his Anglo-Saxon reinforcement, voting as I am to voting by the cocoanut-headed, chocolate-colored typical little coon, Andy Dotsom,

who blacks my shoes every morning. Neither one is fit to perform the supreme functions of citizenship."

Booker T. Washington sent Morrell a note of thanks when he
received the text of the speech.

Belmead had once been a four-thousand-acre plantation owned
by General Philip St. George Cocke. He was reputed to have been
one of the twenty largest slave holders in the South, owning eight
hundred slaves, forty of whom worked the expansive lawns.
According to some of those former slaves and their descendants,
whom the Morrells hired when they purchased the property, Cocke
had committed suicide after returning home for Christmas fur-
lough in 1863. He'd taken a gun, walked to a magnolia tree on the
estate, and shot himself in the head.

Reconstruction, the waning fortunes of the Cocke family, and
the ongoing political and societal upheavals of the region made
this part of "lowland" Virginia more of a backwater than it had
been before; and the land, though beautiful with sloping, verdant
hills and the James rolling peaceably below it, had little access to
the outside world, which meant that its poorest residents had
scant—or no—educational opportunities. Unlike government
mandates that helped defray some of the costs of educating Native
Americans, there were no financial provisions for the impoverished children and grandchildren of former slaves. St. Francis de
Sales, subsequently called Rock Castle by its teachers and students
because it stood in Rock Castle, Virginia, and St. Emma both
addressed that racial inequality. Charles M. Burns designed the
Rock Castle buildings, the largest being nicknamed "the castle"
because of its regal appearance and tall bell tower. Made of bricks
produced on the property and locally quarried stone, it was unlike
anything before constructed on this sleepy bend of the James River.
The students attending were understandably proud of their connection to such an imposing edifice. They may have been poor,
and they may have been the descendants of slaves, but their school
looked as impressive as those in Richmond or distant
Charlottesville.

The Rock Castle cornerstone was laid during the summer of 1895, the same year that Katharine made her final profession; the building was completed and ready for students by the autumn of 1899. The opening was marred when arson destroyed one of the property's barns. Arriving in July to make certain all was in readiness, Mother Katharine now had to worry whether other buildings would be targeted. Wisely, she took out insurance, but that wouldn't prevent other malicious people from starting other devastating fires.

Racial bigotry gained a dangerous aspect of legitimacy when the Supreme Court overturned the Civil Rights Bill in 1884. In 1896, the ruling in *Plessy v. Ferguson* declared the constitutionality of racial segregation in public facilities. "Separate but equal" was the misleading term for a policy that endorsed anything but equality. In Louisiana in 1892 Homer Adolph Plessy, who was seven-eighths Caucasian, attempted to ride in a railway car reserved for whites. Taking his seat, he refused to vacate the car, and was duly arrested. The case began as *Homer Adolph Plessy v. State of Louisiana,* but eventually moved to the Supreme Court following Judge John Howard Ferguson's ruling that Louisiana had the right to regulate railways operating within its state boundaries. The Supreme Court ruled against Plessy, upholding Ferguson's previous decision. Thus were born the notorious Jim Crow laws.

The political climate that Katharine Drexel and the Sisters of the Blessed Sacrament encountered when they began teaching in Virginia didn't dampen their enthusiasm. In fact, Kate's reaction was the reverse. She became combative when provoked. The same steely gaze that was leveled upon novices and postulants who met with her disapproval turned implacable when she encountered those whom she believed were enemies of justice. Anyone who crossed her soon discovered she was mightier than she appeared. And tougher, too.

Besides education, the members of Katharine's order reached out to the area's impoverished residents, visiting homes and providing food and medication and instructing those incarcerated in the nearby state farm prison, an annex of the Richmond Penitentiary. Their ministry wasn't made easier owing to the rats that infested Rock Castle and the region. "Rat Castle" it was dubbed by the Sisters who cowered in their beds at night, and reported that the creatures were stealing their stockings and garters. Brooms were kept at the ready; the more superstitious among the women insisted the beasts were "supernatural rats." Katharine calmly suggested the Sisters purchase a poison called Rough on Rats, and arranged for two large dogs to prowl the place, though one, Mardo, a German shepherd mix that looked like a wolf, inspired as much fear as did the rodents themselves.

The students weren't troubled by the dogs or rats; they were too focused on their lessons, though there was dissension over an early regulation that students remain on the school grounds for the entire course of their education, meaning no visits home. The rule was altered, but it shows Katharine's determination that learning take precedence—no matter the personal cost. One of those initial students was Minnie Canneville, whose older sister, Gertrude, enrolled her. Minnie was a year old when her mother died; Gertrude promised their dying parent to take care of her baby sibling. At sixteen, Minnie started her studies at Rock Castle, while Gertrude hired herself out to work wherever the teachers needed her. Their home became the school and its grounds until Minnie's graduation.

By this time there were over eighty members of the order, and Katharine was spending much of her time traveling between Rock Castle, Santa Fe, and the motherhouse. The government contract system had come under attack by 1898; in the years 1891–1892, there were 3,158 students enrolled; six years later the number was half that. Kate needed all her Washington connections and personal clout to help maintain the extant schools. In 1898, she made a gift of $83,000 to support education facilities not under the auspices of the Sisters of the Blessed Sacrament.

Kate was perpetually in motion when not conferring with Morrell or Walter Smith or Father Stephan (by now a monsignor and director of the Bureau of Catholic Indian Missions), or substituting for teachers in Santa Fe who had contracted typhus or other recurring illnesses, and her own health became a growing concern. Often she didn't take time to eat, or forgot if she had, which engendered worries among her order and supporters. Kate didn't want to admit to being prey to human frailties. Wherever there was work to be done, there she was, which could be disconcerting for the youngest Sisters who viewed her as an august figure, the founder and Mother Superior of their order. Seeing her spend hours among the laundry tubs, mangles, and flat irons in Santa Fe inspired the younger women, but it also intimidated them. How could they follow this example of single-minded devotion? As Katharine's fame as an outspoken proponent for social justice increased, she found her notoriety both a help and hindrance. The public expected someone larger and more authoritative in demeanor. On one occasion, when a stranger was introduced to her, he couldn't help but exclaim, "Oh, I am so disappointed." Her reply was a wry "Everybody is."

St. Emma's Industrial and Agricultural School had become a vibrant institution by 1899. Louise and Edward made regular, extended visits. During their Christmas sojourn in 1899, Louise decided additional purchases were necessary for the festivities; she rushed off to Richmond, dashed back again, developed an upper-respiratory infection and became seriously ill. Lou, for all her audaciousness as a child, had never been physically robust; the force of her character had carried her forward. Now the chubby-faced girl with the fair curls and rosy cheeks had turned into a gaunt woman whose smile revealed hollow circles beneath her eyes. There was

more than a touch of sorrow in her expression. She'd never recovered from Lizzie's death and the death of her baby. Louise and
Edward had no children.

The physical ailment in 1899 affected Louise's emotional
health. When Bernice Cassidy, the Drexel girls' former governess,
died, the information was withheld for several months because it
was deemed dangerous to tell her, although Louise, who'd come to
depend upon the older woman's counsel, complained about missing Bern's visits and letters. From 1900 onward, she and Edward
spent more and more time at their summer home in Bar Harbor,
Maine, although the pressure of life in the social whirl was as great
as it was in Newport, Rhode Island, where the Morrells also maintained a house. Despite Louise's waning physical and mental
health, the couple entertained and were entertained by the
Vanderbilts, Cassatts, Biddles, Chews, and other families who
owned palatial "cottages" overlooking the coastline. Edward, who
sported impressive mustachios and was the image of a hale and
hearty gent, increasingly attended the functions alone while his
wife remained in quiet seclusion at home. Katharine grieved over
her sister's decline. She'd battled her own psychological trauma
and understood the emotional toll; it was impossible to imagine
the youngest and most ebullient of the siblings fading into a sad
middle age. Such appeared to be Lou's future, however. Edward,
despite his political success and the respect of his peers, would
decide not to run for Congress again in 1906. By then Louise's
health would have forced her to quit Washington, leaving Morrell
to live in bachelor quarters until his term expired.

————

By 1900, Katharine had begun a new project, a school for Navajos
in the Arizona Territory. Like the other indigenous peoples, their
treatment at the hands of the government, and the settlers, miners, and trappers who connived to get their land had left them mis-
trustful and angry. Starting in the early seventeenth century, the

Diné, or "the people" as the Navajo called themselves, had had contact with colonists: first with Spaniards, then with Mexicans who enslaved them, and eventually the Americans who wanted to subdue them. It was believed the area was rich with gold. The United States military succeeded in subjugating the tribes in 1864 when Christopher "Kit" Carson and his troops entrapped the Navajo in Cañon de Chelly, which had long been their place of refuge, and forced them, at gun point, on a series of marches known as "The Long Walk"—three hundred fifty miles to Fort Sumner. The land the native peoples left behind was then burned, their crops destroyed, their livestock scattered or killed: all part of a sanctioned policy of extermination.

Kit Carson had already gained fame as an Indian hunter, having previously been a professional trapper and guide. Born in 1809 in Madison County and raised on the Missouri frontier, he participated in the Mexican War, became at Indian agent in Taos, New Mexico, in 1854, fought on the side of the Union during the Civil War in the Southwest, and was breveted brigadier-general of volunteers, then resumed his career as an Indian agent following the war. In 1868, the year of his death, he journeyed to Washington as liaison and translator to Chief Kancache of the Ute tribe in Colorado to meet with Generals Grant and Sherman.

When he died, journalists referred to him as the "Nestor of the Rocky Mountains," the tribute placing Carson within the vaunted sphere of the Argonauts. There would be towns named for him, and memorial tablets erected in Taos and Santa Fe; popular actors like Frank Bradford would add dramatic renderings of Kit Carson's heroic deeds and exploits to their repertoire, and fictionalized accounts of his adventures were serialized for young readers. The consensus was that Carson had been a "grand, old pathfinder, who showed and told Tom Benton, Fremont and the government all they ever knew about this trans-Missouri empire." In addition, he was lauded as a "pacificator."

The Navajo disagreed with that epithet. The "Long Walk" was endured by eight thousand of their men, women, and children. An estimated three hundred died on the forced march to the newly created Bosque Redondo reservation near Fort Sumner; during the four years of their incarceration, additional tribal peoples succumbed because of tainted water or a lack of provisions. Firewood was scarce; the winters were frigid. Following a peace treaty signed by General Sherman, the Navajo were permitted to return to their ancestral home, but they had no reason to believe they would be left in peace. A promise had been made that any Navajo surrendering to Carson's forces wouldn't be harmed, a pledge that had been broken.

When Kate first visited the area in 1900, the Navajo lived on a twelve-million-acre reservation, most of which was desert. Shepherds needed to relocate their flocks often; blindness was a common affliction owing to the winter and summer hogans being poorly ventilated and easily filled with smoke. The United States government's policy toward the indigenous peoples wasn't called genocide, but the tribes had been decimated. Now the Navajo, like the Lakota, were ignored. There were no schools, which made it impossible for them to succeed in the white man's world, keeping the Navajo in a state of perpetual serfdom on largely uninhabitable terrain. Aversion to education was a belief also held by some of the tribal leaders. One, Tall Silversmith, was outspoken in his opposition to Anglo-American schooling. It was only after he and other Navajo headmen visited St. Catherine's in Santa Fe that he changed his mind and decided that the only means of improving living conditions for his people was through education and industrial training.

St. Michael Indian School opened in 1902 under the auspices of the Sisters of the Blessed Sacrament. Building the structure had been a haphazard affair, so had establishing a reliable water system. Honest contractors were scarce, because Katharine's wealth attracted people hoping to defraud her, and there was little enthusiasm among many of the local whites for the project, a scenario replayed at many of the Sisters' schools. Kate, though, was determined that construction would be finished by September 1902.

When she arrived that month, she found workers' shanties everywhere and debris and equipment littering the site. By September 29, efforts were still under way to drill for water; on October 8, the main building was half finished, a Herculean task given that the locally quarried stone had to be transported by wheelbarrow. On Thanksgiving Day, the first students arrived; it was snowy and bitterly cold—the beginning of what would be the most frigid winter in twenty years. On December 3, the school officially opened, although much of it remained incomplete. The students were shy, made nearly mute by the strangeness of their surroundings, and unsure how to react when the black-robed and pale-skinned women insisted they feel at home in a huge place full of openings made of something that looked like ice but was called glass, and with rooms reserved exclusively for sleeping, or studies, or eating. None of the children had left their families or communities before. The school, tile floored and tile roofed, its walls made of cut rocks, and perpetually chilly despite the fireplaces, wasn't like anything their minds could have conjured up.

Navajo family life centered on the hogan: the summer constructions being three-sided, open, and easily transported; the winter counterparts compact and secure enough to withstand heavy snows. All were built to face east. A dedication ceremony was necessary before a hogan could be occupied. If a person died within the dwelling, it was burned and a new one built. The typical dedication began with the man stating, "May it be beautiful, my house. From my head, may it be beautiful. To my feet, may it be beautiful. Where I lie, may it be beautiful. All above me, may it be beautiful. All around me, may it be beautiful. May it be beautiful this road of light, my mother's ancestor." Then the woman would add, "May it be beautiful, my fire. May it be beautiful for my children. May all be well. All my possessions, may they be beautiful. All my flocks, may they increase. May all be well." Fire was equally vital to family life; this was reflected in a chant that extolled the position of women as being the keepers of the hearth: "Beauty extends from the fireside of my Hogan; it extends from the woman."

The Navajo's reverence for loveliness was echoed in a letter Katharine wrote upon her arrival at the unfinished school. Difficulties melted away when faced with the grandeur of the arid landscape. "The sun had sunk an hour behind the red sandstone cliff before we reached the mission. The stillness of the twilight in that ocean of sand stretching far away, melting into the distant horizon, tinged with the red of the departing sun was almost palpable. . . . One seems so alone with God, and so very far away from creatures."

Poetic as the spaces appeared with their giant rock formations, flowering cacti, and those Shelley-like sands stretching "far away," living at St. Michael was a trial. Uncovered buckboards were the norm for travel, but the wagons' springs couldn't ameliorate the severe jouncing caused by the parched and stony ground. Travelers were immediately coated with dust that turned them so white they looked as if they'd been dredged in flour. Dust made their eyes burn and clogged their throats. In the winter, parents couldn't visit sick children because of the snow, nor could the Sisters attend to the needy in the tribal communities. Flash floods were an ongoing peril. The journey from Gallup, New Mexico, then a small mining town where the train stopped, to St. Michael's took four hours and covered a distance of thirty miles. Often the horses were too sick or weary to continue. School and general supplies ordered from St. Louis or Chicago and shipped to Gallup required an additional haulage fee to transport them to the school. Kate and her Sisters were frugal; they found economy a necessity. Letters were habitually composed on the backs of merchants' bills.

Despite the hardships, Katharine and her teachers persevered. They learned to accommodate lessons with the practicalities of Navajo life, closing school so the children could be home to help during the all-important lambing season. Half of each day was given over to studying geography, science, mathematics, music, drawing, and singing; half to industrial training: the boys learning animal husbandry, shoemaking, and carpentry, and the girls home economics, sewing, and weaving. The Sisters hired an expert

Navajo weaver to help the girls learn the subtleties of the craft. The blankets they produced were a critical part of each family's income.

On her annual visit nearly a year after St. Michael opened, Katharine wrote that she "looked up in wonder at God's wonderful ways and thought how little we imagine what may be the result of listening and acting on a desire He puts into the heart."

ten

HIS STEADFAST
GRACE AND LOVE

WHILE KATHARINE FOCUSED HER PASSIONATE HEART ON HER mission, world events reflected escalating turmoil. Reelected in 1900, President William McKinley was assassinated in September 1901. Leon Czolgosz, an anarchist and follower of the firebrand Emma Goldman, shot the president during a reception in Buffalo, New York. Arrested, the perpetrator calmly declared, "I have done my duty."

Initially expected to recover, McKinley was lauded throughout the country while Goldman, who had fled Russian anti-Semitism and whose first job in America as a seamstress earned her a meager $2.50 per week, was confined in a Chicago police station. She was derided as a "fiend in human shape who preached murder and arson." When McKinley lapsed into a coma after murmuring "Nearer, My God, to Thee," and reports surfaced that a similar assassination attempt had targeted Vice President Theodore Roosevelt, the national response became vengeful outrage.

The specter of anarchy engendered an international sense of doom. In the seven years prior to McKinley's assassination, other heads of state had been murdered: President Carnot of France in 1894; Spain's Premier Canovas in 1897; Empress Elisabeth of Austria in 1898; Italy's King Humbert in 1900. King Humbert's assassin was an Italian, Gaetano Bresci, who had been living in Paterson, New Jersey, and who journeyed to Italy specifically to accomplish what he considered a heroic crusade against political and religious tyranny. The violent destruction of inequality was the anarchists' religion; hatred of the rich and powerful, who had kept them in squalid servitude became their creed. Bresci's murder of King Humbert inspired Czolgosz to his own dreams of revenge. Louis Lingg, a Chicago anarchist, famed for blowing himself up before his execution and writing in his own blood "Long Live Anarchy," became a martyr for the cause. The anarchists' victims were ordinary citizens as well as the wealthy. Nerves at home and abroad grew shaky every time an unusual explosion was heard, or an odd-looking man was spotted skulking through the streets. No one felt safe when opera houses were bombed and carriage horses knifed while standing in their traces.

Government reaction to the attack upon its sovereignty became increasingly reactionary and repressive. Real or imagined anarchy was considered the root of all societal conflicts, including workers clamoring—justifiably—for better wages, or the general strikes that became commonplace in every nation. Among the well-to-do, their unquestioned authority now seemed tenuous. When a general strike paralyzed Russia in 1904–1905 culminating in January in "Bloody Sunday" in St. Petersburg, an unarmed gathering of workers approached the tsar's Winter Palace. The protest sought fairer wages and a reduction in workday hours among other petitions. Many in the throng held aloft icons and chanted hymns. They believed the tsar would heed their pleas. Although he wasn't in residence, that didn't prevent the army from firing into the crowd. An estimated thousand people died, which led to clamorous protests throughout Europe and, inevitably, to the Russian Revolution of 1905.

A revolution of another type was under way in the United States. William Dudley "Big Bill" Haywood and like-minded laborers founded the Industrial Workers of the World, the IWW, colloquially known as the "Wobblies." Haywood was as comfortable using his fists as rhetoric. Born in 1869 (the same year as Goldman) in Salt Lake City, Utah Territory, his father had been a Pony Express rider who died when his son was three. Haywood had little formal education. He worked in the mines in Nevada, Colorado, and Montana and was a founding member of the Western Federation of Miners. Later, he authored *Industrial Socialism*. He was convicted of sedition charges in 1918, fled the country while on bail, and became a labor advisor to Lenin's Bolshevik government. At home, he likened capitalism to slavery, and the plight of the working class to human bondage.

Katharine had always been aware of public affairs; after all, she'd employed them to her advantage in the past; and this period of political and economic instability intensified her already ardent commitment. A spiritual shift also became apparent. She grew bolder and more overt in her exhortations that every action she and the Sisters took was part of God's plan.

In the midst of her continuous flow of letters of encouragement—or rebuke—to the Sisters at her far-flung schools, and her careful parsing of each expense: how meat should be economically purchased; how to combat a damp basement; where to store soft coal so that spontaneous combustion wouldn't cause a dangerous blaze; procuring knee pants and jackets for male students; "turning" mattresses and making pillows; even a detailed description of dry-scrubbing a floor by making brushes of wood inserted with corn husks (replete with diagrams), she never neglected her recognition that it was God who was acting through and within her.

In a 1904 Christmas letter to the sisters, she wrote: "When thoughts are on self and what pleases self, self abides in our thoughts. . . . When our actions are for self, self abides in our actions. When our actions are for Jesus, Jesus abides on our actions. When our words are sour and short, self abides in our words. . . .

When our hearts are cold and self-conceited, loving our own ease and satisfactions, our hearts have no room for Jesus." The same letter concluded with her wish that the "Child Jesus may *abide* with you, grow in your thoughts, your words, your hearts, your actions until self no longer lives in you and Christ lives in your *whole* being."

She hadn't lost her trenchant wit, though. During one of her cross-country journeys, a Salvation Army woman was singing at the top of her voice in the railway car. Belting out, "You need the Lord Jesus in your life!" she was interrupted by a boy walking down the aisle selling candy. He supplied the tail end to her verse: "I cannot live without—"

"Chewing gum! Chewing gum!" he shouted, which produced no end of mirth for Katharine.

Nor had the future saint been able to curtail her famous impatience. Every late train, which seemed to be most of them during the long treks west and south, was recorded, as were the often garrulous male travelers who sidled up to her and the Sisters as they shuttled across the nation: one being a young, red-headed priest visiting from Ireland who was desperate for a chat and assumed American nuns were less restricted than those in his homeland; another was an inebriated man puffing heavily on a cigar and hiding his face under a black derby hat. The priest turned out to be a bigot who denounced the extraordinary number of "colored" he encountered in the country. When Katharine explained her order's mission, he was aghast rather than chastened. "It's not so bad with the Indians," he exclaimed, "but those other fellows can't keep the faith!" Katharine dispatched him with a stern reminder about the types and conditions of the people Jesus and His Apostles cared for. The drunk asked her to pray for him before weaving away through the car. She did so, her heart more troubled by his obvious pain than the youthful priest's unchristian ranting.

Racism continued to astonish and grieve her. Despite her practicality and acknowledgment of the world's sordid realities, she simply couldn't fathom why race should engender hatred; weren't

Christians instructed to keep God's commandments and love neighbor as self? During the same period, her brother-in-law Edward Morrell had his own battle with racism when disenfranchisement of African Americans was repeatedly debated in Congress.

"I cannot sit still in my seat and hear the gentleman from Tennessee refer to the Colored Republicans of the south and the Colored race generally as a rope of sand and hills of sand," he told the House of Representatives on April 4, 1904. "If they are so, I would like to ask my friend from Tennessee who made them so. First in bondage where they had no right or privilege, or the ability to exercise any will of their own; since then terrorized by their ex-masters; shot down at the polls if they did not vote as expected or kept away from the polls . . . and now the attempt to deprive them of the right of suffrage." Morrell extolled the hundreds of thousands who had given their lives for freedom and suffrage during the Civil War. He quoted the Fourteenth and Fifteenth Amendments, but his appeals fell on deaf ears. On December 9, 1904, the *Public Ledger* declared "Morrell Against South" when detailing the bill he had introduced to "reduce representation from the Southern States . . . which, after March 4, 1907, denies the right of suffrage to any of its male inhabitants . . . the reduction to be proportionate to the denial of the right of suffrage." Morrell further recommended nullifying past elections owing to disenfranchisement. Nothing came of the measure; African Americans continued to be prevented from voting in the South, either through poll taxes, or all-white primaries, or violence.

———

During the spring of 1904, Katharine took a punishing journey through the deep South in order to witness firsthand the results of approximately $100,000 in funds she had been gradually supplying to build schools and churches. She traveled from New Berne, North Carolina, to Beaufort, Charleston, Savannah, Jacksonville,

Tuskegee, Mobile, New Orleans, Houston, Galveston, and Baton Rouge among other stops. Racial inequality was ubiquitous, and most of the southern bishops either incapable of easing the tension, or turning a blind eye, or, worse, abetting it. A Mrs. Thair of Montgomery, Alabama, expressed her disgust regarding the "ingratitude of the Negro," while in Memphis, the bishop told Katharine that the Negroes in his care were inferior to those in Nashville.

Previously, in 1891, Augustine John Tolton, the first African American ordained as a Roman Catholic priest, had written Katharine in despair from the relative safety of his diocese of Chicago: "I stand alone as the first Negro priest of America. . . . Hence the South looks on with an angry eye. The North in many places is criticizing every act, just as it is watching every move I make. . . . I really feel there will be a stir all over the United States when I begin my church. I shall work and pull at it as long as God gives me life." Protestants ordained African Americans and had done so for decades, as she well knew. Why didn't Roman Catholics? Katharine, being a woman—and a religious—was expected to obey the church fathers' decrees, but their entrenched bigotry galled.

During a retreat years earlier, before she became a postulant, she'd written: "Resolve: Generously and with no half-hearted, timorous dread of the opinions of Church and men *to manifest my mission*. To speak only and when it pleases God; but to lose no opportunity of speaking before priests and bearded men. Manifest yourself. You have no time to occupy your thoughts with that complacency or consideration of what others will think. Your business is simply, 'What will my Father in Heaven think?'"

Guided by her sense of call, she registered her disgust when a female white parishioner claimed that she "was being defiled by sitting next to a Colored lady." (At the time, Katharine was reading Booker T. Washington's *Working with the Hands*.) "Needed! Wanted! The Light of the Holy Ghost!" she wrote, but managed to keep her fury private. Anyone who knew her, though, would have recognized how irate she was. The incident occurred as a result of African American parishioners objecting to being relegated to a church's upstairs gallery, which had been originally built for slaves. In Katharine's assessment, African Americans in the segregated cities operated places of commerce comparable to the white citizens. The groceries and butcher shops, seamstress, tailor, and barbershops, and the neighborhoods in which they were located were fastidiously maintained. The difference was that they were a great deal poorer. The injustice infuriated her.

She tried to temper her outrage, but it was an ongoing battle. "I must keep in check my passions, watch love, anger, fear, hate, sadness, joy, presumptions, hope, etc. that they may be used only by God and for God," she cautioned herself, while understanding she required constant reminders to do so.

———————

The southern trek opened opportunities when the enlightened Bishop Thomas Sebastian Byrne of Nashville, Tennessee, approached Katharine with the idea of building a school for African Americans. He was as determined as she. "This colored question seems a burning, all important one," he told her, adding it was a "marvel it was not commenced fifty years ago."

Together they hatched a plan to purchase a handsome property called Mile End, owned by banker Samuel J. Keith. Byrne believed it could be bought for a moderate price—$18,000—and envisioned an industrial school staffed by Katharine's Sisters. "The good to be done, my dear Mother, is incomparable," he concluded.

Katharine agreed. Through a straw purchaser, Nashville attorney Thomas J. Tyne, negotiations for the land and its "splendid house" (according to Byrne) were begun with Nashville realtor W. P. Ready. Keith got wind that someone with serious funds wanted the place—though he didn't know who—and insisted the asking price was $25,000, which Byrne considered too high. Keith was probably secretly overjoyed to unload it, because the neighborhood was changing and a community of African Americans becoming increasingly prominent. He felt threatened by their presence, and like his peers, employed supposed logic to argue for the benefits of segregation. Nashville was as entrenched in its racism as every other southern city. The *Nashville Banner* regularly depicted people of color as idiots, chicken thieves, and liars, and lampooned them in odious cartoons.

The elevated price was met, and on February 15, 1905, the *Philadelphia Inquirer* ran a small squib indicating that Mother Katharine Drexel had purchased a property from Samuel J. Keith of Nashville and intended to start a Training School for Colored Girls.

When he discovered the identity of the new owner, Keith became apoplectic—as did most of white Nashville who fulminated about plummeting property values in the vicinity of the banker's former residence. Katharine was warned to "insure the property at once," while Keith wrote lengthy letters to the *Banner* charging that he'd been hoodwinked, and asking for the public's aid in rectifying the wrongs done to him. "It is scarcely necessary for me to say that I would not have sold my home place, where I have lived for twenty-five years, to be used as a negro school." When those tactics failed, he vowed that if the sale weren't rescinded he'd destroy the property by permitting the construction of a paper street that had appeared on an earlier deed, thus cutting the place in two. Letters of a threatening nature were also sent to Bishop Ryan and Katharine. She replied in a measured tone that barely concealed her anger.

My dear Sir:

I am just in receipt of your letter of February 17th, transmitted to me from Drexel & Company. I hasten to answer it, and to express to you my regret that you and your neighbors should feel as you do concerning the purchase of the property. I think there is some misapprehension on the part of you and your neighbors, which I should like to remove. The Sisters of the Blessed Sacrament, who have purchased the property, are religious, of the same race as yourself. We will always endeavor in every way to be neighborly to any white neighbors in the vicinity; we have every reason to hope we may receive from our white neighbors the cordial courtesy for which the Southern people are so justly noted.

It is true we intend to open an industrial school and academy for Colored girls, but the girls who will come there will be only day scholars. In coming to the academy and returning to their homes, I am confident they will be orderly and cause no annoyance.

I observed very carefully when in Nashville, that the property we purchased was within very few blocks of numerous houses occupied by Colored families, and therefore, even were the property to be the residence of Colored teachers, which it is not, I think no just exception could be taken to the locality selected.

I can fully realize, I think, how you feel about your old and revered home, around which so many attachments of the past—the sweet relations of home life—hover. I acknowledge that I feel the same about mine, and confess that some time ago, when passing in the trolley cars, when I saw a bill of sale on it, a whole crowd of fond recollections of father and mother and sisters, etc., came vividly to my imagination. Then I more than ever realized how all things temporal pass away, and that there is but one home, strictly speaking, that eternal home where we all hope to meet our own, and where there is no separation any more. As to temporal things, after all, are only to be valued, inasmuch as they bring us and many others—as many as possible—to the same eternal joys for which we were all created.

Keith's response was to publish the letter in the *Banner*, paying for it as advertising space and further inflaming the protest. He also threatened to take the matter to the Supreme Court. Doubtless Katharine's missive was met with the ridicule he intended and her appeal concerning the sentiment of family ties, mocked.

At the same time, a group of supposedly genteel white Nashville ladies tried to elicit her compassion for their plight as homeowners now bereft of all they had "of material value." "You have it in the power to save us," they whimpered en masse, while ignoring who it was Katharine had come to rescue:

> The use of the property as a negro school, not only destroys the property value of that home, but of all the homes now wholly occupied by white people in that locality. That is not all, it arouses racial antagonism. Already the citizens of South Nashville are forming Protective Organizations against negro settlements in their midst.
>
> We are not responsible for the fact that the location of negro residences, institution or settlement is the ruin of real estate in any and every community, North, South, East or West.
>
> It is a well known fact that in Boston, New York, Philadelphia, Chicago, as in Nashville, White people protest and take action . . .
>
> Very respectfully,
>
> Mrs. M. J. McKee, Mrs. J. H. Jenkins, Mrs. Jane Watkins, Mrs. Susan Moore, Mrs. L. D. Palmer, Mrs. Goulding Marr, Mrs. W. H. McLean, Mrs. J. P. Haley, Mrs. Mattie Hart, Mrs. Janet Wheeler, Mrs. John Moore, Mrs. C. E. Thaxton, Mrs. M. Christopher, Mrs. W. A. Hunter, Mrs. Edward Burr, Mrs. G. A Dashiell, Mrs. Orville Ewing, Mrs. Carrie Russell, Miss Addie McLean, Mrs. Janie Christopher, Mrs. Emma Christopher, Mrs. E. A. Pike, Mrs. J. R. Jordan, Mrs. A. L. Rain, Mrs. L. L. Terry, Mrs. Leonard Parkes, Miss Blanche Dashiell, Mrs. J. C. McCrory, Mrs. Jas. L. Morrow, Miss Bettie Christopher, Miss Delia Cotton, Mrs. T. B. Neal.

Katharine was disgusted at the depth of Keith and his supporters' enmity. "They say 'There is another place on the city's outskirts' for our educational work," she fumed to Byrne, who called the agitators "bigots" and Keith "rude and unmanly" while insisting that "the better class is with us." Her answer was terse: "How truly was the Cave of Bethlehem the great educator of the World. . . . My God! how much light can be wasted when the darkness does not comprehend it."

Notwithstanding the power plays to undermine her work, the proposed academy and industrial school opened September 5, 1905, with an enrollment of forty-five in grades four through nine. It would soon outgrow the original Keith house, which would be razed so that additional students could be accommodated.

———

Although she found human behavior in the greater world a cause for grief and anger, the role of nurturing mother to the Sisters in her charge (104 in 1904) increasingly fulfilled Katharine's maternal nature. No matter how far "my daughters" were from the motherhouse or how seldom she conversed with them, missives of advice, counsel, compassion on the death of a relative, or worries about ailments flew daily from her pen. Except when she scolded— and she didn't mince words—her messages swelled with love. Knowing the difficulties the young teachers faced, she needed them to experience God's transcendent grace in every interaction.

Visions of the holy became a recurrent experience despite her taxing schedule. Pausing for a moment if no more, she gave herself to reflections on St. Teresa of Avila and the Apostles like Simon Peter and Andrew who had obeyed Jesus' call. At the Kansas City depot en route to New Mexico in 1905, she observed thousands of people trying to attend the state fair. Everywhere bodies were pushing forward, elbows were jabbing and angry voices demanding tickets or seats on Pullman cars. In the midst of this "heaving mass of humanity," she began counting the number of guardian angels hovering around the swarm. "Adore Him, all ye angels," she sang in silence, then fell into a reverie considering how every facet of the natural world reflected the divine.

When her private visions failed to express her sense of awe and wonderment, she reverted to poetry:

> *This is the Month, and this the happy morn*
> *Wherein the Son of Heav'n's eternal King,*

Of wedded Maid, and Virgin Mother born,
Our great redemption from above did bring;
For so the holy sages once did sing,
That He our deadly forfeit should release,
And with His Father work us a perpetual peace.
That glorious Form, that Light unsufferable,
And that far-beaming blaze of Majesty,
Wherewith He wont at Heav'n's high Council-Table,
To sit the midst of Trinal Unity,
He laid aside; and here with us to be,
Forsook the Courts of everlasting Day,
And chose with us a darksome House of mortal clay.
— John Milton, *On the Morning of Christ's Nativity* (1629)

"God is all," she reminded herself and her Sisters, "and at His summons everything must give way; even joy or happiness count for naught when He calls."

Acting as God's agent was wearing her out physically, however, and her mental state provided no repose. Added to her worries was the fact that Lou had had a complete nervous breakdown during the summer of 1904, and was now under the constant care of specialists in mental disorders. Pleas from the Sisters to take better care of herself went unheeded. Hadn't St. Francis of Assisi achieved his greatest works while living in appalling physical conditions: barefoot in the frigid snow, sleeping on an icy floor? Why should she require cosseting and featherbeds, or sleep when she could pray and plan instead? There were rumors among the order that she'd begun following a regimen of bodily mortification; Katharine being Katharine, though, no one dared question her.

Archbishop Ryan tried to intervene, but he'd become surrogate father as much as spiritual father, and, despite his Irish wit and the forbidding intellect that exposed all small and large deceptions, she was good at cajoling him. He issued a feeble decree proscribing writing while traveling by rail. Katharine cannily misinterpreted the injunction as forbidding "*much* writing in cars"; the qualifying word allowed her to judge what "much" meant. Then she altered her penmanship to cram on more words per page, which increased the strain on her eyes.

> I love to think how small the little foot of Our Lord was on that first Christmas. A little foot does not make big strides; it can only take little steps. In imitating the Divine Babe, let us place ours in His footsteps. Then we shall, with God's grace, grow into the bigger footsteps and make greater strides. If we are faithful in little, we will obtain grace for the big.
>
> The active life of Christ was a life of prayer. When did He pray? It seems always. . . . He prayed before curing the sick, before raising the dead. He passed whole nights in prayer. . . . Before entering the active life, He went into the desert and prayed. . . . If I am to do anything for God, then I must cultivate this inner life of prayer.

Although Katharine was adept at ignoring Archbishop Ryan's dictums when they concerned her physical health, she relied upon him as friend, guide, and mentor. She was closer to him than she'd been to her own father. It was he who had rescued her emotionally following Bishop O'Connor's death when she was an inexperienced novice doubting her ability to live according to her call. It was he to whom she had turned while wrestling with creating the rules for her order. A meeting with Mother Frances Xavier Cabrini had taught her that she must take the document to Rome if she expected action. Mother Cabrini knew whereof she spoke. Born Francesca Cabrini in Italy in 1850, she founded the Missionary Sisters of the Sacred Heart of Jesus, then immigrated to the United States to aid Italian immigrants, and eventually became an American citizen. Establishing schools, orphanages, and hospitals for impoverished Italians first in New York and then throughout the nation, she understood how vital ongoing connections to the Vatican were if she wanted her work to succeed. For Katharine, however, every week away from her ministry was a week she couldn't afford to waste.

Ryan experienced each of her plights as if he shared her burdens. In the case of formalizing the rules, he told her, "We must make up our minds to expect delays," adding "ROMA is MORA, which word means delay." His counsel had proved painfully true when Katharine visited Rome in May 1907, and a monsignor asked whether she was in "any hurry?" Those who knew her would have laughed outright at the question. Katharine kept her peace, waiting until July 18, 1907, when she and Mother M. James sailed for home aboard the *Re d'Italia*, the precious papers at last in hand. She never disclosed what Ryan made of the monsignor's query, but a pointed jest would have been a typical reaction.

Patrick John Ryan was born in County Tipperary, Ireland, February 20, 1831, and ordained a priest in St. Louis in 1853. A dynamic orator and devoted to ending all forms of racial injustice, he became archbishop of Philadelphia on June 8, 1884. He soon made his mark because of his humanity, his large-hearted nature, and his authenticity. He was esteemed by the city's religious and secular leaders, whether Catholic, Protestant, or Jew. His wit was as famous as his fondness for anecdotes. Under questioning during confirmation, a young boy had become confused by the difference between matrimony and purgatory. The boy's priest was outraged, but Ryan cautioned a gentle "Let the boy alone. He may be right. What do you and I know about it anyway?" And once, while waiting at the Broad Street Station in Philadelphia, a man approached him, demanding, "Where in hell have I seen you before?" Ryan, who abhorred profanity, answered a calm but admonishing, "I'm sure I don't know. What part of Hell do you come from?" He had a much-indulged collie named Bob, and often extended his blessing with an unaffected: "I bless you from the bottom of my heart." It's no wonder Katharine revered him as a person.

On January 8, 1911, Ryan eulogized fifteen firemen who had been killed in a leather factory fire. Apparently hale, although he would turn eighty on February 20, he collapsed of "heart feebleness" soon after the memorial service. His condition worsened rapidly; visitors, including Katharine, hastened to his side, while the collie, Bob, repeatedly snuck into the patient's room, barking in dismay and confusion.

For several weeks, the archbishop fought for life, rallying then sinking again. The situation changed daily. When a letter arrived from President Taft, extending his prayers and affection, Ryan's condition seemed to be improving. His instinct was to immediately pen a letter of thanks, from which he was almost forcibly dissuaded, but the effort caused sorrow among those attending him. Ryan had always been a larger-than-life figure. No one could imagine him diminished. Although anticipated, death when it came on February 11 was sudden.

Praise for Ryan's life and work flowed in locally and nationally. Protestant Isaac H. Clothier stated, "His death has removed one of the strongest forces in Philadelphia life." John Wanamaker also paid tribute: "It is plainer and plainer that the kingdom of God is not to be wrapped in a single dogma." Leaders of churches and synagogues sent condolences; newspapers throughout the country lauded him while Katharine grieved in silence, recalling each moment they'd shared, and his steadfast grace and love. She wondered how she and her work would survive without him. So bereft was she that she didn't notice a candle burning close to her while she was lost in prayer. The flame set fire to her coif and white veil. Had Ryan been present, he would have tut-tutted over her absorption before delivering a lesson on tranquility of mind, but he wasn't there to remind her.

Katharine was fifty-three when Archbishop Ryan died. She resumed her work, throwing herself into two new ministries in Harlem and Chicago as a way of overcoming her sense of bereavement. If her pace felt rushed before, it was more so now. Although the Great Migration had not reached its apotheosis, large numbers of African Americans were already deserting the southern states, leaving behind lives as sharecroppers on eroded, soil-robbed farms and journeying north hoping to find labor and a measure of respect. Sweeping the floors of a factory was considered an improvement to spending every day attached to the reins of a mule, or so the new migrants believed.

The truth was grimmer than they could have imagined. Housing was scarce and grossly substandard. An entire family was squeezed into a single room, grandly designated a "kitchenette" in what once had been one of several—or more—rooms in an apartment formerly belonging to a white person. Landlords insisted on weekly rent payments rather than monthly as they did for whites; services and repairs were suspended. If a building was condemned, the inhabitants were immediately turned onto the street. As for labor, every week brought immigrants from Europe and Russia; the newcomers may not have spoken English, but they were white. The menial jobs went to them first. Education for the children and grandchildren of former slaves was haphazard at best.

In July 1912, amid a series of hot, airless days when the garbage and refuse littering the streets turned rank in minutes, and the sun wilted even the hardiest trees, Katharine and Mother M. Ignatius trudged along the streets of Harlem looking for properties that could be refashioned into a school and home for the Sisters. Finding two houses on West 134th Street on opposite sides of the street, Katharine signed an eighteen-month lease on each. One was in deplorable condition and vermin-ridden, but it could be salvaged for the Sisters' living quarters; the other could be utilized as a school until the student population outgrew it. At that point she planned to purchase a new site and expand.

Work immediately began on renovating the buildings with Katharine putting most of her labors into the derelict property, especially in the cellar, which had been overrun with rats and had also served as a communal privy. Her young teachers worked alongside her, but she was the first to begin and last to quit. Having instructed the Sisters time and again on taking precautions when dealing with human and animal excrement and how to avoid infection, she ignored her own counsel.

When the properties seemed nearly habitable, she traveled to Chicago to oversee work on another new school, then departed for Santa Fe. She was ill, but concealed the symptoms and pushed on. In fact, she was very ill. A telegram posted from Albuquerque arrived at the motherhouse: "MOTHER ILL. INCIPIENT TYPHOID. PRAY. KEEP OUT OF NEWSPAPERS."

A subsequent diagnosis indicated full-blown typhoid, bronchial pneumonia, and a functional disturbance of the heart. There was every reason to fear she wouldn't survive.

eleven

GOD AND MAMMON

EDWARD MORRELL JOURNEYED WEST IN ORDER TO ASSESS THE severity of Katherine's illness. The news via telegraph left too many unanswered questions, which was due in part to a desire to keep the press away and therefore continue the focus of the order's work, but also to the inadequacy of telegraph communication. If possible, he intended to bring Katharine home. She would have opposed his plan of hiring a private railway car to transport her back to Philadelphia; years of frugality and self-denial, of resenting the pennies spent on herself rather than the children she served had made her abstemious in the extreme. She took her vow of poverty seriously.

However, she was incapable of protesting, much less putting up a fight. By the time Morrell crossed the country, the symptoms of high nighttime fevers, intestinal ulcerations, and diarrhea had left her emaciated—a common occurrence with typhoid. In true fashion, she'd ignored the early warning signs, assuming her bone weariness was overwork, and her acute abdominal distress caused by hastily consumed meals or none at all, or food poorly prepared during her travels from New York to Chicago and thence west. The lassitude consistent with the disease had evolved into "typhoid coma," a semi-wakeful state that left her prostrated and gasping. When she wasn't staring unseeing from her sick bed, she experienced delirium and extreme physical agitation and muscle spasms that were also symptomatic. Her pulse was quickened and feeble. There was concern that intestinal hemorrhaging had occurred, or that there'd been a perforation of an intestinal ulcer, in which case peritonitis would set in. In 1912, peritonitis brought almost certain death, usually within twenty-four hours.

If she survived, her convalescence would be slow and marred by the probability of relapses. The only treatment at the time that proved reasonably successful was bathing the patient in cool water to reduce fever. Serum therapy was new and untried, and every physician understood that the utmost vigilance was required if the patient were to live, but that all the care in the world couldn't ensure a return to total health.

Morrell took a chance in transferring his sister-in-law to a private carriage and beginning the trek east. He chose the southern route, which though longer, had a flatter rail bed and fewer elevations to ascend and descend. He didn't want the thin mountain air to further compromise her labored breathing. Throughout the journey Katharine vacillated between states of prostration and delirium. Every time she opened her eyes was a miracle; every time she struggled for breath seemed to be the last.

Although those traveling with her didn't recognize their own risk of infection, it was possible they could contract the disease. The case of the notorious Typhoid Mary, a cook who emigrated from Ireland and who spread the illness into every home and institution in which she worked, had only recently received scholarly attention. Typhoid Mary wasn't the only known instance of a seemingly robust and healthy woman sowing the seeds of destruction wherever she went. During the same period in Zurich, family members were infected by the mother, who had long since recovered from typhoid; and a reformatory near Bristol, England, hired a worker who unwittingly spread the disease. But the cases weren't widely publicized among nonmedical folk; and the old prejudices remained: typhoid attacked the poor not the rich.

Those living in tenements contracted the disease because of open or poorly maintained sewers and privies, as did soldiers in encampments. Polluted soil and food could carry the disease; so did flies and dust. The excretions of typhoid bacilli were just as deadly. Changing Katharine's sheets and sponging her with cooling water was a huge risk for those performing the duties, especially in a rail car where washing facilities were minimal.

The days wore on; the travelers prayed continually, as did Katharine's Sisters. When she arrived at the motherhouse on October 19, 1912, the physician summoned to treat her declared her a "very sick woman," suffering from "typhoid, bronchial pneumonia and a functional disturbance of the heart." He further insisted that she needed "great, very great care to get well, and absolute quiet and rest." He insisted that no one except those attending her could see her. Recognizing her supreme mental agitation and continued delirium, he also dictated silence not only in the sick room, but in the corridors and rooms adjoining it. No mass bells were to be rung. His warnings left no argument. "If not we may lose her."

Recovery was fitful and uncertain. Katharine's mind couldn't rest, which further impeded her progress. Rather than give herself into the nurturing care of the Sisters, she struggled to regain control of her mental faculties and chaotic emotions, but the fever's symptoms wouldn't allow her psyche to return to normalcy. She waged war against herself, her frustration at her impotence acute. "I felt so sure God's plans were being fulfilled in me—for certain they were not my plans." But now she had stumbled. Was this God's will? Or the Devil's? Should she submit to a higher intention, and permit death to carry her back to God, or fight for life with all her might? And, why, oh why, wouldn't God answer these questions? Where was His presence; where was His voice? Why did she feel so bereft and helpless? In future, she would write: "Be patient and God will bring all to His glory." But patience under these circumstances was an agony.

Slowly, slowly, she began to heal, although once recovery began she started demanding concessions. She wanted to attend mass, wanted to go outside, wanted to breathe fresh air and feel the sun warming her; especially, she wanted to return to the business of running her order.

She was permitted to attend matins and lauds (though not preside) and allowed to ride in a carriage if the weather was fair. As to the daily letters concerning expenses and other practical matters involving the schools and convents, it was well nigh impossible to keep them from her, but computations that were formerly simple now exhausted her. When she wrote her annual Christmas missive to her Sisters on December 21, 1912, she was still restricted to the infirmary. By the standards of the time, at age fifty-four, she was considered to be in her declining years. Her father had died at sixty-one, her maternal grandfather, Piscator Langstroth, at seventy. Longevity was not in her genes.

———

While Katharine recovered, her Drexel and Biddle cousins devoted themselves to the glittering world of high society, their names listed in every newspaper column devoted to the city's elite: the balls attended, betrothals announced, and marriageable young men and women—and their frocks, "a vision in pink and silver"—described in gushing terms. "Susie Dearest" was one such column in the Philadelphia Inquirer. Sometimes it seemed as if the only people of interest in "Susie's" column were members of the extended Drexel clan.

By now they'd married into the Van Rensselaers, the Dutch colonial family who were included in Mrs. Astor's exclusive "Four Hundred" and whose lineage traced to the early "patroon" of Rensselaerwick, a vast estate south of Albany, New York; the Cassatts, whose name was synonymous with the Pennsylvania

Railroad; and the Fells of the Lehigh Valley Railroad. Margaretta Drexel, granddaughter of Katharine's uncle Tony, had been wed to Lord Maidstone (Guy Montagu George Finch Hatton) in London in 1910, in what was hailed as a "banner event of the London season." Before she married, her visits to Biarritz and sojourns at her parents' London home were faithfully reported. Among the two thousand guests invited to the church and an additional number to the reception on Grosvenor Square were Mrs. Cornelius Vanderbilt and the Duchess of Marlborough. The peerage of the realm was well represented. The new Viscountess's brother-in-law was the African big game hunter Denys George Finch Hatton. Margaretta's brother, Anthony, married Marjorie Gould the same year. She had made her debut the winter prior, and had been "besieged" by "numerous titled foreign suitors"; as the granddaughter of Jay Gould, the Drexel-Gould union cemented spheres of financial power.

The glowing descriptions of the interior of the Gould home at 857 Fifth Avenue with its "sets of old armor" and "rare old oils," its trees of "mauve orchids," its baronial entry hall and equally majestic staircase, or the daily chronicles of society figures "disporting themselves in Paris or in more southerly climes," and George Drexel's yachting sojourns, or the de rigueur presentations at the Court of St. James by Philadelphia's elite made the chasm between Katharine and her extended family impossible to bridge.

Once they had viewed her choice with skepticism mingled with a hefty dose of guilt, now they ignored her. Her behavior was too bohemian, too outré—to use the term of the day. How could they understand her penury and abstinence, or the battles she fought on behalf of the impoverished and persecuted, when they were surrounded by servants, by invitations to cotillions and hunting-lodge house parties, by wedding gifts of pearls, diamond tiaras, and expensive automobiles shipped to the Continent for a couple's use during their honeymoon?

If Katharine felt the loss of her cousins, or of their shared memories of youth, it was momentary. Her work was her passion, the Sisters in her care, and the children they served her family.

"Is this a school?" was the question posed during the early days of Reconstruction by a white member of Louisiana's legislature when he stopped to examine a recently completed school for African Americans. His companion was also white.

"Yes."

"What, for niggers?"

"Evidently."

"Well, well. I have seen many an absurdity in my lifetime, but this is the climax!"

The story originally appeared in *The Report of the Joint Committee on Reconstruction at the first Session, Thirty-ninth Congress*, and subsequently in W.E.B. Du Bois's *Black Reconstruction in America*. The almost universally held belief in the southern states at the time was that educating a "nigger" was not only absurd but that it ruined him. Calling a man or woman a "nigger teacher" was a slur of the highest order. Many whites subscribed to the lawless—though acceptable—attitude that "the damned rascals who attempted to teach niggers would be shot."

By the time Katharine began focusing on education for African Americans in the Deep South, little had altered. On the surface lay a veneer of polite, if grudging, acknowledgment that all peoples were created equal. The veneer was tissue thin. In 1912, while the northern states concentrated on the industrial progress by the automotive industry and aviation, or experimented with and improved mass production techniques, the South remained traumatized by the Civil War and its aftermath. The landed gentry had vanished or married into a rising class of once impoverished whites who had traditionally viewed all blacks as natural enemies. Who would hire a blacksmith when a slave could shoe a horse, or purchase the services of a cook when every plantation had a house slave who performed the role? Once freed, the former slaves and children of slaves were considered even more dangerous, because both groups now competed for the same meager employment.

In 1863, more than 95 percent of the black population in the South was illiterate. During Reconstruction, there was a concerted effort by the Freedman's Bureau to create educational opportunities, but the work was sporadic and often doomed. In rural areas, African American laborers were still chained economically to the former plantations where they'd been enslaved. The cities, wholly segregated, began to swell with freed men and women who fled the dangers of the countryside where it was easy to lynch or murder them with impunity, or entice them to quit family and home with the promise of jobs that then shipped them overseas to the sugar plantations of Cuba, or the Brazilian rubber plantations where they were enslaved again. Secret societies like the Ku Klux Klan, the White League, and the Knights of the White Camellia flourished, creating an odd but lethal fellowship of former gentry and poor whites. "Negro hunts" were commonplace.

William Edward Burghardt Du Bois was born in Massachusetts in 1868; in 1888, he graduated from Fisk University in Nashville, Tennessee. He received his doctorate in history from Harvard in 1895, and taught sociology at the University of Pennsylvania in 1896-1897. Du Bois published the seminal work *The Philadelphia Negro: A Social Study* in 1899 and *The Souls of Black Folk*, a collection of essays in 1903. He was one of the founders of the National Association for the Advancement of Colored People (NAACP), in 1909, and from 1910 to 1934 he directed the organization's publicity and research, sat on the board of directors, and edited the *Crisis*, its monthly magazine.

While attending Fisk, he taught during the summers in rural Georgia, and witnessed firsthand the poverty and enforced ignorance of a people attempting to transition from bondage to freedom. "To be a poor man is hard," he wrote, "but to be a poor man in a land of dollars is the very bottom of hardships." Those whom he taught were a mixture of ages; each student was desperate to learn. They didn't rail against the leaky log hut that had formerly stored corn and now served as a schoolhouse, or the single blackboard resting on the floor, or the backless benches or lack of desks.

The one chair Du Bois used he was obliged to return to the land-
lady each night. This indignity was slight compared to the one he'd
endured when securing his position. Hired by a commissioner on
the same day a white teacher found employment in a white school,
Du Bois was greeted heartily, then asked to remain for dinner,
which he ate alone after the two white men had eaten. "The problem of the Twentieth Century," DuBois declared, "is the problem
of the color line."

On July 10, 1906, three years after the publication of *The Souls
of Black Folk*, Thomas Watt Gregory, who would become the forty-
ninth Attorney General of the United States in 1914, delivered a
paper before the Arkansas and Texas Bar Associations. In it he
commended the work of the Ku Klux Klan. Born in Crawfordsville,
Mississippi, in 1861, and raised on a cotton plantation, Gregory
justified the "Invisible Empire's" creation as being a necessary "revolution" engendered by the "martial law of reconstruction":

> But, if the reconstruction laws were unconstitutional, and
> wrong and vicious in theory, their practical application to the
> situation was infinitely worse; substantially all of the intelligent
> class of the South were disfranchised; the Negroes, not one of
> whom out of every hundred could either read or write, consti-
> tuted almost the entire voting population, carpetbaggers from
> the North and scalawags from the South, composed almost
> exclusively of the very scum of creation, organized and con-
> trolled the Negro vote, held the more lucrative offices and
> began an era of corruption and plunder unheard of before in the
> history of America . . .
>
> The men of the South had seen the last hope from constitut-
> ed authority dissipated; there remained "nothing less than the
> corruption and destruction of their society, a reign of ignorance,
> a regime of power basely used," under which they and their
> wives and children could hope for no protection of life, liberty
> or property, and at this point they gathered for resistance . . .
>
> On Christmas eve in 1865 in the law office of Judge Thomas
> Jones, in the little town of Pulaski, in Southern Tennessee, near
> the Alabama line, six young men, all confederate veterans, con-

cluded to organize a society of some kind; some one suggested
that they call it "Kuklid," from the Greek word Kuklos, meaning a circle, and some other person present said, "Call it Ku
Klux"; the word "Klan" was then added to complete the alliter-
ation . . .

But masked riders and mystery were not the only Ku Klux
devices; carpetbaggers and scalawags and their families were
ostracized in all walks of life; in the church, in the school, in
business wherever men or women, or even children gathered
together, no matter what the purpose or the place, the alien and
the renegade, and all that belonged or pertained to them, were
refused recognition and consigned to outer darkness and the
companionship of Negroes . . .

I have in my possession a letter recently received from one
who in his young manhood was one of the advisers and leaders
of the Klan in East Mississippi, and who subsequently for years
served his State with distinction in the National Congress. I
quote this language of his, worthy of all acceptation:

"No Victim of their displeasure ever suffered without first a
full and ample investigation of his case, ex pâté, 'tis true, but all
the facts were first found out and thoughtfully weighed, for and
against him, and the sentence carefully considered and made
commensurate with the justice and necessity of the case. They
made the punishment suit the crime."

His case made, Gregory concluded: "Whatever may be your
views, I leave the question with you, repeating the proposition
with which I began, that, amid conditions as they existed in the
South from 1866 to 1872, scarcely a man in this audience would
have been other than a Ku Klux or a Ku Klux sympathizer."

twelve

THINK IT, DESIRE IT, SPEAK IT, ACT IT

IN 1915 WHEN KATHARINE BEGAN TO CONSIDER NEW ORLEANS AS a potential site for another school, the Civil War was no hazy memory for southern whites of both the plantation and laboring classes. The deaths and physical incapacitations of fathers, husbands, and brothers were still raw wounds; added to this pain for the once-wealthy was the loss of ancestral lands and the easy, languid livelihoods they provided. That comfortable existence was gone but not forgotten. Preserved in memory as a halcyon age, it gained stature and poignancy to those who felt dispossessed by the Union and Reconstruction. The antagonism was aggravated because the "Yankees" controlled the nation's purse strings, and the only hope the old planter families had of regaining their fortunes was to interact with the Northerners either through business or marriage. During Reconstruction, southern belles sought to escape their impoverished situations and reinvent themselves by choosing northern husbands. The results weren't always happy. Rosalie Eugenia Carter of Virginia joined herself to the Law family of Philadelphia. Her daughter, Eugenia Carter Law, wed Livingston Biddle, one of Katharine's Drexel-Biddle relations. In fits of fury Rosalie habitually referred to her own young children as "damn little Yankees," a condemnation they could never expunge. To Rosalie's dying day, she believed she'd traded the genteel antebellum South for life in an enemy camp.

The city of New Orleans also kept its eyes fixed on the past. Confederate Memorial Hall, officially dedicated in January 1891 and built in the Romanesque style popularized by Louisiana native Henry Hobson Richardson, contained memorabilia from the Civil War—still referred to in the South as the War Between the States. Jefferson Davis was revered and studied along with photographs, paintings, and documents detailing Louisiana's secession and other wartime events. In 1893, when Davis died, an estimated 60,000 people visited Memorial Hall on May 27–28 to pay their respects to Davis' remains, which lay in state in the museum. The building adjoined Lee Circle, adorned with a monument to Robert E. Lee, a twelve-foot statue atop a Doric column sixty feet in height. The striding figure faced north, permanently glaring defiantly at the Union. Jackson Square celebrated Andrew Jackson's triumph during the Battle of New Orleans in 1815. Liberty Place stood at the intersections of Canal, North Peters, and Tchoupitoulas streets; its obelisk, which was erected in 1891 not as a tribute to United States independence from England but to the "Revolution" of September 14, 1874, when the Crescent City White League overcame the detested Republican police and forced the temporary abdication of the Republican government. Federal troops eventually won the day, but Liberty Place immortalized that brief independence from Reconstruction.

Cotton remained king in Louisiana, thus the teeming Cotton Exchange on Carondelet Street, but sugar and molasses were also of prime importance for trade, and gave New Orleans a ranking second to Philadelphia (the nation's chief refiner). The city claimed that it had the largest refinery in the world. Despite that nod to modernity, by the time Katharine began focusing on New Orleans, there was no public sewer system. The open gutters of Toulouse, Chartres, and Salcedo streets overflowed with refuse. During the rains the streets of commercial and residential districts alike became vile, but the residents—even wealthy ones— shrugged off the inconvenience and stench. If their ancestors had deemed the situation acceptable, why should they desire change?

Louisiana suffrage clauses employed a similar, retrograde stance. As anticipated, the clauses ensured the disenfranchisement of most African Americans—males, naturally, as women of any color could not vote. It was necessary for a voter to be able to prove beyond doubt that he could read and write, or prove that he owned property worth at least three hundred dollars, a significant amount. However, illiterate whites could vote if they had done so in any state on or before January 1, 1867; the date for eligibility for their sons and grandsons twenty-one or older was May 12, 1898. Convicts pardoned without an explicit restoration of suffrage clause forfeited the right to vote. Educational opportunities were equally unjust. The school term was longer for white children than black, and their teachers were paid twice as much.

Katharine had traveled to New Orleans prior to 1915; from the earliest days of her order she'd been in communication with the city's fifth archbishop, Francis August Anthony Joseph Janssens, who visited her and her novices in 1891 when she was using her family's former summer home in Torresdale as a temporary novitiate. Born in Holland in 1843, Janssens was ordained to the priesthood in 1867; he arrived in the Diocese of Richmond, Virginia, in 1868; in 1881, he was consecrated bishop of Natchez, Mississippi, and was installed as archbishop in New Orleans in 1888. His nationality put him in a difficult position from the beginning. As the only Dutch prelate among predominantly French priests, his accent—although he was fluent in French—as well as his manner isolated him.

Katharine became a soul mate in whom Janssens felt safe confiding his hopes and failures. "God has blessed your endeavors," he told her while decrying "these miserable prejudices" within his white flock that he found all but intolerable. His doleful eyes and wide, sensuous lips gave him the look of a fin-de-siècle poet and belied the strength of his commitment to empower the ignored and abused, and to prove that God indeed showed no partiality. However, frustrations met every attempt to break down the walls of racism. White parishioners wouldn't supply funds for improving a woefully inadequate orphanage for African Americans, the Ecole des Enfants Indigents, which had been founded by Madame Veuve Bernard Couvent, a free black woman, and where the children were now forced to sleep three to a bed. "I feel sometimes troubled and discouraged" he wrote Katharine, and "Excuse this sorrowing letter," and "You and your community must pray for me." Which she did, recognizing his cries of distress as having echoes in her own soul.

As early as 1892, he asked Katharine's young order to come to Louisiana and teach. She demurred but directed a constant flow of funds for the archdiocese's efforts. "Dear Mother Katharine, I am begging again" became a familiar refrain. She opened her pocket-book over and over again. "If you could read my heart as the Lord does," he told her, "you would know how grateful it feels for your kindness."

A school she had funded in Arnoldsville, Louisiana, met with expected opposition. "The white population there is very ignorant," Janssens informed her. "Before building it they made threats. After building, they tried to burn it down twice and threatened the Sisters. They do not want the negroes instructed and to know more than their children, of whom not one in fifteen can read. . . . I am downcast. I am sick at heart." Threats of arson became fact in other schools.

Janssens also faced resistance among the black Creole population when he finally acquiesced to the whites' desire to assign separate houses of worship for the two races. What would become the *Plessy v. Ferguson* ruling of 1896 was already creating racial chaos. It was natural that African Americans in Louisiana regarded the "separate but equal" approach to their religious life with the same derision as they did their secular life. There was nothing Janssens could do to ameliorate the situation.

Pressured by his white parishioners, he dedicated St. Joseph's Church to serve the African American populace and renamed it St. Katherine's in honor of Katharine's patron saint. Then he retreated from his bold vision of equality for all of God's people, and, instead, put his energies into reducing the diocesan debt, which had reached epic proportions. In that effort, he succeeded, but the emotional burden of a schismatic flock affected his health. At age fifty-three, in 1897, he suffered a heart attack while aboard the steamer *Creole* and died.

Janssens's hope for educational opportunities for Catholic African Americans lay dormant until James Hubert Herbert Blenk became the seventh archbishop of New Orleans in 1906. The two men could not have been more different. Blenk was a pragmatist. For him, Katharine served as an important means to an end, rather than as a friend with mutual hopes and desires. He would never have considered baring his soul to her as Janssens had. Born in 1856 into a large Protestant family in Neustadt, Bavaria, Blenk and his parents and siblings immigrated to New Orleans in 1866; the parents died shortly thereafter. He was then raised by Catholics and converted to Catholicism when he was twelve. Unlike Janssens, he recognized the need to appeal to a diverse populace. Knowing full well that "race feelings run high here, and racial differences cannot be obliterated," he moved cautiously, his eye on the prize, rather than on his desire to follow in Jesus' footsteps. Blenk understood whom to court and when. None of his priests carped about his accent or nationality. His work among his "Dear Colored People" he deemed vital, but he also maintained separate churches for the two races.

In July 1913 Archbishop Blenk invited Katharine to send her Sisters to New Orleans to teach. Again, she held back, waiting for the chance to create her own school rather than engage in archdiocesan politics. In April 1915, the opportunity arose. The campus of Southern University at 5116 Magazine Street was listed for sale. Southern was a land-grant college, and the only institution for higher learning in New Orleans where African American Catholics could study without being required to attend Protestant religious services. When President McKinley visited Southern on May 2, 1901, it was a thriving place. A crowd estimated at five thousand cheered him on when he appeared framed by the high double columns of a building as imposing as he. Since 1913, however, when Southern was forced to relocate to Baton Rouge, the central building—with its grand hall, double stairs, gallery, assembly hall, and sizable stage— an adjacent two-story wood structure that had served as the mechanical department and chemical laboratory, and a three-room cottage had sat deserted.

Land-grant colleges had been established by the Morrill Act of 1862 to remedy the inequity in education between the wealthy and the laboring class; race was not the focus. Section 4 of the act's passage stated: "The leading objective shall be, without excluding other scientific and classical studies, and including military tactics, to teach such branches of learning as are related to agriculture and mechanic arts." Further, the moneys were to be solely dedicated to education rather than creating handsome temples to learning. And most important for the time in which the Morrill Act became law, "No State while in a condition of rebellion or insurrection against the government of the United States shall be entitled to the benefit of this act." Kansas State University became the first land-grant college in September 1863.

In 1890, the Second Morrill Act was passed, its purpose to redress unequal educational opportunities for African Americans: "No money shall be paid out under this act to any State or Territory for the support and maintenance of a college where a distinction of race or color is made in the submission of students, but the establishment and maintenance of such colleges separately for white and colored students shall be held to be a compliance with the provisions of this act."

It was due to the Second Morrill Act that Southern University became a land-grant college in 1890. The area had once housed plantations; a brick building on the property had been built to hold slaves accused of disturbing the peace before sending them out to work in chain gangs. On what was then the outskirts of the city and inhabited mostly by African Americans, Southern University and A & M was conveniently forgotten by the whites until New Orleans' expansion made friction between the two races unavoidable. As had been the situation with Katharine's Nashville school, the new neighbors complained about colored people living and studying nearby. Nor did they approve of whites teaching African Americans. This tension would escalate, producing a bill in Georgia that, if passed, would prohibit white teachers from educating African Americans, and African Americans from working in any school for white pupils. In Louisiana in 1911, Professor V.I. Roy came under censure when he became the president of the State Normal School in Nachitoches, because he'd formerly taught at Southern University, which position demeaned him in the opinion of the white population.

Pressure mounted to close Southern. Some influential white business and civic leaders protested, sending a letter on May 12, 1912, "To the Honorable Members of the General Assembly of Louisiana." They insisted that the area "*was now near the center of the Colored population of the state*," and quoted the latest census, which listed three times as many African Americans living in the south part of Louisiana as in the north. Moving Southern to Baton Rouge would deny access to education to the majority of the state's African American population.

The alliance of blacks and whites failed in their petition; the state legislature voted to move Southern to Baton Rouge. By 1913, the once-bustling buildings were vacant, the lawn fronting the street had grown sere and the graceful live oaks had been neglected. Informed that the place was for sale, Katharine and Mother Mercedes left Philadelphia on April 5, 1915, and hurried to New Orleans where they took a clandestine private tour of the buildings. Katharine had learned a valuable lesson with the purchase of the Nashville property; she kept her identity secret.

With her frugal eye, she noted each broken window—and there were many—as well as the necessity of repainting and plastering, and refurbishment of space for the Sisters' quarters. Despite the need for prudence, the place impressed her. This was no institution erected cheaply for impoverished students. Built in the Italian Renaissance Revival style, it had substance and grandeur; the semi-circular pediments of contrasting stone wouldn't have been out of place in a Florentine palazzo. She made quick sketches of the main edifice while exploring it, looking for telltale cracks over the windows that might denote a compromised foundation. The drawings were made on the back of a book's marbleized endpaper. She had found discarded catalogues of courses offered in a basket in one of the rooms. Naturally, she saved some. The glossy endpaper of red and green hues were the remnants of a university that had hosted a president of the United States.

The Southern board had fixed the sale price at $18,000; it would go no lower. Charles A. Tessier, a well-regarded real estate agent with an office on Carondelet Street near the Cotton Exchange, was called in by Archbishop Blenk to purchase the campus. Blenk worked behind the scenes, talking to the mayor, an architect to corroborate the buildings' solidity, and Tessier. Katharine's name was withheld, as was the impetus for the transaction. When Charles Tessier's negotiation failed, a straw agent bought the property at public auction for the asking price. Variously referred to as "Harry MacInery," "Mr. McEnerny" (by Archbishop Blenk), and "Harry McEnery" in a public announcement of the sale, the name and the several spellings raise questions. The McEnery family was a prominent Catholic one. Samuel Douglas McEnery had served his state first as governor, and then as a senator, dying while in office in 1910. Katharine was informed that "Henry McInery influences the whole state beginning with the Governor and Archbishop."

That part was true, even if the spelling was unreliable. When the *True Democrat* of Bayou Sara, Louisiana, reported the sale on April 17, 1915, no one perusing the notification raised an eyebrow or queried the property's future use: "Southern University square, New Orleans, bought at auction by Harry McEnery for $18,000." It was assumed that the former institution was now in the safe hands of one of the city's leading lights.

The longer paragraph that preceded the sale described "the opening ball game at New Orleans of the Southern League season," and declared that New Orleans defeated Birmingham 7 to 4. The paragraph beneath the purchase reported that the French were in the midst of winning and losing a German trench near Berry au Bac. But the largest story on the page was about Booker Washington, then touring Louisiana. Dr. Washington was quoted as saying, "To the industrious negro, the white man is a friend—I speak particularly of the Southern white man who has and always will be our best friend." The report was entitled "Negroes Get Good Advice."

However the purchaser's name was listed, it didn't take long for the truth to surface. The New Orleans Catholic weekly *Morning Star* reported, "Mother Katharine Drexel is seemingly unconscious of her great work. She is modest and retiring, keeping her own splendid personality and princely donation entirely in the background, and speaking of all the purchases as work contemplated solely as that of the order, of which she is probably the humblest and least assertive member."

There were some who considered her "great work" repellent. By the first week in May, the mayor and city council members were petitioned by angry homeowners, who wanted to pass an ordinance making it impossible for the property to be used as a school for African Americans. Blenk tried to alleviate Katharine's concerns by telling her that "the devil sometimes can stir up an account of opposition"—presumably, as opposed to genuine hostility.

By then she was back in Philadelphia, and could only pray that he was correct. And that his diplomatic manner would win the day. Blenk continued to pull strings, saying that he and her straw agent had chatted amicably on the phone, that he had also discussed the situation at a banquet he'd attended with Mayor Behrman and had the man's assurance that all would be well. Katharine remained apprehensive. Blenk was no Janssens with his candid and open heart. She responded to the archbishop's effort to placate her by reminding him that the deed needed to be finalized, and that she wanted to begin restoring the buildings as soon as possible so the school could open in September. Her communications grew increasingly prickly when the attorney dragged his feet—or was urged to do so by external parties.

Blenk shrugged off her anxiety, telling her the attorney was "bestirring himself." By July 24, the bestirring had produced no results; the property remained without title. Katharine, accustomed to overseeing large financial transactions as well as administering her far-flung schools, which could be found in Massachusetts, New York, Pennsylvania, Virginia, Tennessee, Georgia, Louisiana, Ohio, Illinois, Missouri, Nebraska, New Mexico, and Arizona, was less than pleased with this laissez-faire attitude. Lethargy was a trait she found intolerable.

While she focused on bricks and mortar, Blenk began quibbling with the legal agreement she had drawn up to establish a Sisters of the Blessed Sacrament foundation in New Orleans. He wanted more control of the school than she was willing to give. Katharine didn't back down. She insisted that the order's mother general or her delegate had sole authority over the Sisters' assignments, and that the Sisters of the Blessed Sacrament should be able to raise funds locally if necessary. For an archbishop, her behavior was tantamount to insurrection. Had she not had clout and wealth, Blenk would have reprimanded her, but he was a political animal as well as a man of the cloth.

She revised her original document, having made no real concessions. Blenk pushed back, telling her that "loose and incomplete documents of this kind have given me, both in Porto Rico and New Orleans, a great deal of worry, interfering seriously with the wise and efficient administration of both of the Dioceses." Obviously, he wasn't referring to the tardy title.

When that hurdle was eventually passed, another appeared, at least for the archbishop: Katharine's decision to create a corporation, the Sisters of the Blessed Sacrament for Indians and Colored People of Louisiana. She felt incorporating in the state of Louisiana was a necessity in order to purchase and maintain property for her school. This time, Blenk let his chancellor speak for him. Eighteen months into the process and following letter upon letter of appeal or remonstrance on Katharine's part, and bemused condescension on the part of the chancellor, her patience was at an end. When he smoothly informed her that the paperwork for a corporation would take no more than an hour to draw up, she shot back that the delay of a year and a half was thereby inexplicable. Raised eyebrows, pinched lips, and mutters that northern women were regrettably audacious must have greeted that salvo. Not until May 1916 did Katharine prevail.

Xavier, or "Old Southern" as it was then called, was slated to start registering students on September 13, 1915, its stated mission "to continue to welcome to its advantage pupils of every denomination, and anything like an attempt to force religious convictions of non-Catholics shall be scrupulously avoided." The proclamation concluded, "We hope the story of our work at Old Southern may be found written at the hearthstone of thousands of families throughout the length and breadth of New Orleans."

Due to the delays, the Sisters who made up the first group of teachers, the "Seven Joys" as they dubbed themselves, did most of the cleaning and scrubbing and carting of desks and chairs and classroom necessities. It was hot, dirty work, climbing up and down the stairs hoisting heavy furniture; the "Seven Joys" were attired in habits that hampered their movements, but zeal carried them forward. A limit of no more than fifty students per class in grades seven through ten was soon discarded; an eleventh grade was added. It was clear that more teachers were needed. The air crackled with enthusiasm, as the Sisters prepared lessons in English, mathematics, physical geometry, domestic science, physics, and chemistry, and also planned to expand grades and classes the following year.

The atmosphere thrummed with something more ominous, too. A hurricane was building. Without adequate warning systems, the residents of New Orleans had little concept of the size and power of the storm that was bearing down on them. Passing twenty miles west of the city on September 29, the hurricane sent the barometer to the lowest point yet recorded, and the wind velocity to the highest. The First Presbyterian Church that faced Lafayette Square was destroyed, its tower crushing neighboring residences. The *Times-Picayune* building also sustained severe damage; reporters struggled to get the newspaper to print. Even the sturdiest of businesses and homes sustained severe damage; some were cut in half as though they were dolls' houses; the flimsiest collapsed altogether. A steamship near the river's mouth reported a tidal wave of twelve feet, and that the lower delta was completely submerged.

The "Seven Joys" had never experienced a storm of that magnitude; torrents of rain came through the roof; for a while the women feared it would blow off entirely and that the stout, stone place would be demolished. Half of the domestic sciences building was destroyed when one of the massive live oaks crashed into it. Every room including the dormitory was awash in filthy water; the garden, lawn, and street became a lake full of downed trees, while tree limbs and furniture dropped from the skies. But the women were alive, albeit frightened. Katharine, by then on her annual visitation of the western schools, was desperate to learn if they'd survived. Communications between New Orleans and the outside world had ceased.

Miles of broken levees left communities inundated. In many places the depth of the water was eight feet. Downtown New Orleans was flooded. In lower Plaquemines, only a few houses remained; Myrtle Grove to Pointe à la Hache was washed away completely. Three hundred bodies were eventually recovered; thousands were left homeless with nothing but the wet clothing in which they'd fled; others had been stripped by the water's surge. Food was scarce or nonexistent. By October 3, the stranded and starving begged from passing boats; marooned families clung to whatever scrap of timber bobbed above the surface. The carcasses of horses and cows floated alongside them. Crops were ruined, as were canneries and oyster factories that had provided labor. A sizable portion of the lower delta remained under water. A few hillocks poked above the waters, but otherwise it resembled the surrounding sea. No one could remember a storm of such devastation.

Xavier opened its doors despite the battering the city had sustained. The "Seven Joys" were as indomitable as their Reverend Mother. They delayed school for a day (all other area schools closed for a week or more) and then got down to the business of teaching. Katharine's annual Christmas letter to her convents was ebullient. "My desires," she wrote, extolling the work they were doing, and using capitals to show her enthusiasm: "1. A MOST FIRM FAITH; 2. A MOST CONFIDENT HOPE; 3. A MOST ARDENT CHARITY." A subsequent missive showed equal ardor: "My visit to Xavier was a joy—and you, every one of you, are my joy and a great big joy in God."

The school flourished as she had anticipated. At the first closing exercises in June 1916, the students were exhorted: "We have a world to conquer and we are going to do it by placing a purpose in our lives." Following the expansion of a twelfth grade in 1916, a two-year Normal School program became reality in 1917. Prior to that date, only white teachers were required to have additional education to receive degrees. A year later, the General Assembly of the State of Louisiana decreed that Xavier could "confer such literary honors and degrees and to grant such diplomas as are conferred and granted by any colleges, universities or seminaries of learning in the United States and Europe."

By 1924, college-level courses were part of the curriculum. Katharine noted the transformation: "Praise be to God, the

College has been recognized by the State as a 4 yr. College!!" This was penned on the back of a merchandise return slip in her large, bold, and masculine hand. The girlish style in which she'd been schooled had vanished.

The year 1925 saw the establishment of the College of Liberal Arts and Sciences; a College of Pharmacy became reality in 1927. The same year, the Parent Teachers Association had an unanticipated treat; on a balmy October day, the Sisters chartered the river steamer *Idelwild* to take them on a day's excursion. It was the first time in New Orleans history that African Americans were allowed to participate in this simple pleasure. The group—five hundred strong—stopped at Pelican Plantation for a picnic lunch, the Sisters sitting at a distance so as not to be seen eating in public, but beaming all the while. In 1928, Xavier's first college degrees were awarded.

All this time, Katharine continued to shuttle between her schools and the motherhouse near Philadelphia; not even the influenza epidemic of 1918 slowed her pace, though it did prevent her from detraining and purchasing a meal during a cross-country journey. In the United States, it was estimated that 675,000 people died, while the global figures ran to the millions. For the months that the pandemic raged, no one was safe because the disease attacked the ablest-bodied as well as the elderly and young. Katharine's greater concern was the African Americans in the care of her Sisters who were then nursing the ill in their homes. In one letter, she voiced her anger at being hampered in this ministry: "I am a little disappointed that we cannot give ourselves exclusively for the Colored; and hope since His Grace says there is to be no discrimination in a time like this, there will be none later in schools and hospitals. This will be a strong point for argument in future, which we may find it good to use."

The practical was balanced with the emotional. When one of the Sisters faced a spiritual crisis, Katharine didn't stint with her compassion and counsel. "Why don't you get into the habit of seeing God in the soul of each child you deal with," she advised, adding, "rid yourself of self by not thinking of self." And finally: "In this thought, this desire, this act, is there anything of God's service, God's glory? If so, think it, desire it, speak it, act it."

"Think it, desire it, speak it, act it" had long been her credo. For Katharine, seventy years old in 1928, Xavier University was the result of decades of being God's hands and heart at work in the world. Seeing God in the soul of each child taught, each adult aided was central to her being. The negotiations over land, the construction of buildings, hiring lay teachers to work alongside the Sisters was necessary and good but secondary to her recognition, her *faith*, that God was working through her.

"Lord, it is good for us to be here!" she declared in a letter to the motherhouse following an automobile tour (part of it in an undertaker's car lent for the occasion) of rural Louisiana schools where Xavier graduates now taught alongside the Sisters of the Blessed Sacrament:

> THANKS! THANKS! THANKS! . . . Here in the Southland, intentions keep piling up, and piling up. For there is so much to be done. . . . And in the West and East and North it is the same story "MORE SISTERS! MORE SISTERS!" That is the cry wherever we go . . . the pupils keep piling in . . . . The zeal of these girls [Xavier graduates] is worthy of note. One of them, out of her own salary, is subscribing to a modern encyclopoedia, so as to give her 7th and 8th grade pupils literary information, for they have no books in the school whatsoever, except their school books. Two of her pupils are 19 years of age, and one is 20; they never had opportunity of attending any school before coming to this one.

The journey included Bishop Jules B. Jeanmard of Lafayette whom Katharine invited to join her and Mother M. Agatha (he supplied his car and driver). He agreed enthusiastically; the route covered two hundred fifty miles. On their way to Prairie Bass School, they entered a bayou overgrown with trees. The shade provided respite from the April heat if not from the clouds of insects. The solitary beauty of the place enchanted them, and they decided to eat their box lunches just like any tourists wandering off the beaten path and reveling in nature's riotous glory. Perching on the car's fender, and waving off gnats and biting flies, the bishop munched on his sandwich and sipped warm Coca-Cola while Mother Agatha and "little me" (as Katharine referred to herself) sat in the passenger seats doing the same and passing napkins and condiments back and forth through the open windows. A native of Louisiana, Jules Benjamin Jeanmard would come to national attention in 1954 when he excommunicated two women who attacked a teacher when she integrated her catechism class. He followed that act by reminding his flock that religious instruction was open to all people, and would remain open to all people as long as he was bishop of the diocese.

That leisurely perambulation with Bishop Jeanmard belied the increasingly violent issues of race and the Ku Klux Klan's growing presence. There might have been a lull in activity in Louisiana, but East Texas was another matter. The school in Beaumont where Katharine had established a school in 1916 had an enrollment of 240 in 1920. The prior year, during July 1919, Longview in East Texas had been the scene of "The Great Battle of Longview," according to the *Dallas Express*, an African American weekly newspaper that exposed bigotry on its front pages. What began as a lynching turned into racial war, and Longview, 125 miles from Dallas, came under martial law with three hundred soldiers encamped and trying unsuccessfully to keep peace. Sizable areas of the African American section of the town, including homes and churches, were burned.

In 1921, the same newspaper declared "Texas Leads the Nation in Lynching for the Year of 1920." In one case, lynching occurred because the victim had been "insisting on voting." Even the League of Nations came under attack for being anti-white when U.S. Senator James Alexander Reed, Democrat from Missouri, declared that whites would be outnumbered in the League's voting process, and referred to the body as "a Colored League of Nations," continuing: "How will the senators from the South who represent states which have long contended that the white race alone is fit to control the destiny of the States of America, contend that Liberia, Haiti and other Negro, or semi-Negro nations, should be permitted to sit at the council table of the world and each cast votes the equal to that of the United States?"

During March 1922 the Klan was out in full force in Beaumont. Flogging, tarring, and feathering became commonplace. Murder, especially brutal murder, was in the air. A respected white judge, John Pelt, with known sympathies for African Americans, was abducted from his front porch, driven to a distant location, tarred, feathered, and "returned more dead than alive" according to the Sisters of the Blessed Sacrament teaching in Beaumont. Mother Mary of the Visitation's letters to Katharine rattled with fear. "The church is posted," she wrote on March 21, 1922, quoting the Klan's message:

> To the pastor of this Church—
> We want an end to the services here. We will not consent to any white priests consorting with nigger wenches in the face of our families. We give you one week to suppress it or a flogging and tar and feathering will follow. K.K.K.

"I am certain they will attack the parish," she continued. "We must be prepared for it, for it will surely come. . . . No civic protection can be hoped for, because all the officials here belong to the infamous party."

Katharine had been in Beaumont that very day, but had left before the posting. When she received the dire news, she was in New Iberia, Louisiana. Given her personality, the timing was particularly cowardly: big, beefy men, their faces hidden by white hoods, not daring to confront the woman who had caused them so much trouble. They waited until she was gone.

On March 22, Mother Mary of the Visitation told Katharine that some leading white citizens, including the local rabbi, were trying to help, but it was certain that the sheriff was a member of the KKK. Class issues exacerbated those of race and religion. The Klan hated Catholics and Jews; the fact that a number of African Americans in the targeted church were professionals galled. "These Kluxers are all wrought up and will do much more, I'm afraid, if something very radical is not done to prevent them. The officials here all said they are not members of the Klan, but it is almost certain they are. . . . The lady who was speaking with me today told me a lot of things that she knew officially from her work, but begged me not to speak of it out of the convent."

The Klan staged a noisy nighttime parade near the convent. African Americans, forbidden to purchase firearms or ammunition in the town, had no way of protecting themselves. The children in the Sisters' care—second-graders Alma Perrault, Mamie Trahan, Lorena Brown, Leona Chaison and sixth-grader William Charles—continued to come to school; no one was certain their parents or homes were safe. Katharine sent a guard, but his presence was paltry when faced with the majority of the town's pro-Klan population. Father Alexis LaPlante, the priest, made a good show of denigrating the danger, but it was obvious he was afraid for his life and those of his flock.

Then a miracle occurred. A tornado attacked the area, sweeping a substantial building into the air and shattering it, ripping the hardware store and adjacent properties to pieces, killing six and injuring nineteen while razing a pair of buildings on the outskirts of town that were known Klan meeting spots. Mother Mary of the Visitation believed it was God's punishment, although she understood the danger wasn't past. The Klan had flexed its communal muscle; opposition had been scant.

During the Texas primary election that July, the Klan ticket won by a significant margin, the organization polling 118,000 pro-Klan voters in the Senate race as opposed to 200,000 votes split between four anti-Klan candidates. Earle B. Mayfield, candidate for the Democratic nomination to the U.S. Senate, kept mum about his connections to the "invisible empire," but everyone knew he was the KKK candidate. By the close of 1922, Texas Klan members numbered 150,000.

Katharine's school in Beaumont remained open.

————

At Xavier, an expanding student body necessitated an expanded campus; the library was now too small, and classes were becoming oversized. The Magazine Street neighbors, however, refused to permit the sale of vacant properties to the school. They may not have referred to themselves as Wizards or Cyclops, but they knew they'd been twice deluded about the nature of the institution; and they weren't about to allow more African Americans to live and study among them. Petitions blocked the purchase of empty lots. Katharine had no recourse but to move, but she left Xavier Preparatory School in its original home, foiling the bigots and racists.

In 1929, when financial woes rocked the country, she looked to the unzoned sections of the city and found what she needed, buying land owned by the Hartman Salmon Lumber Co. on Washington, Pine, and Howard streets. The price was an exorbitant $105,000; even removed from residential New Orleans, her mission met with bitter opposition. On the plus side, the property was bracketed by two large streets and had excellent trolley service, making it easily accessible for students. The New Orleans architecture firm of Wogan & Bernard was hired to begin drawing up plans. Katharine wanted the new facility to have a football stadium, men's and women's dormitories, and a students' center. She also insisted on using Indiana limestone. The place would be handsome and spacious; it would provide a superior, higher education to the young women and men attending it.

Having made Xavier co-educational from its founding days, in 1929 Katharine found herself publicly challenging Pope Pius XI's papal encyclical on Christian education, *Divini Illius Magistri*— "The Divine Teacher": "False also and harmful to Christian education is the so-called method of 'coeducation.' . . . The Creator has ordained and disposed perfect union of the sexes only in matrimony, and, with varying degrees of contact, in the family and in society." Aware of this dictum, Katharine visited the Apostolic delegate in Washington, D.C. This was diplomatic, but calculated. She wasn't about to change her belief in educational equality for all.

On the feast day of St. Peter Claver, September 9, 1931, ground was broken for the new institution. The choice of saint's day was fitting. St. Peter Claver (1581–1654), a Spanish Jesuit, spent forty-four years serving the African slaves in Cartagena (present-day Colombia) who'd been imported to work the gold mines in the New World. The port of Cartagena was the capital of the trade. Peter referred to himself as "the slave of the negroes forever."

thirteen

A MIRACLE TO OTHERS

BY THE TIME THE NEW XAVIER CAMPUS WAS DEDICATED IN 1932, Katharine was deeply involved with the work of the NAACP. Recognizing how easy it was for her schools to become lightning rods for racial hatred, she supplied financial help but requested that the institution withhold her name from their newsletters. *The Crisis*, edited by W.E.B. Du Bois, was the organization's official publication. Katharine kept each communication, underlining and double-underlining passages she believed critical to the cause to end discrimination. Advocacy was a natural progression of her hands-on work of building and funding schools. Without radically altered hiring practices or laws ensuring equality, there could be no genuine advancement for African Americans or Native Americans. Whites would remain dominant, racism would prevail, and her students would never experience the same opportunities as white children and youth.

In March 1927, motivated by the Ku Klux Klan's continuing political prowess and by those in positions of authority who from cowardice or apathy turned a blind eye to intolerance, she stepped beyond the role of silent, deep-pocketed advocate, and met with the manager of the Associated Press in New York. Her goal was to lodge a complaint about the way African Americans were treated in the newspapers. Louise, widowed since 1917 when Edward died during a visit to Colorado for his health, accompanied her. As an heiress and wife to a deceased member of the House of Representatives, Louise had status and distinction, but she said little. Katharine controlled the conversation. Her decades of success in overcoming nearly insurmountable obstacles were legendary, as was her avoidance of publicity. The interview must have seemed like a personal coup for the journalist.

Her argument was persuasive. It was common practice for a Negro criminal to be referred to by race, she said, while the ethnicity of a white offender was rarely included. The policy stigmatized an entire population on the country. Change was overdue.

Even if he were not a religious man, the journalist would have recognized an aura of power emanating from this petite woman clad in black. It was quiet, assured; it radiated throughout her being, and was unlike the ego-driven arrogance of the civil activists and statesmen he encountered. Katharine, who'd once been feckless Kitty, was Jesus' apostle, caring for the helpless. "For I was hungry, and you gave me to eat; I was thirsty, and you gave me to drink; I was a stranger, and you took me in: Naked, and you covered me; sick, and you visited me: I was in prison, and you came to me," she might have quoted from Matthew 25, but she didn't need to. The message was stamped on her face; it circled her like a cloud.

Wednesday, October 12, 1932, the day of the dedication of the new Xavier University, was cold and overcast; the heat was turned on for the first time in both the school and convent. The gray chill enhanced the stone solidity of the campus buildings. The architec-

tural firm of Wogan & Bernard (which had worked on Louisiana
State University during its expansion under Governor Huey P.
Long) and the contactor, Bernard J. Glover, had carried out each
of Katharine's wishes—and she had been specific about room proportions as well as appearance. The exterior walls were constructed of buff-hued split-face ashlar trimmed with cut stone, the roofs
dark slate. In this section of the city where structures were a flimsy hodgepodge of rickety wood homes and businesses, Xavier's per-
manence and authority impressed, which was Katharine's intention. The equipment in the science laboratories rivaled that of any
established university; the auditorium seated over five hundred
and was outfitted like the finest Broadway theater.

Some locals considered the campus too fine to waste on teaching "Colored," but that didn't detract from the pomp of the dedication ceremony, or the excitement leading up to it: the rehearsals
for Kipling's rousing *Recessional* and other musical interludes; food
and beverages prepared for a gala reception; and the celebrated
guests who alit from chauffeur-driven cars. The prior Monday,
Louise had arrived with her caregiver and companion, Miss Colby.
Her health remained in doubt; she was nothing like the hoyden
who'd long ago delighted her elder siblings with her antics, but she
was determined to support her sister in her greatest undertaking to
date. Katharine was grateful, but she was too busy to spend time in
family chat.

Remarkable as it seems, all the speeches on that blustery afternoon were delivered by men. Not one woman addressed the audience, although the school's founding had been instigated by one
woman's singular vision. Katharine didn't appear on the podium,
nor did she sit in the audience. Instead, she stood in a window
watching the proceedings, her face nearly invisible in the reflected
light.

Cardinal Dougherty of Philadelphia, bespectacled and rotund
(Louise in private asides to her sister referred to him as "His
Immensity"), had previously made it plain that he believed
Katharine should be canonized for her efforts. Today, he began

with a humorous touch, declaring that "anything Katharine Drexel is interested in should be an object of interest to me," before turning serious and telling his audience that it was long past time for African Americans to come into their own. "Your forefathers were most cruelly dragged from their homes in Africa to be slaves on the tobacco and sugar plantations of this country's blackest chapter in the history of this nation. But God knows how to bring good from evil."

The bishop of Little Rock, Arkansas, the Rt. Rev. John B. Morris, told the crowd,

> Out of two small Colored schools has come the hour of victory we are celebrating. It is a splendid triumph, unique I believe in the history of education that out of two tiny schools has grown the fine college of today and the only Catholic College in America for Colored people. . . . From nothing in 1915 to four splendid schools, one of them the largest parochial school in the Archdiocese with fourteen hundred pupils. . . . Add to this the numerous schools scattered in the rural districts taught by the graduates of St. Xavier's and you have the barest statistics of a feat that is in itself inspiring. . . . It is here that we realize that teaching is not a profession but rather a very sacred vocation that demands more than mere intellectual training, more than technical knowledge of the subject taught. . . . The Sisters of the Blessed Sacrament bring to their classrooms, not knowledge alone and cold, but science, culture warmed and inspired by the flame of Christian charity that makes their own lives seem like a miracle to others.

The band played *The Star-Spangled Banner*; the chorus sang Shubert's *Omnipotence*; the wind whipped the flags, and the red, white, and blue bunting decorating the stage; speeches began and were concluded, the applause following each enthusiastic and prolonged. All the while Katharine as well as her Sisters stood behind the closed windows. If she acknowledged the cheers it was with a private smile that was the quintessence of selflessness.

Discrimination and abuses of African American workers on the Mississippi River Flood Control Project came to Katharine's attention that November through the NAACP. She supplied $1,000 to investigate abuses that turned out to be worse than anticipated: flogged and terrorized laborers were confined to private camps holding government contracts and worked fourteen to sixteen hours per day, seven days a week. Their maltreatment was compounded by the company stores' extortionate prices: condensed milk selling for twenty cents as opposed to eight on the open market; salt pork at fifteen cents as opposed to six. Daily whippings were a given; the tent encampments were filthy and grossly overcrowded. None who were interviewed dared supply names for fear of reprisal. An investigative journalist, George S. Schuyler, known for his exposé of slavery in Liberia, and hired by the NAACP, was thrown in jail in Vicksburg, Mississippi, for asking questions. "Mississippi River Slavery" was what the American Federation of Labor report published in the *American Federalist* deemed the practice.

Katharine wrote to President Franklin Delano Roosevelt voicing her objection:

> I hereby protest against the discriminatory provisions of the Contractors Code, which has been submitted to the NRA [National Recovery Administration], because it does not in any way benefit or improve the condition of the thirty thousand negro laborers on the Mississippi Flood Control Project.
>
> While the Code provides a minimum wage of forty cents an hour it contains a clause that where the minimum wage was less than forty cents an hour in 1932, the present minimum wage shall not be paid. Negroes are not benefited by the maximum provision of the Code. Therefore I offer serious objection to accepting the Code in its present form.
>
> We rely upon you to see that the tenth part of our population shall not be discriminated against in the New Deal.

She sent a telegram reiterating the message.

After that, her focus turned to the Costigan-Wagner Anti-Lynching Bill. Senator Edward Prentiss Costigan (D–Colorado) had been approached by Walter Francis White, executive secretary of the NAACP, who wrote him on November 27, 1933, asking him to introduce a federal anti-lynch law. The law would ensure punishment of lynchers and state officials who abetted them by failing to arrest them. In 1922, the Dyer Bill calling for similar measures had passed the House but was defeated in the Senate by a filibuster led by Southern senators. The NAACP had kept an official count of numbers lynched since 1918, separating them into two categories: those "Taken from Officers and Jails" and those "Not Taken from Officers and Jails." The organization hoped for Roosevelt's support, but his political success relied upon support by Southern Democrats, all of whom were dead set against any anti-lynching legislation. A filibuster killed the measure, and Congress adjourned for the year.

Then came the lynching of Claude Neal in Florida in October 1934. After allegedly confessing to the murder of Lola Cannidy of Greenwood, Florida (Neal's hometown, as well), he was taken first to a jail in Chipley, then moved to Panama City because of threats from an unruly mob. After this he was taken by boat to Pensacola before being moved again, this time to Brewton, Alabama, where an armed mob of approximately one hundred men stormed the jail in the middle of the night. They vowed to turn the prisoner over to the girl's father, who lived some two hundred miles away. Thirty cars paraded the route along Highway 231, Neal prominently displayed in the first. A radio station in Dothan, Alabama, announced "a lynching party to which all white people are invited."

A jeering throng of men, women, and children gathered to watch. Over the space of ten to twelve hours, Neal was systematically tortured. His penis and testicles were cut off; he was forced to eat them and assure the crowd that he liked the taste. His fingers and toes were removed one by one; hot irons were applied to his entire body, which was also slashed with knives. When the mass of

spectators became bored, Neal was hung by a rope until he nearly
expired, after which he was dropped to the ground again, and the
torment resumed. Finally he was tied to an automobile and dragged
over the highway to the Cannidy home, where a woman drove a
butcher knife through his heart. By then the witnesses numbered
in the thousands; children were among those who attacked the
dead man's body with sharpened sticks. His fingers and toes were
kept as souvenirs; photographs of the corpse hanging in the court-
house square in Marianna, Florida, sold for an exorbitant fifty cents
apiece. Neal's family's home was burned to the ground. No black
person in Marianna felt safe during the subsequent days. Police
presence was nonexistent. According to the NAACP, Neal was the
5,068th person lynched in the United States since 1882, and the
forty-fifth since FDR became president.

Katharine began a campaign of protest, sending the president
letters from each superior of each Blessed Sacrament convent. All
were composed at the motherhouse, submitted for signatures, and
mailed from the appropriate county and state; no two were alike.
Roosevelt was barraged with outraged appeals. Without supplying
numbers, Katharine also made certain that he understood how
important every institution was; the subliminal message was that
Democratic votes were at stake, and that those votes had northern
affiliations.

Dear Mr. President,

The recent disgraceful occurrence in Florida, the torture by
fire and lynching of a Negro prisoner is the sixteenth lynching
in our Country since June.

As a Sister of the Blessed Sacrament for Indians and Colored
People, in charge of this Negro school in Montgomery
[Alabama], I beg you as our revered President, to put a stop to
these crimes by bringing about the speedy passage of the
Costigan-Wagner Anti-Lynching Bill.

Katharine's own missive was dated December 24, 1934, as they
all were. It was imperative that the president discuss Costigan-

Wagner during his opening address to Congress on January 3, 1935:

> The recent shameless abduction from one State to another of a defenseless Negro prisoner and his subsequent barbarous lynching in Florida, by a mob regardless of law and order, is a blot on the America we love and upon our common humanity.
>
> Therefore that such a disgraceful episode may never occur again, as president of Xavier University in New Orleans, a Catholic college for Negroes with an enrollment of 539 students, I most respectfully urge you to bring about the speedy passage of the Costigan-Wagner Anti-Lynching Bill.
>
> In these days that try men's souls, the reputation is justly yours that no request brought to you is disregarded.

Congress dragged its feet on the bill that year, too. Roy Wilkins of the NAACP interviewed Senator Huey P. Long about the lynch law for the February 1935 *Crisis*, but Long "ducked" the discussion, preferring to focus on his candidacy for president. When questioned about a lynching the day prior in Franklinton, he said, "That one slipped up on us." Long appeared barefoot and in his pajamas for the 9:30 A.M. interview, padding around the room or into the bathroom to brush his teeth. He didn't curb his racist tone when addressing Wilkins, who was African American. "I can't do nothing about it," he protested. "No sir. Can't do the dead nigra no good. Why, if I tried to go after those lynchers it might cause a hundred more niggers to be killed."

Wilkins pressed, pointing out that Long controlled the state—which he did, having moved on from governor to the United States Senate after hand-picking his successor. "Yeah, but it's not that simple" was the rejoinder. "I told you there are some things even Huey Long can't get away with. We'll just have to watch out for the next one. Anyway that nigger was guilty of coldblooded murder."

When Wilkins reminded Long that the Louisiana Supreme Court had granted the man a new trial, the senator remained adamant. "Sure we got a law which allows a reversal on technical points. This nigger got a smart lawyer somewhere and proved a technicality. He was guilty as hell."

"Every Man a King" was Long's slogan and the title of his auto-biography, though it was clear the axiom excluded African Americans. Middle-class by sheer determination, Huey Pierce Long loathed the old planter class that had maintained control of Louisiana politics since Reconstruction. He railed against Standard Oil, "the world's greatest criminal," and special interest groups that lined their pockets while shutting down locally owned independent companies and robbing Louisiana of income. He'd fought the battle against big business since he was twenty-four. His popularity among poor whites was unshakable. But, as Roy Wilkins had concluded in his interview, Long "wouldn't hesitate to throw Negroes to the wolves if it became necessary." Their support didn't count, because as Long stated, "They don't vote in the South."

The assumption among Southern whites that African Americans were inherently bad or less than human led to Long's assassination, as reported to Katharine by Mother Agatha from the convent at Xavier University. On September 8, 1935, in Baton Rouge, Dr. Carl Weiss pulled a gun on Long, shot him, then was killed by the senator's bodyguards during the ensuing melee. That was the official story.

However, according to Mother Agatha, whose missive back to the motherhouse jittered with numerous "they say's," the rumors in circulation in New Orleans claimed that Long had insulted his nemesis Judge Benjamin Pavy by insisting he had "colored blood in his veins." Pavy's son-in-law, Carl Weiss, a respected ear, nose, and throat doctor, became so incensed at the charge that he confronted Long the following day, punching him in the face. The bodyguards pulled their weapons; it was they who shot Long by accident, or so Mother Agatha had heard, and Weiss was killed to cover up the mistake. Apparently, the undertaker corroborated the story, saying that Weiss's revolver was of too small a caliber to cause the fatal wound—or so it was reported to Katharine. True or not, Mother

Agatha's worries weren't concerned with whether it was Weiss or a trigger-happy guard who fired the fatal shot, but that the entire incident had started as a racial slur.

––––––––––

Roy Wilkins, concluding his *Crisis* interview, called Huey Long a "colorful character." The senator's well-crafted image certainly projected that persona: the straight-talker who never minced words but who could drop his southern slang in a heartbeat and speak like any Harvard-educated gent. What Long couldn't do— nor did he attempt to—was conceal a legacy of racial mistrust and hatred.

That hatred was nothing new, of course, nor was it confined to the South. Race riots had occurred in northern industrial cities— Chicago being one of the most infamous in July 1919. Closer to Katharine's motherhouse in Bensalem, the city of Chester, Pennsylvania, had been the scene of a lethal riot in 1917, also in July. The Great Migration, the relocation of hundreds of thousands of African Americans trying to escape the poverty and depredations of the South, put the new arrivals into competition for jobs: the lowest on the economic rung (in the case of Chicago, the Italians) kicking wildly at anyone attempting to climb the same ladder. In Chicago, a mob attacked an African American hospital. In the Italian district, an African American riding a bicycle was beaten, stabbed, shot sixteen times, after which gasoline was poured on his corpse, setting it ablaze. There were reports of whites firing "indiscriminately at blacks."

After three days of mayhem, twenty-eight were left dead, five hundred wounded. The Chester incident saw less loss of life, but only because it was a smaller city. The animosity of those who had barely become "haves" toward the encroaching "have nots" was fierce wherever laborers gathered, vying for insufficient employment. In Detroit, the UAW (United Auto Workers) created a policy whereby only whites could qualify as skilled labor.

———

Despite acknowledged racial tensions in the North, the Sisters of Blessed Sacrament who arrived to teach at Xavier soon realized that they were in alien territory. They were Catholic when the Ku Klux Klan despised Catholicism, and mostly from northern states with accents Louisianans inherently mistrusted. Worse was that they were at Xavier to teach people whom the majority of southern whites believed didn't merit or need education. Deserving special mention of the many Sisters who taught at Xavier are Sister M. Lurana Neely, an artist and early member of the university's art department, and Sister M. Elise Sisson, who joined Xavier's music faculty in 1934. Their students flourished because of the women's quiet war on intolerance.

Sister M. Lurana designed the Xavier shield, which depicts a lion, the symbol of courage, and a green field representing God. The motto DEO ADJUVANTE NON TIMENDUM, "If God be with us, nothing is to be feared" imparts a different message today than it did when lynching was commonplace, and when being derided as "uppity" by attempting to rise above one's station and become something other than a peanut or cotton picker or sharecropper or maid or waiter could prove fatal.

Sister M. Elise was born Lorraine Sisson on November 10, 1897, in New York. She'd aimed at a career in opera, and had studied with her "beloved" Carl von Praeger at the Paris Conservatory; with Muzia Modelewski at the Conservatory of Petrograd; and Mme. Von Unschuld, who was court pianist to the late queen of Romania. Her photographs from that period are glamorous: curly brown hair and a romantic glint in her eye, but nothing suggests the ingénue in her face or pose. Instead, she looks like a force to be reckoned with, which she was.

Like the younger Katharine, she bridged two worlds; one being her connections with the elite of the music community, the other her vocation. After the death of her mother, who'd been a long-time invalid, Sisson abruptly shifted focus. Without medical bills to pay, she decided to give herself and her artistic talents to God.

She was unshakable in her belief that grand opera shouldn't be a whites-only realm. Upon retiring from her teaching duties at Xavier, she co-founded Opera Ebony in 1973, and Opera South in Jackson, Mississippi, in 1975.

During the early years those achievements seemed unlikely if not downright absurd. "I remember coming down here in 1934 totally unaware of the significance of segregation and the situation here," she said in an interview for the *Times-Picayune* in April 1981. "Segregation was a term I was familiar with up North, but ignorant of the effects of it." Sister M. Elise soon learned that African Americans were barred from attending musical performances in municipal auditoriums and concert halls. Audiences and casts were segregated, a fact she discovered when Walter Herbert of the New Orleans Opera asked her to train Xavier students for the prisoners' chorus in *Aida*; he rescinded the request because whites wouldn't attend an interracial production.

Sister M. Elise persevered, creating a program in Grand Opera at Xavier, and staging full-length operas: *Carmen* in 1936, *Faust* in 1937, then *Il Pagliacci, Tales of Hoffman, Il Trovatore, Aida*. The university's art department created the scenery. In 1941 the Metropolitan Opera news wrote a full-page acclamation of the university's production of Carl Maria von Weber's *Der Freischütz*. Among Sisson's students during her decades at Xavier were LaVergne Monette, Debria Brown, Emma Goldman, Gwendolyn Wright, Raeschelle Potter, Mervin Wallace, and Annabelle Bernard. Bernard performed with great success in Germany and married German tenor Karl-Ernst Mercker. She credited Sisson as being a guiding force in her life and professional career while daring her to attempt what seemed impossible: breaking the color barrier. "When the curtain falls," Bernard-Mercker's obituary quoted her as saying, "our response to God will not be what part we played, but how well we played the part assigned to us."

These words mirrored Sisson's understanding of her own divine gifts. With her ubiquitous black purse, she commanded the most commanding of divas who towered above her, clutching lavish bouquets from their admirers, their makeup flawless, their gowns resplendent.

In temperament, Sister Lurana Neely was Sisson's opposite. Born in Kansas City, Missouri, June 9, 1918, Emily Clara Neely had a small, sweet face that was regularly described as "angelic." She was calm and abidingly gentle even while encouraging her students to reach beyond societal limitations. John T. Scott, a MacArthur Foundation "genius grant" awardee of 1992 and former student, said of her during his 2004 memorial speech entitled "A Love Letter to a Friend":

> How do you describe someone who always saw potential where others saw despair? Who believed the only limitations in life are the one we impose on ourselves? One who made opportunities where none existed and prepared her students to make the most of each one . . . knowing that "good enough" was never good enough, and only the BEST was acceptable.
>
> A teacher who had the ability to see the slightest glimpse of a creative seed in a student and make it blossom into a full garden . . .
>
> Waving her magic spirit she taught us how to transform the gym into an "Opera Hall" or a classical ballroom . . .
>
> She made us realize that media in the arts was like language and there was nothing wrong with being linguistically proficient. This she did by example, a musician, a calligrapher, a sculptor, a printmaker and a draftsman, not to mention one of the finest teachers I've met in a lifetime.
>
> She taught us to look everyone in the eye as equals: enter all competitions with the intention of winning, for being second best was not an option. She felt we had been in that situation far too long.
>
> Finally, I thought long and hard about what do you say to someone who has given so much to so many with so much love for so long . . . you say I'll pass it on.

Scott, who was born in 1940, received his first commission when a sophomore; Neely made it a habit of contacting architects looking for artists to decorate their new buildings. After four decades of teaching at Xavier, Scott died in Houston in 2007, having fled there from Hurricane Katrina. He passed along Neely's gifts and his own prodigious ones.

fourteen

SIT STILL OFTEN IN
THE PRESENCE OF GOD

IN 1935, THE GREAT DEPRESSION STILL CAST ITS PALL, ESPECIALLY on the nation's poor. A riot in Harlem in March left the area "like a war ravaged country" according to the Sisters of the Blessed Sacrament who taught there. What began as a simple act of a boy stealing a bag of candy turned into a massive conflict involving looting, retaliatory gunfire, and death. "Our people were the first to feel the depression," the order's yearly Annals recorded, "and the last to recover." The impoverished throughout the country faced the same situation, putting additional stress on the Sisters' students and their parents. There seemed no end in sight to the financial catastrophe. In the West, along with a prolonged drought that had instigated near daily bankruptcies and foreclosures, mountainous and unpredictable dust storms had started paralyzing the region. The Sisters in South Dakota wrote about the devastating attacks of nature when they sent home news to the mother-house. They didn't realize they were experiencing what would become known as the Dust Bowl. In May 1934, twelve million tons of desiccated earth funneled from the Great Plains roared eastward, eventually falling on Chicago, New York, and Washington, D.C. Children in the Plains area were regularly diagnosed with "dust pneumonia." Cattle, already bony due to the lack of vegetation, were blinded and suffocated by the relentless, roiling sand.

The largest "Duster" to that point hit April 14, 1935, which was Palm Sunday and would thereafter be called "Black Sunday." Originating in North Dakota, it slammed its way across South Dakota, Nebraska, Colorado, Kansas, Oklahoma, and into Texas. Estimated at two hundred miles wide and two thousand feet high with winds as strong and loud as a tornado's, and black as the blackest night, it buried or half-buried dugout houses, barns, chicken coops, farm implements, livestock, corn and wheat fields, and anyone or anything unlucky enough to be caught in its path. The cars of those attempting to flee shorted out due to static electricity that was potent enough to knock a grown person to the ground. In the monster's wake were dunes of barren sand where once had been arable fields. By Friday, April 19, the dust of farm and ranch and hardscrabble town rained down on the nation's capital.

At the time Katharine was in the South, visiting her schools and missions. To those who hadn't experienced it, the Black Sunday storm was considered an aberration, like an unexpectedly savage hurricane or tornado season. Katharine's itinerary left her little time to ponder nature's vagaries, however, because her schedule that year was grueling. She seemed to have no cognizance of restrictions due to age. Perhaps, like her grandfather, she willfully ignored those diminutions in her desire to get the job done, or maybe, the advancing years impelled her to work harder and faster. Since March, she had been touring Nashville, Montgomery, New Orleans, Beaumont, Port Arthur, and stops along the way. In February she'd been in Boston where the children presented a play about her and the order's work. One girl acted the part of a Native

American: "They saw in the Indian the child of God, the brother of Christ, and they toiled and slaved and died on our behalf."

The line contained more truth than the young actor knew. The Sisters' unsparing natures and equally demanding regimens were taking a toll on their health. Some of the original Sisters were now middle-aged and older and starting to suffer from cancer and other deadly diseases. So was Katharine, although she couldn't or wouldn't admit physical limitations. "It is a miracle to me how dear Reverend Mother keeps up under such constant strain and rush," Sister Miriam confided to Mother Mercedes after Katharine's visit to Beaumont in the beginning of May. That famous stamina was soon to end.

By May 7, Katharine was in Gallup, New Mexico, changing trains yet again as she made her way to the Northwest. She'd already passed through some of the country destroyed during "Black Sunday." Despite the blighted land and the human lives and hopes equally blasted, and her own grief for those afflicted, the journey to her western schools revived her. Chatting with students and teachers, donning an apron and boiling up a vat of rice, or chopping bushels of cabbage to make sauerkraut was the simplest and most direct method she knew of spreading God's love. Although she'd become an exemplary administrator, her soul required this facet of her mission. "Energized, invigorated, excited" was what she felt.

Everything she'd done and was continuing to do was for "the children" or "the boys and girls," terms she applied to ten-year-olds as well as twenty-year-olds. At the age of seventy-seven, she was welcomed as if she were a grandmother come to share a bit of fun. Like a grandmother, she fretted over an outbreak of infantile paralysis in Boston, or the purchase of a car (subsequently dubbed "Sancta Maria") for the Sisters in Houck, Arizona, or where to buy reasonably priced curtain rods, or how the now chronically unemployed could find jobs, or restoring her daughters' physical health. "I am with you in spirit," she wrote to one ailing Sister, adding: "How I would love to be with you, dear daughter, to nurse you!" To another who was grieving, she advised: "They tell me you are brave. Our Lord likes courage. Get it from Him." Then added a practical: "A little bird tells me you don't eat much."

Faith, though, remained paramount. As she aged Katharine felt more and more driven to fill the younger Sisters' hearts and minds with her own intrinsic belief in God's enveloping love. "Sometimes in religion our hearts are filled with many things, things crowded into our hearts, and there is little room for Him. We cannot hear our Lord when the poison of the world is in our hearts. Let us try to listen to the throbbing of His Heart when He tells us: Do not be afraid." The Sisters were set extraordinary standards:

> Having willingly answered the call of our Divine Lord to be Religious, we are therefore obliged to strive intensely and enthusiastically to acquire that personal holiness, that sanctity which the religious state demands. It would be a great spiritual disaster if any Religious were to think that nothing more is demanded of her than just ordinary goodness. Whether we realize it or not, we shall constantly be growing in power with God for men and with men for God.

"Ordinary goodness" was an unknown attribute among the Sisters of the Blessed Sacrament. Like Katharine, their lives were consumed by their vocation. They were intrepid, courageous, and single-mindedly devoted to embracing members of society who remained the outcasts of the nation. From northern tenement to southern sharecropper's shack to the hogans of the West, they toiled and taught, cheered, healed, and comforted. When they died, the family members who gathered to mourn were other Sisters. It would have been a lonely existence—and at times it could be—were it not for their understanding that they were Jesus' apostles.

Katharine's 1935 visitation to the Northwest was as hectic as her southern one. She returned to the motherhouse on June 7 in order to attend the formal unveiling of her portrait by Lazar Raditz, a well-known society artist. Although she'd reluctantly agreed to sit for it, the finished object caused her no little embarrassment. Her cousins commissioned large oil paintings of themselves, but they also possessed summer and winter homes and expensive motorcars and wardrobes that filled entire rooms. Frugality—even during the Depression—was unknown to them. Katharine requested that the portrait in its thick gilt frame be kept in an inconspicuous place.

On September 14, she was back in Albuquerque. From then on, she was a blur of movement. Reaching Houck, Arizona, she found Sister Stanislaus in excruciating pain, and suffering from what was presumed to be cancer. Katharine brought her to the hospital in Gallup, then immediately continued on to St. Michael's School where she grew dizzy, lost her balance, and fell while dictating letters to her companion, Mother Mary of the Visitation. A second attack at St. Catherine's School was worse. The young government doctor attending the school's children diagnosed hardening of the arteries. Katharine didn't bother to describe the prior attack, ignored his warnings, and refused the prescribed bed rest, even when he told her the condition might be very serious. Furthermore, she made him promise not to disclose what had happened. After that she returned to Gallup where she decided that Sister Stanislaus should be taken to Chicago to see a specialist.

In Chicago, she collapsed again but declared that Sister Stanislaus' care was a priority and so accompanied her to a sanitarium in St. Louis. By then it was early November. Mother Mary of the Visitation was sick with fear. Every day Katharine seemed to be moving faster rather than slower. She hurried through train stations, disembarking during pre-dawn hours to board a connecting railway, and receiving and responding to correspondence on the run. One letter described the "terrific problem" Xavier was having finding facilities in which to hold dances or play basketball. "Loyola," Katharine read in a report from the Sisters in New Orleans, "would have been burned to the ground" if the all-white school's team had played Xavier's. The news didn't improve her health. Nor did the message's conclusion: that not a student would remain enrolled at Loyola if the school ever dared play against Xavier.

In St. Louis she suffered her worst attack yet. Her face became a dull red color; her feet turned ice cold. Alerted to the by-now familiar danger signs, Mother Mary of the Visitation feared a cerebral hemorrhage. The local doctor agreed, adding that paralysis or thrombosis were distinct possibilities. He was blunt with his prognosis. She had obviously suffered several heart attacks. If she didn't cease all activity at once, she wouldn't last long.

Without Katharine's knowledge, Mother Mary telegraphed the motherhouse. Louise wired money for the women to travel in the drawing-room section of the train. Katharine was too sick to argue with Lou's extravagance, but was incensed nonetheless. Here was a woman who reused every scrap of paper, wore her shoes until the soles cracked and the leather could no longer be repaired, and ground pencils into nubs she could barely hold. Her vow of poverty was as sacred as her promise to be a servant and mother to those in her care.

If she grumbled about Louise's cosseting, or tried to cajole her caregivers into thinking she'd be right as rain given a couple of days' rest, Mother Mary of the Visitation and the Sisters waiting anxiously in Cornwells Heights were firm: Katharine required care. Immediately.

She was permitted to leave St Louis and return to the motherhouse on December 7, 1935. She would never leave the grounds again.

––––––––

Her Christmas message that year was dictated from her infirmary bed. "Let us take courage; let us start anew. . . . This courage He imparts to us for the asking, not only on Christmas morning but every morning."

It could have been herself she was encouraging, because
Katharine was clearly irked by her weakened state. After having
led such a vital existence, she was frustrated by being confined to
a bed or a wheelchair or a few brief strolls. When she had had
typhoid fever, the cure had seemed tortuously slow, but there had
been a cure. A failing heart, however, could never be restored to
health. She would have to accustom herself to being an invalid for
the rest of her days, but, oh, the adjustment was hard.

Her Meditation Slips and Retreat Notes fill a combined twenty-two binders in the archives at the motherhouse. Katharine's
impatience at her own impatience is a continual theme as she
struggled and struggled and struggled afresh to achieve peace with
her new mode of life.

> Very difficult to keep patient when invalid.
> I must strive to imitate our Lord's patience.
> Just before meditation I burst forth in *words of real impatience.*
> Almost a frantic impatience [with her night nurse]. I
> reproved her emphatically.
> Dear Jesus, never let me say a word without first having *a
> word with you.*
> I do not think I was impatient today. Deo Gratias.

While Katharine strove to accept her limitations, her Sisters did
as well. They had long been accustomed to her vivacity and charismatic personality; her bouts of pique injured them because they
understood how disturbing the behavior was to this woman they all
revered and loved. Then, too, no one knew when the end might
come. As quiescent as everyone attempted to keep her, and as passive as Katharine attempted to be, focusing on meditations entitled
"Preparation for Death," the uncertainty was omnipresent. In early
1936, she suffered another heart attack, then in 1937, resigned as
Superior General.

The change was necessary, of course, but it was devastating to
every Sister whether at the motherhouse or far afield. Katharine
who had shepherded, inspired, and fought on behalf of the

oppressed would never do so again. The closely knit community had lost the leadership of its original champion and guide. When Mother M. Mercedes assumed the role of Superior General and Katharine knelt and promised obedience in a soft but clear voice, the chapel erupted in sobs. Katharine was true to her word, and Mother Mercedes, who'd been friend, confidant, and fellow laborer, made an apt successor to the Order's mission.

April 1943 brought another blow to Katharine's compromised health when it was discovered she had breast cancer. A mastectomy was performed using only local anesthetic owing to fear of further heart damage. Needless to say, she was in agony. "Grabbed hold of the nurse's arm and hurt her so much," she chastised herself in May. She wanted to keep her pain and suffering private, but could not. She prayed to become more accepting, and spent sleepless hours focusing on illness as a special grace. Still, though, her body ached; pain was a constant.

Several months later, on November 5, 1943, Louise suffered a cerebral hemorrhage and died. Katharine couldn't contain her grief. Her mind began to wander. She imagined she saw Johanna and her father, envisioned shivering children needing aid, and tried to pluck off her own warm blanket and give it to these phantoms. Nothing would convince here that the images were a fiction. She insisted the children were in the room with her and speaking to her, telling her to arise and resume her work on their behalf. She couldn't believe no one else could hear them. Her nurses were unable to convince her that she'd been dreaming or hallucinating, but perhaps they were wrong and Katharine right. Perhaps, she'd entered that thin universe where mystics meet God and God's anointed. Henceforth the children and their needs never deserted her. Nor did they cease communicating with her.

World War II was very much on her mind by then. When she could write clearly and lucidly—which wasn't always certain—the news from abroad tortured her. "There is a Hell," Katharine wrote in August 1941. "There is no such thing as love there, nor pity. . . . A mother curses the son and vice versa. Hear the yells of despair.

Think of the terror in the inn in Gallup with those drunken delirium tremens men in the bar room fighting all night!!! Eternity of this!! War, confusion, fighting!! Eternity of this!!"

Xavier University's annual gift to Katharine was a folio-sized tome bound in marbleized paper containing photographs and chapter headings rendered in calligraphy, and a summary of the news from Xavier's various schools and departments. Along with reports and personal messages, there were images of Xavier graduates enlisted in the armed forces. In the Yearly Book of 1941, James Morrow, Class of '39, smiles from the page while wearing his midshipman's uniform. Stationed on the USS *Utah*, he was killed in the attack on Pearl Harbor, December 7, 1941.

> Praying for valiant soldiers in the shadow of death. . . .
>
> Think of the valiant soldiers now being slaughtered on the battlefield this June 23 [1944] . . . I ask the salvation of all the citizens who are bombed and dying. Help the suffering, agonized relatives of the soldiers and the defeated; I especially commend to Your care the children of all nations. I am now thinking of all the prisoners—religious, male and female—release them, O Blessed Mother, all.

There was consolation in letters from alumni and parents. Vivian S. Chavin of Jacksonville, Florida, contacted Katharine to tell her that her son Nelson W. V. Spaulding would be graduating in June 1941, and that he intended on becoming a medical doctor. "I am writing to let you know how thankful I am for the wonderful university of Xavier." Edmund Burke, who had sung Mephistopheles in *Faust*, also expressed his thanks, telling Katharine that the university had been a "particularly hard struggle for me, I wish to express my gratitude and thankfulness to all who may have been influential in aiding me directly or indirectly." Some sent telegrams: "The students at Xavier cannot rest in solitude until you know our gratitude for your personal interest in the Negro youth. Long may you live Mother Katharine Drexel and may there ever be sunshine in your path." A former Holy

Providence student declared, "I am always one of Reverend Mother's children." The war, though, created perpetual fear that these bright, young lights of their generation wouldn't survive the conflict that had engulfed the globe. Sometimes it seemed to Katharine that the world was coming to an end. "Can an omnipotent God allow so many evils?" she wondered repeatedly.

As her outward shell diminished, her soul intensified its inner quest. "Father," she prayed, "make me just as You wish me to be." She marked favorite passages from the Gospels and the Acts of the Apostles, and devoted hours to studying religious tracts and the lives of the saints, among whom Teresa of Avila had a special place in her heart. *The Mystical City of God*, written by the seventeenth-century Spanish abbess and mystic Maria of Agreda, was a four-volume work she read in its entirety.

Like Katharine, Maria had been thrust unwillingly into a leadership position. The abbess' sagacity earned her the respect of King Philip IV, who visited the convent in Agreda and corresponded regularly seeking her advice on national affairs. In the midst of her practical duties, she had a vision of Jacob's ladder climbing into heaven. A voice instructed her to ascend. Having reached the top rung she saw Mary, clothed with the sun and crowned with stars— similar to the description in the Book of Revelation. The abbess was commanded to write a history of the life of the Mother of God, which she did. Fearing she wasn't equipped for the task and that her effort had been an act of self-pride she destroyed the work— against the wishes of the Church Fathers, then rewrote it, an activity that consumed the rest of her life, and that drew her into deeper contemplation and mysticism. Katharine was hungry for Maria of Agreda's guidance, and for the grace that had overwhelmed the Virgin Mary when she accepted the angel Gabriel's announcement. As Katharine reflected in one of her retreat notes, Mary hadn't "wasted time asking why." She'd simply accepted what God had called her to do and be.

"I should endeavor to enkindle within my soul the fire of the Holy Spirit." Katharine resolved. "I have only to ask. I must open my mouth and pant. I must open wide the mouth of my heart."

Without the busyness of the world, confined to small, familiar spaces, her mind devoted itself to the Holy. Around her the convent maintained its work, Sisters came and went as schools were re-staffed. There were meetings, discussions, letters written, visitors received, bills paid, and food prepared, but there settled over the stone walls and tile roofs, over the lawns and shade trees and garden a deep sense of peace. In the distance the Delaware glinted, shimmery blue in summer, ice-gray in winter. The river carried the mountains' melted snows and the spring rains that fell on farm and field, town and city down toward the sea, bringing with the returning tides the ocean's tangy brine: a continuum of exchange and renewal.

"The life we draw from the Resurrection is a continual dying and perpetual rising from the tomb." Katharine now understood. "To die to self-love that I may live to God alone is the great business of the Spiritual life."

Recognize our Lord in His mysteries, in His virtues, His kindness, His amiability, His tenderness, His bounty, His sacrifice.

Sit still often in the presence of God, lost in acts of faith and love and hope, in acts of praise and adoration and thanksgiving.

One of the most characteristic signs of unusual action of Divine grace within a soul is an ardent and persistent desire to strip off one's selfishness, to forget oneself more and more and more, to be consumed entirely in order to be united with God by pure and perfect love.

I love to think how small the little foot of Our Lord was on that first Christmas. A little foot does not make big strides; it can only take little steps. In imitating the Divine Babe, let us place ours in His footsteps. Then we shall, with God's grace, grow into the bigger footsteps and make greater strides. If we are faithful in little, we will obtain grace for the big.

"Listen to Jesus," she exhorted herself over and over. "Listening" and "hearing" were a constant theme.

"Begin at length in real earnest to love and serve God. Take for your rule of life the example of Jesus Christ," Katharine wrote in

March 1946, but she'd started that work more than a half century before.

———

Mother Katharine Drexel died March 3, 1955. To those whose lives she had touched—even in the smallest measure—she was considered a saint. Following her funeral Mass Archbishop Ryan said of her, "I shall never live to see it, but Mother Katharine will be someday to come most certainly a canonized saint of the Church." Archbishop O'Hara agreed. "All of us felt we were attending the funeral of a saint." The words *saint* and *saintly* were on everyone's tongue whether ordained or lay, rich or poor. *The Catholic Standard and Times* referred to her as "One of the most remarkable women in the history of America." The auxiliary bishop of Philadelphia, Joseph McShea, who delivered the funeral sermon, said, "First and foremost, in youth and old age, in health and in sickness, with friends and with strangers, the beloved soul of Mother Katharine was activated, inspired and impelled by an insatiable love of God."

Those were the public accolades. They arrived, as did the mourners, from across the nation. Personal recollections continued to flow into the motherhouse. They described Katharine's humility, grace, perspicacity, vision, and love. Some were long and eloquent, some halting and tongue-tied. They came from Sisters, former students, priests, and prelates. One was a story dating from 1916 when a young priest, Nicholas Perschl, was assigned to take Katharine and her companion on a four-hundred-mile tour of the Southwest. Father Perschl described how they had traveled by Model T; he'd been at the wheel acting as chauffeur and guide. The roads were riddled with gullies; the car lurched dangerously, its top speed being thirty-five miles an hour, although that was a rarity.

Pausing to eat in the desert night, Father Perschl produced a battery-operated lantern while the coyotes yipped and darkness descended. He was very anxious to impress this unusual foundress of her own order, and very nervous about his—and the dining spot's—shortcomings. Although he well understood that she had taken a vow of poverty, he was equally aware of the manner in which she'd been raised. Hoping to better accommodate her, he'd brought a folding table and two rickety chairs whose legs sank into the sandy earth. Katharine seemed undeterred, but he was filled with misgivings about his role as host. The meal he served consisted of beans and chile con carne and a flat, pale round thing the one-time heiress and Philadelphia socialite didn't recognize as edible. The table manners she'd learned at her parents' and aunts' and uncles' homes came to her aid.

"Pardon me, Father," she said, holding up the thing to the light, "is this a doily?" The doily was a tortilla.

Amidst all the outpourings of grief from Oregon to South Dakota, Wisconsin to Louisiana, Indiana to Ohio to Uganda and British Honduras, a message from Mother Irenaeus of McKeesport, Pennsylvania, speaks to the essence of Katharine's life and legacy: "I think God waited until the Community was ripe for this to happen. He has a group of God-fearing women at the helm. Women of sound judgment, strong character, fearless, but giants in their trust in God."

Afterword

IN 1964, NINE YEARS AFTER MOTHER KATHARINE DREXEL'S DEATH, the Cause for her Beatification was introduced by John Cardinal Krol, archbishop of Philadelphia. She was declared Venerable by Pope John Paul II (now Saint Pope John Paul II) on January 26, 1987, and beatified on November 20, 1988. She was canonized on October 1, 2000. In addition to her documented Heroic Virtues, the requisite two miracles involved healing from deafness; Robert Gutherman and Amy Wall were cured after their families prayed for intercession to Mother Drexel.

Saint Katharine Drexel's shrine in Bensalem, Pennsylvania (near Philadelphia), is a place of pilgrimage. Her tomb lies beneath the main altar of St. Elizabeth's Chapel (built in honor of Elizabeth Drexel Smith), where the Sisters of the Blessed Sacrament still worship. Although reduced in numbers, the Sisters continue the work of empowerment, education, and social justice Katharine began among Native Americans and African Americans. Their ministry also takes them to Haiti.

Saint Katharine Drexel's feast day is March 3.

NOTES

CHAPTER I: HEREDITY

2: I left my native place. Francis Martin Drexel, "The Life and Travels of F. M. Drexel, 1792–1826," Drexel University Archives. Two copies exist: one handwritten; one transcribed and typed.

4: *Familien Buch*. Dornbirn, Austria, Town Hall.

7: I never had any inclination for mercantile affairs. Drexel, "The Life and Travels of F. M. Drexel, 1792–1826."

10: but by no means stay. Ibid.

10: quantity of cheese per week. Ibid.

12: creating his own maxims. Boies Penrose, "The Early Life of F. M. Drexel, 1792–1837," *Pennsylvania Magazine of History and Biography* (October 1936): 343–344.

13: The family before her death treated me like a son. Ibid., 344.

14: I did not escape his infamous tongue. Ibid., 345.

16: I embarked on the Peruvian Brig Confianza. Francis Martin Drexel, "Journal from Guayaquil, Pacific Ocean, to Different Parts of Chili." Drexel University Archives.

18: Arrived the 10th in the morning. Ibid.

18: that damned Dutchman. Penrose, "The Early Life of F.M. Drexel, 1792–1837," 357.

18: his expenses were $3,260. Ibid. 357.

19: The address given was 18, Calle de Tiburcia. Ibid.

20: Robert E. Wright, *The First Wall Street: Chestnut Street, Philadelphia, and the Birth of American Finance* (Chicago: University of Chicago Press, 2005), 149.

21: the fury of a chained panther biting the bars of his cage. Reginald C. McGrane, ed., *The Correspondence of Nicholas Biddle Dealing with National Affairs, 1807–1844* (Boston: Houghton Mifflin, 1919), 196.

22: This worthy President thinks that because he has scalped Indians. Ibid. 221.

22: merely thro' a lack of courage. Drexel, "The Life and Travels of F.M. Drexel, 1792–1826."

22: Our Lord likes courage. Get it from Him. ASBS Writings of M.M. Katharine. Number 691.

CHAPTER 2: A CHILD OF PRIVILEGE

27: attend her funeral on Sunday morning at 9 1/2 o'clock. "Mortuary Notices," *North American and United States Gazette*, January 1, 1859, 2.

27: Each heart has its own Necropolis. Daniel Jay Sprague, "Guardian Angels," *Godey's Lady's Book* (November 1858).

29: If his wife declared. As told to the author by her grandfather, Livingston L. Biddle.

29: Drexel descendants carried on the tradition. As told to the author.

32: we believe the negro unfit for it. Sydney George Fisher, *The Laws of Race, as Connected With Slavery* (Philadelphia: Willis P. Hazard, 1860).

35: Assassinated on this spot. Abraham Lincoln, *Collected Works of Abraham Lincoln* (New Brunswick, NJ: Rutgers University Press, 1953), vol. 4, 241.

36: "Brave Boys, Are They." Henry C. Work, 1861.

36: "Our Captain's Last Words." Ibid.

37: This community is deprived of one of its most valued citizens. *North American and United States Gazette*, June 10, 1863, 1.

37: Miss. P. A. Donnelly. Ibid.

39: End of the War!! *North American and United States Gazette*, April 10, 1865, 2.

39: Lee Finds His Waterloo. *Philadelphia Inquirer*, April 10, 1865, 1.

40: very fine acting there tonight. "Assassination Plot," *North American and United States Gazette*, April 19, 1865, 1.

41: The transition from jubilance to grief and woe. "The Great Tragedy," *Philadelphia Inquirer*, April 17, 1865, 1.

41: Nation Mourns. Ibid.

CHAPTER 3: KATIE

43: Never let the poor have cold feet. ASBS Meditation Slips, Volume 4, 65.

43: Thou shalt love thy neighbor as thyself. Matthew 22: 37–39.

43: For I was hungry. Matthew 25: 35–36.

43: "How it Would Be, if Some Ladies Had Their Own Way." *Harper's Weekly*, May 16, 1868.

45: Dear Louise. Sister Consuela Marie Duffy, *Katharine Drexel: A Biography* (Cornwells Heights, PA: Mother Katharine Drexel Guild, 1977), 29.

45: "Nadal." ASBS Writings of M.M. Katharine, Number 3211.

45: a frail, fair, delicate, little thing of twelve. Ibid.

45: moral qualities of the peerless Catherine. Ibid.

47: excepting also any other child or children he may have had by her.

Lou Baldwin, *Saint Katharine Drexel: Apostle to the Oppressed* (Philadelphia: Catholic Standard and Times, 2000), 21.

50: Garden for young Plants; enter. ASBS Writings of M.M. Katharine, Number 3212.

50: which seemed to come from someone near me. Ibid.

51: WANTED GARDENERS. Ibid.

51: having impetuous ideas. ASBS Writings of M.M. Katharine.

52: "When May Diamonds Be Worn?" "Ladies Fashions," *Sunday Morning Times*, March 10, 1872, 1.

52: Emilie Drexel's marriage. "City Affairs—The Centennial Commission: In Town," *North American and United States Gazette*, March 8, 1872, 1.

52: Tony contributed to the purchase of a house intended for Grant's retirement. Dan Rottenberg, *The Man Who Made Wall Street: Anthony Drexel and the Rise of Modern Finance* (Philadelphia: University of Pennsylvania Press, 2006), 78.

54: President Grant, his wife, and daughter, Nellie Grant, were at the wedding. ASBS Annals, Volume 1, 40–41.

54: shipwrecks, they are so very exciting. Ibid.

54: "Peace Policy." *State of the Union Addresses by United States Presidents: State of the Union Addresses of U.S. Grant*, December 5, 1870, http://www.presidency.ucsb.edu (accessed August 6, 2013).

55: ku klux. "By Telegraph and Mail," *North American and United States Gazette*, March 7, 1872, 1.

55: Ibid.

55: *State of the Union Addresses by United States Presidents: State of the Union Addresses of U.S. Grant*, December 4, 1871, http://www.presidency.ucsb.edu (accessed August 6, 2013).

55: Ibid.

57: the crank of our engine broke on the tenth day of our voyage. ASBS Writings of M.M. Katharine, Numbers 2985–2990.

57: I have been having a really splendid time . . . *Scott's Poetical Works*. Ibid.

58: jolly row on the Thames. Ibid.

59: we had the greatest difficulty in getting them. Ibid., Number 3216.

59: meaning of the word punctuality. Ibid., Number 2990.

59: Life is discipline. Sister Marie Elizabeth Letterhouse, *The Francis A. Drexel Family* (Cornwells Heights, PA: Sisters of the Blessed Sacrament, 1939), 124, 125.

60: that her Pa had been governor of Siberia. ASBS Annals, Volume 1, 91.

61: I enjoyed myself. Ibid., 92.

61: Bernese Oberland. ASBS Writings of M.M. Katharine, Number 3217.

62: Paintings . . . have opened up to us a new world of pleasure. Ibid., Number 3221.

62: They are very fond of balls they are so "awfully jolly," etc., etc., etc. Ibid., Number 3222.

62: offer up all yr actions to God. ASBS Writings of M.M. Katharine, Number 1.

63: all the vices of his Pa exaggerated. ASBS Writings of M.M. Katharine, Number 3224.

CHAPTER 4: A YOUNG LADY OF PHILADELPHIA

67: all modern languages are spoken. Russell F. Weigley, ed., *Philadelphia: A 300-Year History* (New York: W. W. Norton, 1982), 462.

68: I am happy to say that our New Year's Eve commenced. ASBS Writings of M.M. Katharine, Number 3202.

69: conversation did not become general . . . Miss A. Antello. Ibid., Number 5448.

70: Good gracious! What a scramble there was to get me dressed. Ibid., Number 5451.

71: A silence ensued. Ibid., Number 5452.

71: To outsiders I do not wear well. Letterhouse, *The Francis A. Drexel Family*, 178.

71: beautiful seaside plantation. Ibid., 158.

72: best horses in America run. Ibid., 169.

72: Stunning. ASBS Writings of M.M. Katharine, Number 1521.

72: deep water either with the Beaux. Letterhouse, *The Francis A. Drexel Family*, 171.

72: Englishman steal your hearts. Ibid., 178.

73: left me very indignant. Ibid., 160.

73: At least his depressed manner. Ibid., 165.

76: melancholy whist. Letterhouse, *The Francis A. Drexel Family*, 215.

CHAPTER 5: AN HEIRESS

80: The complete list is as follows: Cathedral of St. Peter and St. Paul, Conferences of St. Vincent de Paul of the Archdiocese of Philadelphia, St. Joseph's Church (on Willings Alley), St. John's Orphan Asylum, St. Joseph's Hospital, St. Mary's Hospital, Sisters of St. Francis, Philadelphia Theological Seminary of St. Charles Borromeo, St. Joseph's College, House of the Good Shepherd, West Philadelphia Industrial School, St. Bonifacius Church, St. Joseph's Hospital (Reading, PA), St. James

Parochial School, St. Peter's Church, Roman Catholic Society of St. Joseph for Educating and Maintaining Poor Orphan Children, Little Sisters of the Poor, Sisters of Mercy, St. Vincent's Orphan Asylum, LaSalle College, Sharon Hill Academy, Lankenau Hospital, Institute of Ladies of the Sacred Heart of Eden Hall, St. Catherine's Female Orphan Asylum, St. Mary Magdalen de Pazzi's Asylum for Italian Orphan Girls, St. Anne's Widows' Asylum, and the Institute of Ladies of the Sacred Heart of Philadelphia.

83: I send these few lines to bid you goodbye. ASBS, Anthony J. Drexel, H50 A3.

84: We had hoped for a more decided cure. Letterhouse, *The Francis A. Drexel Family*, 255.

85: The whole pass is most somber. ASBS Writings of M.M. Katharine, Number 2951.

85: Inferno. Farther on Purgatorio. Ibid.

85: Why did a creator require a handmaid? Ibid.

86: I am afraid you are traveling too fast. ASBS, Anthony J. Drexel, H50 A3.

87: impregnated with rancid oil. Letterhouse, *The Francis A. Drexel Family*, 286.

87: jumping from boulder to boulder. Ibid., 287.

88: I have no doubt the absence of restraint has its charms. ASBS, Anthony J. Drexel, H50 A3.

88: prayer-dry. ASBS Writings of M.M. Katharine, Number 2262.

89: COUNT PILA. Ibid.

89: "Why not, my child, yourself become a missionary?" Duffy, *Katharine Drexel*, 100.

90: Desperadoes. ASBS, Letter to Katharine Drexel from O'Connor, June 6, 1877, H10B 41.

90: all the rage. ASBS Writings of M.M. Katharine, Number 19.

91: God protect you from that fate that would involve such a title. ASBS Letter to Katharine Drexel from O'Connor, June 6, 1881, H10B 41.

91: venturesome to rashness. Ibid., June 3, 1882.

91: interior trials. ASBS Writings of M.M. Katharine, Book IV.

91: "Strictly Private—The Holy Ghost Speaking to My Soul." ASBS Writings of M.M. Katharine, Numbers 1?7.

91: Choose a secret place to thyself. Ibid.

91: Try not to be so scrupulous. Ibid.

92: How many of us make a sacrifice to God? ASBS Writings of M.M. Katharine, Number 7.

92: gourmand. ASBS Writings of M.M. Katharine, Number 33.

93: Reasons for entering religion. ASBS Writings of M.M. Katharine, Numbers 3207–3208.

94: saying that he desired but my happiness. ASBS Letter from Katharine Drexel to O'Connor. May 21, 1883, Number 28.

95: further in your examination. ASBS Letter to Katharine Drexel from O'Connor, May 26, 1883, H10B 41.

95: Think, pray, wait. ASBS Letter to Katharine Drexel from O'Connor, August 5, 1883, H10B 41.

96: What am I to do *now*? ASBS Letter from Katharine Drexel to O'Connor, January 27, 1884, Number 33.

96: we left others for her. Ibid.

96: under the rule of a cranky superioress. Ibid.

96: be content with the rule of life I've given you. ASBS Letter to Katharine Drexel from O'Connor, February 15, 1884, H10B 41.

97: Please tell me, dear Father, what I should do. ASBS Letter from Katharine Drexel to O'Connor, August 1, 1885, Number 41.

97: Not to enter. ASBS Letter to Katharine Drexel from O'Connor, August 29, 1885, H10B 41.

99: the most illuminating religious book of the century. Walter Rauschenbusch, "Appreciation of the Press," *A Theology for the Social Gospel* (New York: Macmillan Company, 1917).

99: the true followers of Jesus. Ibid., 108, 109.

100: clutching for food that was already unfit to eat. Jane Addams, *Twenty Years at Hull House* (New York: Signet Classics, 1961), 44.

103: it is the Great Father's fault. *Philadelphia Inquirer*, June 8, 1870, 1.

103: "The Speech of Red Cloud." *Philadelphia Inquirer*, June 10, 1870, 4.

104: let me live in as big a house. *Philadelphia Inquirer*, June 7, 1870, 1.

104: Pennsylvania's beauties doubly appreciated after a dose of prairie. Letterhouse, *The Francis A. Drexel Family*, 325.

Chapter 6: Renouncing Millions

106: would break you down in no time. ASBS Letter to Katharine Drexel from O'Connor, June 24, 1887, H10B 41.

109: "common assault." Common indeed! Deirdre McMahon, "The Condition of Women and the Ripper Case," paper delivered at Drexel University, October 29, 2011.

110: instruct a better and broader womanhood, a braver and more intelligent manhood. Edward D. McDonald and Edward M. Hinton, "Drexel Institute of Technology 1891–1941: A Memorial History" (Camden: Haddon Craftsmen, 1942), 29–30.

111: restless because my heart is not rested in God. ASBS Writings of

M.M. Katharine, Number 52.

111: uncommonly handsome. "Married by the Archbishop," *New York Times,* January 18, 1889.

112: you could do in religion. ASBS Letter to Katharine Drexel from O'Connor, March 14, 1888, H10B 41.

112: I want a missionary order for Indians and Colored people. ASBS Writings of M.M. Katharine, Number 55.

112: "ladies" of her social class. ASBS Letter to Katharine Drexel from O'Connor, December 21, 1888, H10B 41.

113: No wedding that has occurred in Philadelphia has equaled this in widespread interest. "Married by the Archbishop," *New York Times,* January 18, 1889.

114: How would it do to enter a Novitiate on May 5th? ASBS Writings of M.M. Katharine, Number 57.

114: You have the means to make such an establishment. ASBS Letter to Katharine Drexel from O'Connor, February 16, 1889, H10 B 41.

114: The responsibility of such a call. ASBS Writings of M.M. Katharine, Number 59.

115: I was never so quietly sure of any vocation. ASBS Letter to Katharine Drexel from O'Connor, February 28, 1889, H10B 41.

115: if she does not undertake it, it will remain undone. ASBS Letter to Katharine Drexel from O'Connor, March 16, 1889, H10B 41.

118: "Renouncing Millions," *Public Ledger* (Philadelphia), May 8, 1889.

CHAPTER 7: SISTER M. KATHARINE

122: for the order you are establishing? ASBS Writings of M.M. Katharine, Number 65.

122: If you expect an angel. ASBS Letter to Katharine Drexel from O'Connor, June 16, 1889, H10B 41.

122: The work will be God's work. Ibid.

122: You don't know how to teach. I'll teach you. ASBS Writings of M.M. Katharine, Number 86.

123: fifty thousand dollars a year as a fund for its support. ASBS Letter to Katharine Drexel from O'Connor, July 20, 1889, H10B 41.

123: renounce now and forever my opinion and judgment. ASBS Writings of M.M. Katharine, Number 73.

125: "A Brilliant Wedding," *New York Times,* January 8, 1890.

127: vague apprehensions that have entered your mind. ASBS Letter to Katharine Drexel from O'Connor, November 7, 1889, H10B 41.

129: I draw on your reserve stock. Letterhouse, *The Francis A. Drexel Family,* 413.

131: sacred goal. ASBS Writings of M.M. Katharine, Number 47.

131: needed for her canonization. Ibid.

CHAPTER 8: HERE AM I; SEND ME

133: "Kate Drexel's Big Projects," *Philadelphia Inquirer*, December 19, 1890, 1.

133: "Great Week for Women," *Philadelphia Inquirer*, February 23, 1891, 2.

134: sugar paper . . . sugar talk. "Council at Pine Ridge," *Philadelphia Inquirer*, June 20, 1889, 2.

135: so-called prophet or Messiah. "Death from the Dance," *Philadelphia Inquirer*, November 22, 1890, 1.

135: You must not be afraid of anything. Ibid.

137: sunken Vesuvius. "The Awful Massacre," *Philadelphia Inquirer*, December 31, 1890, 1.

138: fight against his own people if the mission came to harm. Duffy, *Katharine Drexel*, 168.

139: "Miss Drexel's Final Vows," *Philadelphia Inquirer*, February 13, 1891, 1.

140: costly. "St. Elizabeth's House," *Philadelphia Inquirer*, July 16, 1891, 8.

141: "Oh how audacious I was in those days." ASBS Annals Volume 3, 188.

143: "neglect and abandonment of the Indian and Colored Races." ASBS Annals 1891.

143: an old Stage Coach. Letter from Katharine Drexel to Mother Inez, June 1891, ASBS Writings, Number 91.

143: Western specimen. Ibid.

143: tall broad backed barren hills. Ibid.

144: We shook hands with William Shakespeare, the Indian interpreter. Ibid.

147: Miss Drexel is spending too much money on these Colored people. ASBS Annals 1891, 47.

147: not a single child in school! ASBS Writings of M.M. Katharine, Number 3158.

147: to be built at St. Stephen's Mission Wyoming. Ibid., Number 3159.

148: An industrial school. Ibid., Number 3160.

148: fat and well. Ibid., Numbers 1539, 1891.

149: The country—I think it is Ohio. ASBS Annals 1894, 7.

149: You are coming to take St. Catherine's. ASBS Annals 1894, 8.

150: heavy broom and lye. ASBS Annals 1894, 11.

150: grey sand hills of Albuquerque. ASBS Annals 1894, 14.

150: the wind sends a fine sand. Ibid.

150: WATCH YOUR LUGGAGE. ASBS Annals 1894, 27.

152: wholly untrue. "Debs Makes an Address," *Philadelphia Inquirer*, July 6, 1894, 2.

153: rough types . . . conversation . . . what women should listen to. ASBS Annals 1894, 46–48.

154: Well, it seems when the strikers didn't kill us. ASBS Annals 1894, 49.

154: I am certain we are riding to our deaths. Ibid.

154: most noble. Ibid.

154: did anyone ever see such styles? Ibid., 69.

155: three wild Apaches, as wild as wild can be . . . break every window in the house. ASBS Annals 1894, 97–98.

156: If we have died to self in life. ASBS Annals 1894, 71.

157: *begging* for poor outcasts. ASBS Annals 1894, 83.

CHAPTER 9: LISTENING AND ACTING

159: you shall not crucify mankind on a cross of gold. "Bryan on the Fifth Ballot," *Philadelphia Inquirer*, July 11, 1896, 1.

159: Civilized America. Ida B. Wells, "Southern Horrors: Lynch Law in All of Its Phases," *New York Age*, 1892.

161: three-fourths of a million can neither read nor write. ASBS Speech of Hon. Edward de V. Morrell, 12.

162: Neither one is fit to perform the supreme functions of citizenship. Ibid., 17.

164: supernatural rats. ASBS Annals 1898–1899, 67.

165: Oh, I am so disappointed. ASBS Annals 1895, 10.

166: missing "Bern's" visits and letters. ASBS Annals 1898–1899, 37.

167: grand, old pathfinder. "Kit Carson's Grave," *Philadelphia Inquirer*, February 15, 1876, 8.

169: May all be well. Berard Haile, OFM, "Why the Navajo Hogan?" "Primitive Man," *Quarterly Bulletin of the Catholic Anthropological Conference* 15, nos. 3–4 (July–August 1942).

169: it extends from the woman. Ibid.

170: The sun had sunk an hour behind the red sandstone cliff before we reached the mission. . . . One seems so alone with God. ASBS Writings of M.M. Katharine, Number 146.

171: looked up in wonder at God's wonderful ways. ASBS Writings of M.M. Katharine, Number 167.

CHAPTER 10: HIS STEADFAST GRACE AND LOVE

172: I have done my duty. "President M'Kinley, Shot Down by an Anarchist," *Philadelphia Inquirer*, September 7, 1901, 1.

172: preached murder and arson. *Philadelphia Inquirer*, September 14, 1901, 5.

172: Nearer, my God, to Thee. "Last Sad Offices About the Bedside," *Philadelphia Inquirer*, September 14, 1901, 1.

175: our hearts have no room for Jesus. ASBS Writings of M.M. Katharine, Number 193.

175: Christ lives in your *whole* being. Ibid.

175: Chewing gum! Chewing gum! Ibid., Number 205.

175: but those other fellows can't keep the faith! Ibid., Number 183.

176: deprive them of the right of suffrage. ASBS Edward Morrell Speech, April 4, 1904.

176: to the denial of the right of suffrage. "Morrell Against South," *Public Ledger*, December 9, 1904, ASBS.

177: ingratitude of the Negro. ASBS Writings of M.M. Katharine, Number 2950.

177: I shall work and pull at it as long as God gives me life. Duffy, *Katharine Drexel*, 249.

177: What will my Father in Heaven think? ASBS Retreat Notes of M.M. Katharine, Volume 1, 75.

177: NEEDED! WANTED! The Light of the Holy Ghost! ASBS Writings of M.M. Katharine, Number 175.

178: I must keep in check my passions. ASBS Original Annals 1907, 9.

178: marvel it was not commenced fifty years ago. ASBS Annals 1905, 24.

178: The good to be done, my dear Mother, is incomparable. Ibid., 24.

179: insure the property at once. Ibid., 7.

179: to be used as a negro school. Ibid., 19.

180: My dear Sir: I am just in receipt of your letter of February 17th. ASBS Original Annals 1905, 15.

181: The use of the property as a negro school. ASBS Original Annals 1905, 38–40.

181: They say "There is another place on the city's outskirts." Ibid., 23.

181: the better class is with us. Ibid., 24.

181: when the darkness does not comprehend it. ASBS Letter from Katharine Drexel to Byrne, July 14, 1905, H10A Box 19.

182: heaving mass of humanity. ASBS Writings of M.M. Katharine, Number 208.

183: God is all, and at His summons everything must give way; even joy or happiness count for naught when He calls. ASBS Meditation Slips of M.M. Katharine, Volume 11, 66.

183: *much* writing in cars. ASBS Writings of M.M. Katharine, Number 226.

184: I love to think how small the little foot. ASBS Meditation Slips of M.M. Katharine, Volume 7, 4.

184: The active life of Christ was a life of prayer. ASBS Original Annals 1904–1905, 38.

185: ROMA is MORA, which word means delay. Ibid., 69.

185: any hurry? Duffy, *Katharine Drexel*, 284.

185: What do you and I know about it anyway? ASBS Annals 1911, 61. (Obituary from *Public Ledger*, February 12, 1912.)

185: What part of Hell do you come from?" ASBS Annals 1911, 66.

185: I bless you from the bottom of my heart. Ibid., 11.

186: strongest forces in Philadelphia life. Ibid., 51.

186: the kingdom of God is not to be wrapped in a single dogma. Ibid., 53.

188: MOTHER ILL. ASBS Correspondence of M.M. Katharine, H10A Box 17. F.1.

CHAPTER 11: GOD AND MAMMON

191: very sick woman. ASBS Original Annals 1912, 80.

191: If not we may lose her. Ibid.

191: I felt so sure God's plans were being fulfilled in me. ASBS Writings of M.M. Katharine, Number 328.

192: Be patient and God will bring all to His glory. ASBS Writings of M.M. Katharine, Number 474.

192: a vision in pink and silver. "Susie Dearest," *Philadelphia Inquirer*, December 19, 1909, 4.

193: banner event of the London season. *Philadelphia Inquirer*, June 9, 1910, 1.

193: besieged . . . numerous titled foreign suitors. "Marjorie Gould to Wed A. J. Drexel, Jr.," *New York Times*, January 19, 1910.

193: sets of old armor and rare old oils, its trees of mauve orchids. Ibid.

193: disporting themselves in Paris or in more southerly climes. "Margaretta Drexel to Sail for Home," *Philadelphia Inquirer*, April 3, 1910, 2.

194: is this a school? W.E.B. Du Bois, *Black Reconstruction in America 1860–1880* (New York: Free Press, 1998), 645. (Originally published as *Black Reconstruction* [New York: Harcourt Brace, 1935].)

194: the damned rascals who attempted to teach niggers would be shot. Ibid., 646.

195: more than 95 percent of the black population in the South was illiterate. Ibid., 638.

195: "Negro hunts" were commonplace. Ibid., 68.

195: to be a poor man in a land of dollars is the very bottom of hardships. W.E.B. Du Bois, *The Souls of Black Folk* (New York: Dover Publications, 1994), 5. (Originally published: Chicago: A. C. McClurg, 1903.)

196: The problem of the Twentieth Century is the problem of the color line. Ibid., Forethought.

197: scarcely a man in this audience would have been other than . . . a Ku Klux sympathizer. Thomas Watt Gregory, "The History of the Original Ku Klux Klan," paper read before the Arkansas and Texas Bar Associations, July 10, 1906. http://www.kkk.bz/whenan.htm (accessed August 4, 2013).

CHAPTER 12: THINK IT, DESIRE IT, SPEAK IT, ACT IT

200: God has blessed your endeavors. ASBS Letter to Katharine Drexel from Janssens, February 29, 1892, H10B 30.

201: these miserable prejudices. ASBS Letter to Katharine Drexel from Janssens, March 2, 1894, H10B 30.

201: the children were now forced to sleep three to a bed. ASBS Letter to Katharine Drexel from Janssens, January 14, 1892, Box H10B 30.

201: I feel sometimes troubled and discouraged. ASBS Letter to Katharine Drexel from Janssens, May 28, 1892, Box H10B 30.

201: Excuse this sorrowing letter. ASBS Letter to Katharine Drexel from Janssens, January 9, 1892, Box H10B 30.

201: You and your community must pray for me. Ibid.

201: Dear Mother Katharine, I am begging again. ASBS Letter to Katharine Drexel from Janssens, October 9, 1892, Box H10B 30.

201: you would know how grateful it feels for your kindness. ASBS Letter to Katharine Drexel from Janssens, February 17, 1893, Box H10B 30.

201: The white population there is very ignorant. ASBS Letter to Katharine Drexel from Janssens, October 7, 1893, Box H10B 30.

202: race feelings run high here, and racial differences cannot be obliterated. ASBS Letter to Katharine Drexel from Blenk, March 25, 1909, Box H10B 04.

202: Dear Colored People. Ibid.

203: No State while in a condition of rebellion or insurrection. Transcript of Morrill Act (1862). Chap. CXXX.—AN ACT Donating Public Lands to the several States and Territories which may provide Colleges for the

Benefit of Agricultural and Mechanic Arts. http://www.ourdocuments.gov (accessed March 19, 2013).

204: That no money shall be paid out under this act. Second Morrill Act of 1890, Act of August 30, 1890, ch. 841, 26 Stat. 417, 7 U.S.C. 322 et seq. http://www.csrees.usda.gov (accessed August 4, 2013).

204: To the Honorable Members of the General Assembly of Louisiana. AXU, SBS of Louisiana Corporation Minutes Book, Volume 1, Box 1, File 1.

205: Harry MacInery. ASBS Original Annals 1915, 51.

206: Henry McInery influences the whole state. AXU Sister Patricia Lynch, "Odds & Ends," Part 1.

206: Southern University square, New Orleans, bought at auction. *True Democrat* (Bayou Sara), April 17, 1915, Library of Congress, Chronicling America, http://chroniclingamerica.loc.gov (accessed August 4, 2013).

206: the opening ball game. Ibid.

206: winning and losing of a German trench near Berry au Bac. Ibid.

206: "Negroes Get Good Advice." Ibid.

206: Mother Katharine Drexel is seemingly unconscious of her great work. ASBS Original Annals 1915, 51.

206: the devil sometimes can stir up an account of opposition. ASBS Correspondence of M.M. Katharine, May 16, 1915, Box H10A 19.

207: bestirring himself. ASBS Letter to Katharine Drexel from Blenk, June 29, 1915, Box H10B 04.

208: interfering seriously with the wise and efficient administration of both of the Dioceses. ASBS Letter to Katharine Drexel from Blenk, July 24, 1915, Box H10B 04.

208: to continue to welcome to its advantage pupils of every denomination. ASBS Annals 1915, 127.

208: We hope the story of our work at Old Southern. Ibid.

210: A MOST ARDENT CHARITY. ASBS Christmas letter from M.M.K., December 20, 1915, Xavier Prep Annals, 1915–1944.

210: a great big joy in God. AXU Letter from Katharine Drexel, October 15, 1916, Xavier School and Convent Early Annals, Box 1, Folder 1.

210: "We have a world to conquer." AXU Closing Exercises June 15, 1916, Xavier School and Convent Early Annals, Box 1, Folder 1.

210: "confer such literary honors and degrees" ASBS Xavier Prep Annals 1915–1944.

211: Praise be to God. AXU M.M. Katharine Correspondence, Misc. March 28, 1928.

211: I am a little disappointed that we cannot give ourselves exclusively for the Colored. ASBS Writings of M.M. Katharine, Number 424.

212: think it, desire it, speak it, act it. Ibid., Number 383.

212: Lord, it is good for us to be here! AXU M.M. Katharine Correspondence, May 5, 1930.

212: never had opportunity of attending any school before coming to this one. Ibid.

213: little me. ASBS Original Annals 1930, 97.

213: Great Battle of Longview. "The Great Battle of Longview, Texas," *Dallas Express*, July 19, 1919. http://chroniclingamerica.loc.gov (accessed August 4, 2013).

213: insisting on voting. "Texas Leads the Nation in Lynching for the Year of 1920," *Dallas Express*, January 8, 1921. http://chroniclingamerica. loc.gov (accessed August 4, 2013).

214: a Colored League of Nations. "Missouri Senator Assails League Proposals," *Dallas Express*, May 31, 1919. http://chroniclingamerica. loc.gov (accessed August 4, 2013).

214: The church is posted. ASBS Letter to Katharine Drexel from Mother Mary of the Visitation, March 21, 1922, H10 A Box 26.

215: begged me not to speak of it out of the convent. ASBS Letter to Katharine Drexel from Mother Mary of the Visitation, March 24, 1922, H10 A Box 26.

217: False also and harmful to Christian education is the so-called method of "coeducation." "Encyclical of Pope Pius XI on Christian Education to the Patriarchs, Primates, Archbishops, Bishops, and Other Ordinaries in Peace and Communion with the Apostolic See and to all the Faithful of the Catholic World." Given at Rome, at St. Peter's, the thirty-first day of December, in the year 1929, the eighth of Our Pontificate. http://www.vatican.va (accessed August 4, 2013).

CHAPTER 13: A MIRACLE TO OTHERS

219: The policy stigmatized an entire population on the country. ASBS Correspondence of M.M. Katharine, March 25, 1927, H10A 27, f.4.

221: But God knows how to bring good from evil. D. Cardinal Dougherty "Blessing," AXU, Xavier School and Convent Early Annals, Box 1, Folder 1.

221: The Sisters of the Blessed Sacrament bring to their classrooms. Rt. Rev. John B. Morris "Sermon," AXU, Xavier School and Convent Early Annals, Box 1, Folder 1.

222: Mississippi River Slavery. ASBS H80 B Box B, NAACP.

222: We rely upon you to see that the tenth part of our population shall not be discriminated against in the New Deal. ASBS Katharine Drexel letter to FDR, September 16, 1933, H 10 A 26.

223: Taken from Officers and Jails . . . Not Taken from Officers and Jails. Library of Congress Manuscript Division, NAACP Collection.
223: Lynching of Claude Neal. Walter White, "The Lynching of Claude Neal," Library of Congress Manuscript Division, NAACP Collection, 1C352.
224: Ibid.
224: the speedy passage of the Costigan-Wagner Anti-Lynching Bill. ASBS Letter from Mother M. Dorothea to FDR, H40 B5 Box 2, F.4.
225: In these days that try men's souls, the reputation is justly yours that no request brought to you is disregarded. ASBS Letter from Katharine Drexel to FDR, December, 24, 1934, H10 A 26.
225:That one slipped up on us. Roy Wilkins, "Huey Long Says—An Interview with Louisiana's Kingfish," *Crisis*, February 1935, Library of Congress Manuscript Division, NAACP Collection.
225: Why, if I tried to go after those lynchers. Ibid.
225: Anyway that nigger was guilty of coldblooded murder. Ibid.
226: He was guilty as hell. Ibid.
226: wouldn't hesitate to throw Negroes to the wolves if it became necessary. Ibid.
226: They don't vote in the South. Ibid.
226: they say's. ASBS Original Annals 1935, 357.
226: The undertaker corroborated the story. Ibid.
227: whites firing indiscriminately at blacks. "Whites and Blacks Continue Fighting in the City Streets," *Philadelphia Inquirer*, July 30, 1919, 1.
228: beloved Carl von Praeger. ASBS Sr. M. Elise Sisson, H 30C Box 7A f.3.
229: Segregation was a term I was familiar with up North, but ignorant of the effects of it. ASBS Sr. M. Elise Sisson, H30C Box 7C, 7D.
229: how well we played the part assigned to us. *Times-Picayune*, February 1, 2005. http://files.usgwarchives.net/la/orleans/obits/2005 /2005-02.txt (accessed August 8, 2013).
230: John T Scott, "A Love Letter to a Friend," ASBS Sr. Lurana Neely, H30C Box 1.

CHAPTER 14: SIT STILL OFTEN IN THE PRESENCE OF GOD
232: like a war ravaged country. ASBS Original Annals 1935, 63.
232: Ibid.
233: dust pneumonia. Timothy Egan, *The Worst Hard Time* (Boston: Houghton Mifflin, 2006), 5.
233: Black Sunday. Ibid., 198.

234: they toiled and slaved and died on our behalf. ASBS Original Annals 1935, 27.

234: keeps up under such constant strain and rush. ASBS Original Annals 1935, 135.

234: Energized, invigorated, excited. ASBS Original Annals 1935, 259.

234: the boys and girls. ASBS Katharine Drexel Correspondence, December 27, 1935, H10A BOX 26.

234: How I would love to be with you, dear daughter, to nurse you. ASBS Writings of M.M. Katharine, 690.

235: A little bird tells me you don't eat much. ASBS Writings of M.M. Katharine, 691.

235: Do not be afraid. ASBS Original Annals 1930, 231.

235: be growing in power with God for men and with men for God. ASBS Letter from Katharine Drexel to the Sisters, January 10, 1935, Original Annals 1935, 2.

236: would have been burned to the ground. ASBS Original Annals 1935, 356.

237: Let us take courage; let us start anew. ASBS Original Annals 1935, 425.

238: Very difficult to keep patient when invalid. ASBS M.M. Katharine Meditation Slips Volume 6, 4.

238: I must strive to imitate our Lord's patience. M.M. Katharine Meditation Slips Volume 6, 15.

238: I burst forth in *words of real impatience*. M.M. Katharine Meditation Slips Volume 8, 40.

238: I reproved her emphatically. M.M. Katharine Meditation Slips Volume 8, 42.

238: Dear Jesus, never let me say a word without first having *a word with you*. M.M. Katharine Meditation Slips Volume 8, 56.

238: Deo Gratias. M.M. Katharine Meditation Slips Volume 6, 128.

238: Preparation for Death, M.M. Katharine Meditation Slips Volume 8, 1?5.

239: Grabbed hold of the nurse's arm, May 17, 1943. M.M. Katharine Meditation Slips Volume 6, 73.

240: War, confusion, fighting!! Eternity of this!! M.M. Katharine Meditation Slips Volume 6, 90.

240: Praying for valiant soldiers in the shadow of death. M.M. Katharine Meditation Slips June 7, 1944. Volume 6, 27.

240: Release them, O *Blessed Mother, all*. M.M. Katharine Meditation Slips Volume 6, 42.

240: wonderful university of Xavier. ASBS Original Annals 1941, 29.

240: aiding me directly or indirectly. ASBS Letter to Katharine Drexel H10 B 58, No. 10.

240: may there ever be sunshine in your path. ASBS Telegram to Katharine Drexel H10 B 58, No. 2 (from Albertine Anderson).

241: one of Reverend Mother's children. ASBS Original Annals 1955, 147 (from Martha Selby, Philadelphia).

241: Can an omnipotent God allow so many evils? M.M. Katharine Meditation Slips Volume 4, 35.

241: make me just as You wish me to be. M.M. Katharine Meditation Slips Volume 1, 2.

241: Mary hadn't wasted time asking why. ASBS M.M. Katharine Retreat Notes Volume 3, 109?110.

241: open wide the mouth of my heart. M.M. Katharine Meditation Slips Volume 4, 72.

242: continual dying and perpetual rising from the tomb. M.M. Katharine Meditation Slips Volume 8, 12–13.

242: the great business of the Spiritual life. M.M. Katharine Meditation Slips Volume 1, 53.

242: His sacrifice. M.M. Katharine Meditation Slips Volume 6, 87.

242: adoration and thanksgiving. M.M. Katharine Meditation Slips Volume 5, 23.

242: pure and perfect love. M.M. Katharine Meditation Slips Volume 5, 18.

242: we will obtain grace for the big. M.M. Katharine Meditation Slips Volume 7, 4.

242: Listen to Jesus. M.M. Katharine Meditation Slips Volume 8, 22.

242: Take for your rule of life the example of Jesus Christ. M.M. Katharine Meditation Slips Volume 5, 36.

243: canonized saint of the Church. ASBS Original Annals 1955, 117.

243: the funeral of a saint. ASBS Original Annals 1955, 32.

243: women in the history of America. ASBS "In Memoriam" Document from Xavier Prep.

243: insatiable love of God. ASBS Original Annals 1955, 25.

244: is this a doily? ASBS Original Annals 1955, 87.

244: giants in their trust in God. ASBS Original Annals 1955, 97.

BIBLIOGRAPHY

PRIMARY SOURCES

Drexel University, W.W. Hagerty Library, Philadelphia, PA
  Archives of Drexel University

Sisters of the Blessed Sacrament, Bensalem, PA
  Archives of the Sisters of the Blessed Sacrament—ASBS
    Writings of M.M. Katharine
    Retreat Notes of M.M. Katharine
    Meditation Slips of M.M. Katharine
    Correspondence of M.M. Katharine

Xavier University of Louisiana, New Orleans, LA
  Archives of Xavier University—AXU

SECONDARY SOURCES

Addams, Jane. *Twenty Years at Hull House*. New York: Signet
  Classics, 1961.
Agreda, Sor. Maria de Jesus, de. Translated by Fiscar Marison. *The
  Mystical City of God: The Divine History and Life of the Virgin
  Mother of God*. Hammond: Theophilita/W. B. Conkey, 1914.
Baldwin, Lou. *Saint Katharine Drexel: Apostle to the Oppressed*.
  Philadelphia: Catholic Standard and Times, 2000.
Custer, Elizabeth. *Boots and Saddles; Or, Life in Dakota with General
  Custer*. New York: Harper & Brothers, 1885.
Dorrien, Gary. *Soul in Society*. Minneapolis: Fortress Press, 1995.
Drexel, Francis Martin. "Journal from Guayaquil, Pacific Ocean, to
  Different Parts of Chili." Drexel University Archives.
———. "The Life and Travels of F.M. Drexel, 1792–1826." Drexel
  University Archives. Two copies exist: one handwritten; one tran-
  scribed and typed.

Du Bois, W.E.B. *Black Reconstruction in America 1860–1880*. New York: Free Press, 1998. (Originally published as *Black Reconstruction*. New York: Harcourt Brace, 1935.)
———. *The Souls of Black Folk*. New York: Dover Publications, 1994. (Originally published: Chicago: A.C. McClurg, 1903.)
Duffy, Sister Consuela Marie SBS. *Katharine Drexel: A Biography*. Cornwells Heights, PA: Mother Katharine Drexel Guild. 3rd Printing, August 1977.
Egan, Timothy. *The Worst Hard Time*. Boston: Houghton Mifflin, 2006.
Fisher, Sydney George. *The Laws of Race, as Connected With Slavery*. Philadelphia: Willis P. Hazard, 1860.
Harrison, Eliza Cope, ed. *Philadelphia Merchant: The Diary of Thomas P. Cope*. South Bend: Gateway Editions, 1978.
Letterhouse, Sister Marie Elizabeth SBS. *The Francis A. Drexel Family*. Cornwells Heights, PA: Sisters of the Blessed Sacrament, 1939.
Lincoln, Abraham. *Collected Works of Abraham Lincoln*. New Brunswick: Rutgers University Press, 1953.
Long, Huey. *Every Man a King*. New Orleans: National Book Company, 1934.
Lynch, Sister Patricia SBS. *Sharing the Bread in Service: Sisters of the Blessed Sacrament, 1891–1991*. Bensalem: Sisters of the Blessed Sacrament, 1998.
McGrane, Reginald C., Ph.D., ed. *The Correspondence of Nicholas Biddle Dealing with National Affairs, 1807–1844*. Boston: Houghton Mifflin, 1919.
Moon, Francis C. "Franz Reuleaux: Contributions to Nineteenth-Century Kinematics and Theory of Machines." Abstract. Ithaca: August 2001 (Revised February 2002).
Penrose, Boies. "The Early Life of F.M. Drexel, 1792–1837." *Pennsylvania Magazine of History and Biography* (October 1936).
Philadelphia: A 300-Year History. Russell F. Weigley, ed. New York: W.W. Norton, 1982.
Rauschenbusch, Walter. *A Theology for the Social Gospel*. New York: Macmillan, 1917.
Rottenberg, Dan. *The Man Who Made Wall Street: Anthony Drexel and the Rise of Modern Finance*. Philadelphia: University of Pennsylvania Press, 2006.

Scharf, J. Thomas, and Thompson Westcott. *History of Philadelphia, 1609–1884.* Philadelphia: L. H. Everts & Co., 1884.

Twain, Mark, and Charles Dudley Warner. *The Gilded Age: A Tale of Today.* Hartford: American Publishing Company, 1873.

Workshop of the World: A Selective Guide to the Industrial Archeology of Philadelphia. Oliver Evans Chapter of the Society for Industrial Archeology. Philadelphia: Oliver Evans Press, 1990.

Wright, Richard. *12 Million Black Voices.* New York: Thunder's Mouth Press, 2002. (Originally published: New York: Viking Press, 1941.)

Wright, Robert E. *The First Wall Street: Chestnut Street, Philadelphia, and the Birth of American Finance.* Chicago: University of Chicago Press, 2005.

ACKNOWLEDGMENTS

Enormous thanks to those who encouraged and aided me as I was writing Saint Katharine Drexel's story:

My husband, Steve, who never flagged in his enthusiasm and support—

Alan Nevins, my literary agent, who believed in the project since its inception—

Irwin Lachoff, Associate Archivist Xavier University, New Orleans—

Cornelia S. King, Chief of Reference and Curator of Women's Studies at the Library Company of Philadelphia—

Marcia J. Rogers who supplied me with a trove of books and maps focused on historic Philadelphia—

Thanks also to Bruce H. Franklin of Westholme Publishing, copy editor Noreen O'Connor-Abel, and cover designer Trudi Gershenov.

And, most of all, my abiding gratitude to Dr. Stephanie Morris, Director of Archives at the Sisters of the Blessed Sacrament. My many hours in the archives were a researcher's delight. Stephanie was the epitome of thoroughness and knowledge and aid. I felt that we were on a joint journey of discovery into the life of an extraordinary woman.

INDEX

About the Author

CORDELIA FRANCES BIDDLE is a direct descendant of Francis Martin Drexel, grandfather of Saint Katharine Drexel. She is an independent scholar and novelist. She has been an adjunct professor at Drexel University's Pennoni Honors College since 2007 and was the recipient of the Pennoni Honors College Outstanding Teaching Award in 2012. In addition, she has taught creative writing at the University of the Arts, Temple University Center City. Her most recent works of fiction are: *Without Fear, Deception's Daughter,* and *The Conjurer.* The novels are set during the Victorian era in Philadelphia and explore women's issues and the chasm between rich and poor. Biddle's other works are the historical novel *Beneath the Wind* (Simon & Schuster, 1993) and the *Crossword Mystery* series penned with her husband under the nom de plume Nero Blanc, all published by Penguin Putnam. As a journalist, she has contributed to *Town and Country, Hemispheres,* and *W,* and won a Society of American Travel Writers Lowell Thomas award for *Three Perfect Days in Philadelphia.* She was a contributing writer to the film *Philadelphia: The Great Experiment,* and author of the one-man show: *This Community of Faith: Hopes, Dreams, Trials and Resolution* performed by Sam Waterston in celebration of the 250th anniversary of St. Peter's Church (Philadelphia). She also contributed to *St. Peter's Church: Faith in Action for 250 Years* (Temple University Press, 2011). She has recently completed a new historical novel, and is currently writing a biography of financier Nicholas Biddle. She is a member of the Authors Guild.